MORE
HARM
THAN
GOOD

MORE HARM THAN GOOD
DRUG POLICY IN CANADA

SUSAN BOYD,
CONNIE I. CARTER &
DONALD MACPHERSON

FERNWOOD PUBLISHING
HALIFAX & WINNIPEG

Editing: Jessica Antony
Cover design: John van der Woude
Printed and bound in Canada

Published by Fernwood Publishing
32 Oceanvista Lane, Black Point, Nova Scotia, B0J 1B0
and 748 Broadway Avenue, Winnipeg, Manitoba, R3G 0X3

www.fernwoodpublishing.ca

Fernwood Publishing Company Limited gratefully acknowledges the financial support of the Government of Canada through the Canada Book Fund, the Manitoba Department of Culture, Heritage and Tourism under the Manitoba Publishers Marketing Assistance Program and the Province of Manitoba, through the Book Publishing Tax Credit, for our publishing program. We are pleased to work in partnership with the Province of Nova Scotia to develop and promote our creative industries for the benefit of all Nova Scotians. We acknowledge the support of the Canada Council for the Arts, which last year invested $153 million to bring the arts to Canadians throughout the country.

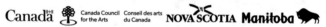

Library and Archives Canada Cataloguing in Publication

Boyd, Susan C., 1953-, author
More harm than good : drug policy in Canada / Susan Boyd, Connie
I. Carter, and Donald MacPherson.

Includes bibliographical references.
Issued in print and electronic formats.
ISBN 978-1-55266-850-4 (paperback).--ISBN 978-1-55266-862-7 (epub).--
ISBN 978-1-55266-863-4 (kindle)

1. Drug control--Canada. I. Carter, Connie, author
II. MacPherson, Donald, 1952-, author III. Title.

HV5840.C3B693 2016   363.450971   C2015-908519-5
                            C2015-908520-9

CONTENTS

ACKNOWLEDGEMENTS

The authors are grateful to the Policy Working Group and the Steering Committee of the Canadian Drug Policy Coalition for assistance with the original report (Carter and MacPherson 2013). The following persons provided detailed reviews of the report: Lynne Belle-Isle, Walter Cavalieri, Irene Goldstone, Philippe Lucas, Michaela Montaner, Caroline Mousseau, Bernie Pauly, Susan Shepherd, Ron Shore, Kenneth Tupper and Dan Werb. We also extend our gratitude to key informants representing organizations from across Canada who wish to remain anonymous.

The original report from which this book draws was made possible by the support of the MACAIDS Fund, the Open Society Global Drug Policy Fund, private donors and Steve Chapman. The Canadian Drug Policy Coalition also wishes to thank the Faculty of Health Sciences at Simon Fraser University and the Centre for Applied Research in Mental Health and Addiction (CARMHA) for their assistance with the report.

We wish to thank Catherine van Mossell for editing and formatting some of the book manuscript, at Fernwood Publishing, Wayne Antony for his excellent feedback, and Jessica Antony for her precise editing. Finally, we would like to thank all of the staff at Fernwood Publishing for supporting the publication of our book.

PREFACE

This book draws from a 2013 report on Canadian drug policy written by Connie I. Carter and Donald MacPherson of the Canadian Drug Policy Coalition. The report provided the original framework for this book. However, this book is significantly different. First, we invited Susan Boyd to contribute to the book. We then expanded on a number of pertinent areas and added new sections to better reflect the state of drug policy in Canada today. We updated the scholarly literature and provided text boxes and cases to illuminate sections of the book. We also provided a more comprehensive theoretical framework for the book, drawing from critical and feminist sociological perspectives. All three authors contributed equally to the project and, in sum, the book took on a life of its own.

1

DRUGS AND
DRUG POLICY

Although substance use has been a part of human societies for thousands of years, the range and types of substances available for psychoactive (that is, mind-altering) purposes has grown exponentially since the early twentieth century. Along with these changes, our understanding of substance use has also changed, as have our approaches to curbing its use. Since the early twentieth century the predominant means that many Western nations have used to curb substance use is through prohibition and criminalization, entailing the extensive use of the criminal justice system and international cooperation to detect and suppress drug trafficking. The twentieth century was marked by the development and spread of these drug laws and heavy sanctions against the use of some substances. Through the three main U.N. conventions on drug control, these approaches have been implemented around the globe. Although prohibition has long had its critics, at the end of the twentieth century and into the beginning of the current century, new voices, including the leaders of some countries, have emerged to challenge prohibition as the only and the best method of addressing the harms of substance use. There are numerous reasons for the growing number of voices opposed to strict prohibition; some of these reasons include the well-documented negative effects of prohibition on efforts to scale-up much needed public health services for people who use drugs, along with increasing evidence that drug laws and sanctions undermine the human rights of some groups of people. Not the least significant among these concerns is the growing realization, documented by sound evidence, that prohibition has failed to deliver on its promises, including curbing drug use and its harms and ensuring increased public safety and national security. One of the most damning critiques of prohibition lies in the increasing body of evidence that suggests that it is in fact responsible for some of the harm associated with drugs that accrues to individuals, families, communities and nations.

The focus of this book is a critical analysis of Canadian drug policy. This volume takes a critical look at the current state of Canadian drug policy and raises key questions about the effects of Canada's increasing involvement in and commitment to the "war on drugs." This book is meant to be a primer on Canadian drug policy that will be useful to a variety of audiences, including students, lay readers, policy makers and health, law and social service workers.

In this book we use a number of approaches. As we discuss more fully below, our analysis of Canadian drug policy is shaped by critical sociological and feminist perspectives on drugs. Some of the information in this book was gleaned from interviews with key informants from across the country who helped identify crucial issues facing people who use drugs. Many of these informants work in harm reduction or treatment programs; some work as policy advisors and some are responsible for research programs; most importantly, some are people who use drugs and have first-hand experience of the issues we discuss in the following pages. We also drew on the extensive body of research on substance use and drug policy produced mainly by Canadian and other scholars, as well as on a review of Canadian drug policy documents. We have excluded consideration of alcohol and tobacco, not because they are unimportant but because they deserve more in-depth consideration that we can provide in this book.[1]

WHAT IS DRUG POLICY?

A key focus of this book is the concept of "drug policy." Drug policy can seem like an amorphous concept, but it is an overarching set of guidelines, policies and laws that shape the decisions that governments and other groups make about how to spend public monies, the types and levels of services to offer and the laws and criminal justice activities to be undertaken by police, courts and correctional systems. Drug policy is not found in one particular aspect of government policy. Rather, it cuts across a number of domains, including policing, justice, law-making, the use of military force, interpretation of law and the decisions of judges. Our approach takes a critical and sociological lens to drugs and drug policy.

As we will discuss in more detail later on, drug policies are usually based on a process of problematization whereby a specific issue is identified as a problem and solutions are proposed based on how the problem is formulated (Bacchi 2009; Fraser and Moore 2011a, 2011b). Illegal drug use, for example, is often formulated as a problem, regardless of the type or amount of drugs that people use. People who use illegal drugs are often portrayed in simplistic terms either as lacking personal discipline or as victims of "evil" drug pushers. Proposed solutions to this "problem" often take the form of drug policies. These policies are usually based on a given diagnosis of the "drug problem" (criminalization of drugs, enforcement strategies focused on "drug pushers") accompanied by a plan for amelioration of this problem (what is to be done).

Canadian drug policy is a multijurisdictional phenomenon crossing many of the traditional boundaries between social, criminal, economic and other policy domains. Typically we understand drug policy to be a matter of criminal law, including policing, justice, law-making, the use of military force, interpretation of law and the decisions of judges. But drug policy decisions can cut across a number of other public policy domains such as health, housing, social assistance, education and immigration and citizenship. Where, for example, social housing does not allow people who use drugs to live in a facility, this is a drug policy decision. Health care systems also make key drug policy decisions when they determine the level of services they will provide to people who use drugs. Decisions to expel youth from school when they are caught using drugs, or to use drug-sniffing dogs to inspect students' possessions are also drug policy decisions.

In Canada, contemporary drug policy is expressed formally in part through federal law, namely the *Controlled Drugs and Substances Act*, which attempts to control the distribution and prevent the use of stimulant, depressant and "hallucinogenic" compounds that can be abused. Despite such attempts at control, Canada spends enormous amounts of public funds annually to prevent the illegal purchase and/ or distribution of prohibited drugs both inside Canada and beyond its borders. Drugs continue to be available despite these efforts. Indeed, the availability and purity of many common illegal drugs has increased in the last thirty years (Wood et al. 2012: 37).

WHAT ARE DRUGS?

In this book we do not assume that there is a common understanding of drugs. In contrast, we define what drugs are. Drugs are "chemical compounds that affect activity in the brain and body" (Here to Help 2013: 1). Any drug that changes the way we feel, think and behave is a psychoactive drug (that is, mind altering). These drugs include not just illegal ones such as cannabis, cocaine and heroin, but also drugs like alcohol and nicotine, both of which are available through legal, regulated markets. Mind-altering drugs also include completely unregulated ones like caffeine, as well as drugs available over-the-counter such as Tylenol and aspirin, and drugs only available by prescriptions such as a wide range of anti-psychotics, anti-depressants, benzodiazepines, some opioid-based painkillers and some medications like Ritalin, prescribed for conditions such as attention deficit and hyperactivity disorder (ADHD). As drug researchers Fraser, valentine and Roberts (2009: 123) state, our culture is a scientific and biomedical one, saturated with legal and illegal drugs.

Different drugs affect humans in different ways. Some drugs are stimulants that speed up the central nervous system at the same time as they produce pleasurable sensations. Drugs such as caffeine, amphetamines, cocaine and crack cocaine fall into this category. Other drugs can depress the functioning of the central nervous system, including alcohol and opioids (heroin, codeine, methadone and prescribed painkillers such as hydromorphone and vicodin, for example) (BC Partners for Mental Health Addictions Information 2013). Still others work in different ways on both brain and body such as hallucinogenic drugs like peyote and ayahuasca.

Humans have used drugs to alter their mood for thousands of years and most of these drugs were plant based. Since the nineteenth century the array of drugs available has increased tremendously due to colonial expansion, global travel, the emergence of synthetic drugs and the modern-day pharmaceutical industry (Boyd 2015: 25). These drugs can cause pleasurable sensations, but can also affect humans by negatively altering our relationships, health and sense of worth (Here to Help 2013: 1). Drug consumption varies across a spectrum. Drug use can have benefits (such as the prescribed use of opioid-based drugs for pain relief or peyote consumed during a Native American Church of Canada ceremony). Drugs can also be used for religious and ceremonial purposes or to broaden consciousness. As well, some people become dependent or addicted to a drug. However, the consequences or outcomes of drug use "vary according to one's position in social structure" (Reinarman and Granfield 2015: 16). Systemic race, class and gender biases shape our Canadian criminal justice system (Balfour and Comack 2014; Chan and Chunn 2014; Razack 2002). For example, the consequences of arrest for possession of cannabis may differ for a poor Aboriginal youth who has to rely on Legal Aid than for an upper-class white youth whose family can afford to pay for top-notch legal support.

One of the insights of sociological theories of drug use is that the effects of a drug are not simply a matter of the pharmacology of a given drug. The way a drug affects a person can depend on the type of drug, the user (age, gender and drug use history, including tolerance, mental health and overall physical health, for example) and the context of use (how much, how often and method of use, for example ingestion, smoking, injection, the atmosphere of the setting and with or without other drugs) (BC Partners for Mental Health Addictions Information 2013). The times, places and activities associated with using drugs contributes to the risks of drug use. In other words, the risks of drug use do not stem only from the drug itself. The reasons people use drugs are also important to understanding their risks (for example, using drugs because of curiosity versus using drugs to protect oneself from life's difficulties and deficits).

All plant-based and human-produced drugs can affect the brain and all drugs carry risks, including drugs prescribed by physicians. Alcohol is one of the most commonly used drugs. Because of the nature of this drug (relative toxicity), and the many contexts in which it is used, it is also one of the most impactful drugs on human health and social life (Nutt, King and Phillips 2010). Drugs produced in illegal settings carry unique risks because of lack of quality control in the production and distribution of these drugs (Here to Help 2013: 2). There is a tendency to lump all illegal drugs together as somehow more dangerous than drugs that are available over-the-counter in pharmacies or by prescription. But drugs like prescribed opioid-based painkillers can also be risky given the potential for users to become dependent or overdose on these medications. In fact, the use of prescribed opioids for non-cancer pain has increased significantly in the last ten years accompanied by increased numbers of overdoses and requests for treatment for dependency (Fischer, Jones, Krahn and Rehm 2011). This book explores these themes and more in relation to Canadian drug policy.

In Chapter 2 we illuminate our theoretical framework, drawing on sociological and feminist perspectives. We also introduce readers to Carol Bacchi's approach to critical policy analysis — how policies "give *shape* to 'problems'" (2009: x, italics in original). We examine theories about the origins of drug use and "critical addiction studies." In Chapter 3 we provide a brief history of Canadian drug law and policy. Chapter 4 highlights drug use in Canada, drawing from survey and qualitative research. In addition, the harms and benefits associated with drug use are examined. Chapter 5 explores the failure of federal drug policy, including the emergence of the National Anti-Drug Strategy in 2007 and its impact. Chapter 6 investigates the "war on drugs" and the impact of criminalization, including the 2012 *Safe Streets and Communities Act*. In addition, drug arrests and incarceration are explored. Cannabis regulation and alternatives to prohibition (such as decriminalization and legal regulation) are discussed. Chapter 7 examines the international drug control system, global efforts towards drug reform and Canada's involvement on the international stage. Chapter 8 provides an overview of services and supports for people who use drugs. Effective programs and initiatives are highlighted and obstacles to services are considered. Chapter 9 focuses on harm reduction services in Canada. Successful programs and initiatives are discussed and challenges to harm reduction are illuminated. Chapter 10 provides a short conclusion about Canadian drug policy and the global movement for drug policy reform.

Note

1.   For examples of this work, see CCSA 2012b.

2

SOCIOLOGICAL APPROACHES TO DRUGS AND DRUG POLICY

OUR APPROACH

In order to understand the "problem" of drugs and drug policy in Canada, we draw from sociological perspectives on social constructionism. Social constructionism "makes visible the social dynamics that help constitute conditions as problems" (Fraser and Moore 2011a: 3). In this book we argue that social problems, such as the "drug problem," are socially constructed. Social constructionist analyses also draw our attention to the institutionally based claims-makers who shape our understanding of drugs as a social problem, such as the Royal Canadian Mounted Police, municipal police forces, politicians, physicians, researchers and others. Daily, spokespeople in Canada use a variety of forums, including radio, newspapers, television, films and numerous websites and social media forums to make claims about drugs as a social problem. These claims-makers help to define the nature of the "drug problem" and they also offer solutions to this problem that correspond with their institutional priorities and concerns (Best 1995). Social constructionist scholarship also draws our attention to the contradictory nature of claims about "social problems" (Reinarman and Levine 2000). This is no less the case with drugs. Even a cursory examination of websites devoted to this topic will reveal competing and contradictory ideas about drugs. These same sites will also offer contradictory analysis of why drugs are a problem and how we should respond to this problem. The voices behind these claims and counter-claims often compete with each other to define the drug problem, but they are also challenged by others' voices, including spokespeople from groups supporting drug policy reform, academics and groups of people who use drugs.

This book also draws on sociological perspectives to explore how our ideas about drugs have deeply rooted cultural and historical origins. The meanings associated with substance use, for example, are not necessarily a result of inherent unchanging qualities of drugs but develop through interactions between human beings over time. In other words, how we understand what a drug is and how it affects people are products of cultural and social systems that shape the meaning and experience of a substance (Conrad and Barker 2010). Thus, ideas about drugs are produced by humans in daily interactions in political, social and cultural contexts. The notion that some drugs are good and some are bad, for example, is not necessarily based on the supposed health or social harms of a drug but is related to the history of claims made about that substance. Indeed, as is the case in Canada, many of these socially constructed ideas about drugs have been codified into laws that govern how we may access and use these same drugs.

Criminalized drugs are most often those substances that a variety of institutionally based groups condemned in a specific historical era. As we will discuss more fully below, specific substances like opium, heroin and cocaine were criminalized in the early 1900s in Canada. Prior to and following the legal prohibition of these substances, ideas about drugs were under considerable public debate, debates that shaped how we understand these drugs and their effects to this day. For example, concepts of addiction are not static. Addiction, "*both* in its conceptual and material senses, is produced by the times" (Fraser and Moore 2011a: 7, emphasis in original). Noted sociologists, such as Craig Reinarman and Robert Granfield, show us that the concept of "addiction is a recent invention" (Reinarman and Granfield 2015: 1). These same researchers draw our attention to how a term like addiction is continually reworked as new claims-makers arise to define and redefine this concept.

CRITICAL SOCIOLOGICAL AND FEMINIST PERSPECTIVES

Since the early writings of Howard Becker in the 1950s, critical sociologists who examine crime and deviancy argue that "deviance is not a quality of the acts the person commits, but rather a consequence of the application of rules and sanction to an 'offender'" (Pfhol 1994: 345). These sociologists argue that no act is inherently deviant; rather in specific historical eras, certain behaviours such as using, producing or selling specific drugs like marijuana or cocaine are deemed criminal through a complex interplay between laws, politics and other social phenomena. These sociologists challenge the idea that that criminal behaviour is either a rational individual choice or stems from individual pathology. These scholars argue that ideas about what constitutes crime are political and social artefacts of human activity. Nor do they accept that punishment will deter crime. Rather, these critical sociologists are interested in how inequitable exercises of power and the existence of profound forms of social inequality shape and produce crime and deviancy. They are interested in how social factors both limit and constrain individuals and the interplay between the individual and society (Mills 1975).

Critical scholars have also shown us that our theories about why crime occurs and what constitutes "deviancy" are not neutral; nor are our criminal justice systems. Similar to drug categories, these theories and our social systems are the result of social and political activities by humans. Some groups of claims-makers "are likely to prefer some theoretical perspectives over others" (Pfohl 1994: 8). In Canada, the national police organization, the Royal Canadian Mounted Police (RCMP), for example are a key proponent of law-and-order perspectives when it comes to illegal drugs (harsh drug laws and prison sentencing to deter and punish crime).

Critical sociologists also critique the systems and practices we use to detect and limit crime, such as policing, courts and prisons. They have made excellent contributions to our understanding of the socio-historical origins of our laws, and their accompanying systems of social control, including the role of policing, the courts and corrections (prisons, community service, and so forth). These researchers have illuminated how social status — race, class, gender, sexuality — shape

---

Deviant Behaviours

Are certain types of behaviours naturally deviant in all societies? Critical sociologist Stephen Pfohl responds:

Homicide is a way of categorizing the act of killing, such that taking another's life is viewed as totally reprehensible ... Some types of killing are categorized as homicide. Others are not. What differs is not the behavior but the manner in which reactions to that behavior are socially organized. The behavior is essentially the same: killing a police officer or killing by a police officer; stabbing an old lady in the back or stabbing the unsuspecting wartime enemy; a black slave shooting a white master or a white master lynching a Black slave; being run over by a drunken driver or slowly dying of a painful cancer caused by a polluting factor. Each is a type of killing. Some are labeled homicide. Others are excused, justified, or viewed, as is the case of dangerous industrial pollution, as environmental risks, necessary for the health of our economy if not our bodies. The form and content of what is seen as homicide thus varies with social context and circumstance (Pfohl 1994: 345–46).

encounters with criminal justice agents (Boyd 2015; Balfour and Comack 2014; Comack and Balfour 2004; Mosher 1998).

Policy

In this book, our discussion of drugs and addiction draws from the perspectives outlined above and from our overriding interest in Canadian drug policy. Since 2007, drug policy in Canada has rapidly changed. As we write, new policies seem to be created daily. Although it is outside of any book to capture every drug policy shift, this book provides a comprehensive framework to understand current policy and tools to interrogate new drug policies.

In the introduction we examined how claims-makers identify social problems and offer solutions to "problems" that correspond with their institutional priorities and concerns. We also noted how "social constructionism makes visible the social dynamics that help constitute conditions as problems" (Fraser and Moore 2011a: 3). Thus, we ask the question: How do ideas about substances, and the people who use them, shape policy? What solutions and policies are advanced to solve the problem of illegal drugs? Feminist scholar Carol Bacchi (Bacchi 2009, 2012) draws on a social constructionist approach to policy problems and the work of Michel Foucault, whose writings illustrate how concepts like mental illness and sexuality emerged historically as objects for thought through a process he identified as "problematizations" (Bacchi 2012: 8). In contrast to many of the social constructionist approaches identified above, Foucault was not interested in whether claims about social objects like drugs are accurate. Instead, Foucault, like Bacchi, focuses on how claims or certain problematizations of social phenomena come into being through a range of techniques and tactics. Bacchi has developed Foucault's work on problematizations to explore how social problems such as drugs are problematized and how solutions are actualized in policy. Bacchi asks a set of questions that help analysts explore how problems are represented in specific policies. She suggests that analysts explore the assumptions that "underlie this representation of the 'problem'"; how this representation "of the 'problem' have come about"; what is "left unproblematic" in this representation of the problem; what are "the silences" and "can the 'problem' be thought of differently?" Then she asks, "what effects are produced by this representation of the 'problem'" and "how/ where has this representation of the 'problem' been produced, disseminated and defended? How could it be questioned, disrupted and replaced?" (Bacchi 2009: xii).

All of these questions can be applied to the "drug problem" in Canada. In relation to drug policy, Bacchi might ask what are the taken-for-granted ideas that pervade Canadian drug policy and what are the ideas that shape the responses governments and others propose for the "problem of drugs." Bacchi's approach asks us to then work backwards to understand the key concepts and explicit binaries that shape the meanings attached to the "drug problem." Drug policies are often character-ized by a similar set of binary ideas, including: addicted/non-addicted, good/bad drugs, illegal/legal drugs, responsible/irresponsible use, controlled/out of control drug use, moral/immoral and risky/non-risky. Bacchi's approach then entails an examination of how specific representations of drugs, ideas about addiction and reports on drug trafficking and other drug crimes contribute to our understanding of how the "drug problem" can be remedied.

In her analysis of drug policy in Australia, Bacchi argues that the war against drugs "is primarily a war against 'evil' traffickers and only secondarily against users" (Bacchi 2009: 89). She shows her readers that the Australian focus on drug traf-ficking "produces" the problem of illegal drugs as a "supply-side 'problem.'" Efforts to address Australia's "drug problem" are then directed at reducing the supply of drugs on the assumption that this will make the problem go away. As she notes, this approach completely ignores both the reasons why people use substances and the harms that stem from prohibition itself (ibid: 89). In this volume we contend that there are both similarities and differences in Canada's approach to drugs, a topic we will return to later in this book. Bacchi also argues that policy makers assume that policy *solves* social problems. In contrast, Bacchi's work shows how policies "*give shape* to 'problems'; they do not *address* them (Bacchi 2009: x, ital-ics in original). By examining how problems are "produced (and re-produced) through the language of drug policy, we also begin to see how policy problems can be reframed and thought about differently, because policy problems are not fixed, objective ideas" (Lancaster and Ritter 2014: 82). Thus, as we will discuss more fully in these pages, international and Canadian drug policies give shape to, and are central to, the problem of illegal drugs.

Although many critical scholars provide a gender analysis or draw from feminist scholarship, most often feminist scholars focus more specifically on issues that relate to women. For example, Carol Bacchi's (1999: 204) early work illuminates how policy, policy making and the "problem of women's inequality is discursively constructed." She argues that "feminists' problematizations reflect deeply held cul-tural assumptions" and are specific to "historical, economic and cultural locations" (Bacchi 1999: 205). Early on, feminist scholars also argued that the regulation of women centres on "reproduction, mothering, double standards of morality, [and] social and legal subordination" (Smart and Smart 1978: 3). The regulation of women is also shaped by conflicting and contradictory socially constructed ideas about who women are, which women are considered to be good, and what roles women should fulfil in their homes, employment and in broader social and politi-cal activities. Some of these feminist scholars have turned their attention to drug laws and policies and have illustrated how perceptions about women's drug use and how legal, social service, medical and governmental responses to women who use drugs are often different than for men (Boyd 2015; Flavin 2009; Paltrow and Flavin 2013). In relation to criminal justice, feminist scholars also draw attention to the intersection of race and the "gendered contexts" that often bring girls and women into conflict with the law; some of these contexts include the feminization of poverty, the impact of colonization on the lives of Indigenous women, racism, and state, domestic and sexual violence. These contexts affect how women are treated by legal and criminal justice systems (Comack 1996: 38–39). Women who use criminalized drugs, especially cocaine and heroin, are often considered to be more deviant than their male counterparts and have "long been constructed as the 'Other,' who is outside the norms of proper moral and gendered female behavior" (Boyd 2015: 15). These feminist scholars have explored how, nationally and internationally, drug prohibition and drug policy negatively affects women engaged in or suspected of drug production and selling or using criminalized drugs (Kensy et al. 2012). These same scholars are often at the forefront of activism and scholarship about the intersection of the war on drugs and women's reproductive autonomy (Paltrow and Flavin 2013).

Feminist scholarship about pregnant women and mothers suspected of substance use has been particularly adept at drawing on a range of insights to explore how women's reproductive capacity intersects with drug laws and policies. Many of these scholars have used an anti-racist approach to show that when it comes to drug crime (and all criminal offences), poor, Indigenous, racialized and non-heterosexual women are often treated as more deviant, immoral and dangerous to their children and society than middle- and upper-class white women and men. Thus, these marginalized women are seen as more deserving of punishment. Feminist researchers are not homogenous; thus their contribution and critique of drug policy is diverse (Boyd 2014; Paltrow and Flavin 2013; Haines-Saah et al. 2013; Ford and Saibil 2010; VANDU Women's Care Team 2009).

THEORIES ABOUT DRUG USE AND ADDICTION

The Moral Model

Theories about why people use and become dependent on psychoactive drugs are subject to much debate. There are several predominant models that attempt to explain not only why people use drugs but also why use translates into dependency. These models broadly include: moral/criminal, medical and critical addiction studies. The moral model of drug use emerged alongside early efforts to prohibit some drugs and remains a chief way that many people understand illegal drug use: all illegal drug use is bad and using drugs to alter one's perceptions is the result of poor decision making and lack of personal discipline. In this theory, dependency on drugs or addiction is the result of poor choices and bad behaviour. Since drug use is thought to be a bad habit resulting from poor personal discipline, the major methods of curbing it should be punishment. Increasingly we see, however, that punishment does not stop people from using drugs. This was abundantly clear during the 1920s and 1930s in North America during alcohol prohibition. Despite laws that banned the use and trade in alcohol, consumption continued. Alcohol prohibition also helped to fuel a criminal underground and to foster disrespect for the law.

This model also underscores the contemporary war on drugs, a multi-billion-dollar effort in North America first initiated by U.S. President Richard Nixon in 1971 (and pursued by Canadian politicians and law agents). The result has been very limited success at curbing drug use, alongside the implementation of laws and justice practices that have resulted in the U.S. having the highest rate of incarceration in the world. The other downside is that the moral model results in profound forms of discrimination and marginalization of people who use drugs, particularly people without sufficient economic resources. Because of fear of judgment and arrest, people avoid seeking help with their drug use, which results in unnecessarily harmful health and social outcomes of drug use.

One of the other problematic outcomes of the moral model is the insistence by many that there is an inevitable relationship between drug use and criminality. Because people are forced to seek drugs from illegal markets, it has been easy to assume that these same people are also criminals. As we will illustrate in the chapter on the history of Canadian drug policy, in the first half of the twentieth century, the RCMP played a large role in promoting the notion of the "criminal addict" by influencing magazine and newspaper articles and through film and radio (S. Boyd 2013, 2014). Indeed, because drug use is judged by the moral model to be a failure of personal will, abstinence and punishment are seen as the cure for these failures. The moral model also supports the notion that drugs all by themselves pose public safety threats to communities, individuals and nations. Where criminalization fails to stop people from using and selling illegal drugs, police and others sometimes claim that policy makers have failed to provide sufficient public resources to support police, courts and prisons (Boyd and Carter 2014: 83–84) Thus, they argue that harsher laws, longer prison sentences and more policing resources will lower drug use rates and drug production and trafficking.

Disease Model

The medical- or disease-model of drug use came to prominence in the mid-twentieth century — although tenets of this model have existed since the 1700s, especially in the temperance writings (Musto 2002). This theory posited that the origins of drug dependency lie in the biological and neurological processes of the body and brain, rather than in the failures of the soul. The rise of the medical model parallels the consolidation of the power of physicians over health care. In the late nineteenth and early twentieth centuries, members of the newly established medical profession strengthened their tenuous position by advocating that specific fields such as addiction were in their rightful domain of expertise. Thus, traditional healers were excluded and other emerging professions were marginalized from the field of addiction at that time. However, as drug historians Charles Terry and Mildred Pellens (1970) argue, physicians also contributed in part to misinformation about addiction, especially their theory that withdrawal from drugs and continued abstinence leads to a cure for drug addiction.

Not only does the disease or medical model understand addiction as a biological problem, but this model also suggests that it is a progressive and permanent disease. Relapse to drug use is understood to be a normal part of recovery and sobriety. One of the impetuses for the development of the medical model was the search for another, less moralistic approach to drug use problems. The development of the "disease" of addiction helps to shift blame away from the person and instead sees people with drug problems as deserving of treatment. In fact, this model remains very much in currency today, sometimes referred to as a medicalized approach to addiction, or a twelve-step program. The powerful research granting agency, the U.S. National Institute of Drug Abuse, has officially designated addiction as a "disease of the brain" and draws from neuroscience to support its claim (Campbell 2007). This model, however, has key shortcomings. For instance, this model "entails detaching brains from bodies and from the social contexts in which bodies and brains develop" (Reinarman and Granfield 2015: 6).

Research has not illustrated conclusively that there is a genetic basis for drug addiction, nor have other biological determinants been conclusively defined. As noted above, typically the disease model also defined addiction as a "chronic, relapsing" illness. Although relapse from abstinence is common for many people, disease labels can also operate as a trap. It is difficult to overcome this diagnosis once it has been placed on individuals. No doubt biology plays a role in addiction, but there are many documented cases of people who "spontaneously" recover from addiction when they decide to give up drug use on their own (BC Ministry of Health Services 2004). Sociologist Craig Reinarman (2011: 178) argues that the adoption of the medical model of addiction is a "mixed blessing" because it individualizes drug use and the social and cultural contexts of use "fall out of view." Secondly, he argues that defining addiction as a disease prevents individuals from understanding their drug use in any other way and ultimately the model rejects human agency. Reinarman points to the limitations of the medical model and discusses how it makes other services more difficult to establish, such as harm reduction services (needle exchange and safer injection sites and so forth). These services are often portrayed as "enabling" drug users and thus contributing to their addiction.

Medical/Criminal Model

The moral/criminal and medical models of drug use do not exist wholly separately from each other. Canadian scholars have convincingly argued that, although the moral/criminal model is still predominant in Canada, it exists alongside a medical approach to drug use. In Canada following WWII the medical profession began to more fully assert their influence in the field of addiction. One of the results of this development was the emergence of the treatment movement, a development we will discuss in more detail later. For now, it is enough to point out that as a result of medical influence, publicly funded drug treatment services were established from the 1960s on for people who used illegal drugs. But these treatment programs existed in tandem with harsh drug laws and people who were addicted to criminalized drugs often found themselves sentenced to prison for drug possession and low-level street selling. Reinarman argues that although the medical model of addiction has led to expanded drug treatment services, it is also used to justify prison time, so criminal justice regulation has increased (Reinarman 2011). For example, participants in Canada's drug treatment courts can be sent to prison if they cannot ultimately achieve abstinence while in the program. Reinarman also (2011: 182) points out that there is an inherent contradiction in an approach that combines criminal and medical approaches to drug use — how can punishment be effective if addiction is a health concern characterized as a permanent biological disease and relapse is integral to the disease? As we pointed out earlier in the chapter, ideas about drugs are often contradictory. As we will illustrate later on, the criminal/medical model continues to shape Canadian drug policy.

Critical Addiction Studies

A variety of newer discoveries and practices have led to an emerging consensus about a more holistic approach to drug use. This approach draws heavily from the sociological perspective described earlier in this chapter. Craig Reinarman and Robert Granfield introduce the concept of "critical addiction studies," a sociological analysis of addiction that provides a holistic and multi-disciplinary approach. They point to the social, political and cultural factors that shape our ideas about addiction. In the text box below, we outline their six basic principles that "characterize this approach to addiction" (Reinarman and Granfield 2015: 16–17).

Critical addictions studies would suggest that drug use is affected by a variety of factors such as biological processes, individual traits and key issues in the social environment, including events throughout the life course. This approach also recognizes that people use drugs for a variety of reasons and with varying outcomes. It acknowledges that there can be benefits to drug use, even illegal drug use. These benefits could be physical, mental, emotional, social and spiritual. It also recognizes that drug use can be pleasurable (Moore 2008). Manning (2007: 4) illuminates how "drug consumption is a popular cultural practice." For example, he points to shifts in drug consumption in the late 1980s and early 1990s and young peoples' positive accounts of rave culture and marijuana use. Manning (2007: 4) emphasizes the normalization of some drug consumption and how popular culture representations of illegal drug use has moved from the "sub-cultural to the mainstream." These accounts differ from earlier notions of problematic or criminal use of illegal drugs and a solely medical model of addiction. A critical perspective acknowledges that illegal drug use is also mediated by race, class, gender and the law. Thus, not all drug use is viewed equally, nor are the consequences of drug use experienced equally.

A critical addiction perspective also recognizes that all drugs carry risks depending upon the context of use, dosage and history of other drug use, for example. Most people do not experience significant problems because of

their drug use, some do develop drug problems and others may experience clear benefits from using illegal drugs (Reinarman and Granfield 2015). This perspective

Critical Addiction Studies: Six Basic Principles

1. Historical and cultural specificity: "Concepts of addiction are social constructions, built by actors and deployed by institutions that have specific cultural locations, interests, and ideologies, all of which evolve over time."
2. The contextual is integral: "Addiction cannot be understood as merely the behaviour patterns of an individual, as if they were the product of personal choices or personality characteristics alone, but also must be conceptualized as collective probabilities that are woven into the social fabric." Thus, "mass consumption culture, and globalizing neo-liberalism to subculture, countercultures, and the repertoires of intoxication, both pleasurable and problematic" shape drug use.
3. Addiction is sociologically contingent and indeterminate: "There are multiple trajectories into, within, and out of addiction."
4. Social inequality and differential consequences: "Attend to the uneven probabilities of onset, trajectories, and consequences of addictive behaviors that are associated with race, class, gender, and other axes of social inequality."
5. Multi-disciplinary and multi-vocal investigative strategy: "Attending to the voices of those who experience addiction and society's responses to it is essential, as they are the primary sources of subjugated knowledge about addiction, including the routes into addiction, informal social controls that reduce risk, strategies for controlled use, and natural recovery."
6. Consequentialist conceptualization of policy: "Seek to imagine more humane alternative drug policies that can integrate rather than ostracize problem drug users and better reduce drug related harm" (Reinarman and Granfield 2015: 16–17).

on drug use also recognizes that only a small portion of drug use becomes problematic. Indeed, many people use currently illegal drugs on an occasional basis and suffer no harms. But this perspective emphasizes that notions of harm and problematic use are also social and cultural and that they vary from one historical period to another. Contemporary perceptions of harm are still mainly defined in the public realm by professionals in the health care field and law enforcement and policy makers. Rarely do people who use drugs get the opportunity to publicly influence the way we perceive drugs.

The important point we wish to emphasize is that the harms and benefits of drug use can be compounded and in some cases wholly created by drug policy. The unique pharmacology of any drug is only part of the story. As the principles of critical addiction studies suggest, a user's mindset and the environment of use also shape the effects of drugs; drug policies and drug laws are key components that also shape the environment of use. Social factors like homelessness, imprisonment and encounters with law enforcement have been found to exacerbate the harms of drug use. Use of injection drugs in public, for example, can lead people to rush and/or disregard practices of safer use because of fear of police or public detection, leading to infections and overdose (Fischer et al. 2012). And the reasons people use drugs in public are likely related to lack of housing and/or available private spaces. It is also important to not conflate the harms of drug use with the harms created by policy itself. For example, research suggests that where syringe distribution programs are either criminalized or limited by municipal bylaws, needle sharing and the transmission of blood borne diseases are much higher (Bernstein and Bennet 2013: e63). In Chapters 5 and 6 we will discuss in detail the harms of drug policy.

3

A BRIEF HISTORY OF DRUG LAWS AND POLICY IN CANADA

The early history of drug policy and laws in Canada reveals that the moral/criminal model of drug use was predominant. Historians have demonstrated that drug law in Canada has not been a benign phenomenon aimed at safeguarding the health of Canadians, but a tool of social control directed unevenly at some groups of people (Fischer et al. 2003: 267). Numerous studies on the adoption of Canada's first federal drug legislation convincingly argued that the regulation of drugs such as opium had more to do with anti-Asian sentiments than with concerns about the pharmacological effects of this drug (Carstairs 2006; Fischer et al. 2003; Grayson 2008).

In the early part of the twentieth century, drugs such as opium were associated with a variety of supposed social ills, including interracial relationships, white slavery, degradation and loose sexual morals. The historical literature on Canadian drug policy suggests that periods of heightened concern about drugs were often driven by a combination of newspaper campaigns, as well as interest and advocacy group activities, resulting in changes to Canada's drug policy laws (Boyd 2015; Carstairs 2006; Grayson 2008; Martel 2006; Valverde 1998). Drug prohibition in Canada did not begin until the passage of the *Opium Act* in 1908 (however, alcohol prohibition for those labelled Status Indian began in 1868). Prior to this point, nineteenth-century opiate use, alcohol consumption and tobacco smoking were "widely embedded in social custom" and practised by white citizens in Western nations (Berridge 2013: 12). At that time, anyone could buy, without a prescription, a wide array of opiate, cocaine and cannabis-based products, such as tinctures, creams, pills, patient medicines and powders (ibid.: 15).

Following a notorious race riot in Vancouver's Chinatown in 1907, an event that was fuelled by the race and class concerns of white workers against Chinese labourers at that time, Canadian politician (and later Prime Minister) William Lyon Mackenzie King was sent to Vancouver to investigate the causes of this riot. King's report on this riot borrowed from racist newspaper accounts that claimed that smoking opium led ordinarily moral and upstanding white Canadians to ruin in the opium dens thought to be run exclusively by Chinese Canadians. His report also included the testimony of prominent anti-opium reformers who made similar claims about the effects of opium. Following this event, King is quoted as declaring, "We will get some good out of this riot yet" (Boyd 1984: 115; Comack 1986). King's report to the federal government recommended that opium prepared for smoking and powered and crude opium be criminalized. In response, Parliament passed the *Opium Act* in 1908. The Act regulated crude and powdered opium and opium prepared for smoking and made it an offence to import, manufacture, offer to sell or sell or possess to sell opium for non-medical reasons. Thus, early on law enforcement focused on closing opium dens and regulating those associated with the smoking of opium — almost exclusively Chinese residents living in Canada (Boyd 1984). Even as opium was prohibited, many other Canadians still consumed opiates in patent medicines such as cough syrups and laudanum.

The *Opium and Drug Act* of 1911 criminalized other opiates and cocaine derivatives, prohibited opium smoking and created the offence of possession of these drugs or of being found in an opium den. This Act granted exceptional powers to police and the burden of proof was placed upon the person charged with a drug offence. This "reverse onus" clause became a standard legal practice in Canadian drugs laws. The prohibition of cannabis in 1923 was likely related to a racist scare about the drug promoted by one of Canada's social reformers of the time, Emily Murphy, given that few Canadians used this drug and fewer knew of its existence (Carstairs 2006; Fischer et al. 2003; Solomon and Green 1988). In fact, there were no arrests related to cannabis in Canada until 1937, causing some Canadian scholars to call the criminalization of cannabis "a solution without a problem" (Giffen, Endicott and Lambert 1991: 182).

By 1927, Colonel C.H.L. Sharman had assumed the role of chief of the Division of Narcotic Control, a position he held until 1946. Sharman was a civil servant with "an extraordinary amount of influence and power. The control apparatus he headed came to have a virtual monopoly over the decision making processes from enactment to enforcement to the international role" (Giffen, Endicott and Lambert 1991: 146). Sharman managed to consolidate the power of his office and assert control over how drugs were understood by the professions and by readers of Canadian magazines and newspapers. He promoted his views that drugs led to criminality by sending information to the editors of the *Canadian Medical Association Journal,* who used Sharman's claims in their editorials. He also presented lectures to medical students, advocated with legislators for harsher penalties and worked closely with the RCMP to enforce Canada's growing number of drug laws (Giffen, Endicott and Lambert 1991: 158). By the end of the 1920s, the image of the drug user in Canada had shifted from a morally weak individual to a "fiendish criminal obsessed with the need to addict others and motivated by lust and greed." Illegal drug use was defined as a law enforcement problem that must be remedied with increasingly punitive consequences (Solomon and Green 1988: 100).

As early as 1928, the Division of Narcotic Control increased its surveillance of supposed drug users and kept comprehensive files right up until the early 1970s on "Addicts," "Traffickers" and "Doctors" (Carstairs 2006). The effects of the surveillance for poor and working-class people who used criminalized drugs were long prison sentences, whipping and deportation (Carstairs 2006; Giffen, Endicott and Lambert 1991; Grace 1958; Stevenson et al. 1956). Police could search the private residences of suspected drug users without a warrant, and there was a reverse onus of proof, meaning that offenders had to prove in court that they were innocent (rather than being assumed innocent until proven guilty).

In the 1930s, a series of changes to Canada's drug laws included prohibiting codeine other than for medical use and amendments that helped to ensure that many different kinds of drug use became criminal acts. In 1938, the *Toronto Star* carried a story entitled, "Marijuana smokers seized with sudden craze to kill: Officer warns insidious weed is even supplied school children." This article signalled an increased media interest in a relatively unknown drug. Media claims about cannabis suggested it was associated with murder and that it could send people "to the insane asylum" (Giffen, Endicott and Lambert 1991: 184, 186). In the late 1930s, a bill that proposed to make marijuana cultivation an offence precipitated the first full debate on marijuana in Parliament (Giffen, Endicott and Lambert 1991). By 1938, the federal Division of Narcotic Control concluded that drug treatment was ineffective, a conclusion echoed by the Royal Commission to Investigate the Penal System in the same year (Carstairs 2006: 152). Thus, unlike other countries, publicly funded drug treatment was not available to Canadians at this time. Nor were Canadian doctors allowed to issue prescriptions for non-medical use, such as providing narcotics to treat addiction. In fact, from 1911 on they could be arrested and charged with illegal prescribing (Giffen, Endicott and Lambert 1991: 341).

In the 1940s, RCMP reports continued to promote the view that criminality and drug use were intimately linked. Despite these continued efforts to consolidate control of drugs in the criminal justice system, reformers such as E.E. Winch of the Co-operative Commonwealth Federation (CCF) party rallied support for a medical approach to "narcotic addiction" (Giffen, Endicott and Lambert 1991: 363). Calls for reform in B.C. stemmed from concern about a small group of white poor and working-class heroin users living in Vancouver. Following WWII and the closure of the opium dens and deportation of Chinese residents, drug use in Canada shifted from smoking opium to injection drug use of heroin and morphine, and to a lesser degree cocaine (Boyd 2013, 2014; Paulus 1966). Police began profiling a relatively small group of visible white heroin users in Montreal and Vancouver. (Carstairs 2006; Stevenson et al. 1956). In the post-war period during the late 1940s, this surveillance was part of efforts by police to subject people who used heroin to intense surveillance.

In the early 1950s, calls for a medical approach to drug use precipitated the emergence of a "treatment movement" in Vancouver. This movement, comprised of a wide range of politicians, medical professionals and social workers, called for publicly funded drug treatment and narcotic maintenance programs, and an end to minimum sentences for drug possession (Giffen, Endicott and Lambert 1991: 359–404). At the time, no public drug treatment provisions were set up for individuals who used or were addicted to newly criminalized drugs such as heroin or morphine (without a prescription). Nor were drug substitution treatments (that is, morphine and other opioids) and drug maintenance therapy available for people addicted to narcotics in Canada as they were in Britain and the U.S. (Acker 2002; Brecher et al. 1972; Lart 1998; Musto 1987). In fact, the Division of Narcotic Control maintained primary control over Canadian drug policy. As noted above, Canadian doctors were not allowed to prescribe drugs for maintenance purposes to people identified as "addicts" (Giffen, Endicott and Lambert 1991).

Historians point out that it was not unusual in the 1950s for illegal drug-using Canadians to have experienced extensive histories of police surveillance and incarceration in Canada's prisons (Carstairs 2006). But increasing medical interest in this issue was reflected in the findings of the Senate Special Committee on the Traffic in Narcotic Drugs. The Committee, appointed in 1955, investigated a recent flurry of newspaper articles detailing a supposed rise in youthful heroin use in the eastside of Vancouver in the early 1950s, especially among vulnerable young girls (Carstairs 2006: 153). The Committee found this scare to be groundless and went on to examine a variety of drug-related issues, including whether addiction could be treated and the supposed contagiousness of addiction from one person to another. Testimony at Committee hearings from law enforcement officials emphasized the criminality and contagious nature of addiction. These officials also supported the compulsory confinement of people addicted to drugs and they refuted the validity of drug maintenance programs (Giffen, Endicott and Lambert 1991: 373–388).

The report of the Special Senate Committee supported the setting up by the provinces of better medical treatment, including follow-up and support services.

Vancouver treatment advocates were disappointed by the conclusions of the Committee, calling the final report "a nothing report" that would do little to solve Vancouver's addiction problem (Giffen, Endicott and Lambert 1991: 388). Despite the efforts of law enforcement officials, a nascent treatment approach was established in Canada. By 1959, the Narcotic Addiction Foundation (NAF) of B.C. had begun a limited methadone withdrawal program. This program of methadone maintenance was one of the first of its kind in North America along with a maintenance program at the Addiction Research Foundation of Ontario in 1960 (Fischer et al. 2003: 191; Giffen, Endicott and Lambert 1991: 399; Peachy and Franklin 1985: 291).

In the early 1960s, Canada revised and consolidated its various drug laws, resulting in the 1961 *Narcotic Control Act*. This legislation gave Canada the distinction of enacting some of the harshest drug laws of any Western nation. Part I of the Act provided for life imprisonment for trafficking offences, a minimum of seven years for illegal importing and exporting, elimination of the minimum six-month sentences and summary indictment proceedings for possession and removal of whipping for all offences. The search and seizure powers part of the Act, in place since 1929, did not change significantly. Part II of the Act provided for committal to custody and treatment of individuals proven to be "addicts"; release would then be determined by the National Parole Board. Custody would be followed by ten years of supervision and parole could be revoked if the individual was found to be using drugs again. However, this section of the Act was never carried forward. The schedules for this Act included fourteen groups of drugs and eighty-nine of their preparations, derivatives, salts and alkaloids (Giffen, Endicott and Lambert 1991: 439). This legislation also permitted the use of methadone for opiate dependence but only under a doctor's care (Peachy and Franklin 1985: 291).

The 1960s saw massive shifts in the social climate in Canada, including increased recreational drug use of cannabis. The same period saw increasing numbers of arrests and convictions for drug offences. In 1961, 495 people were convicted of a drug charge in Canada. By 1969, 2,367 people were convicted of drug charges in that year (Giffen, Endicott and Lambert 1991: 593). Between 1964 and 1973, the number of charges related to cannabis also rose, from 78 to 37,668, and the number of convictions, from 28 to 19,929 in Canada. By 1970, an estimated 850,000 Canadians had used marijuana at least once (Giffen, Endicott and Lambert 1991: 495). In 1969, partially in response to increasing concerns about the numbers of young white middle-class citizens who could potentially receive prison sentences for possession and to lessen the burden on prosecutors and courts, an amendment to the *Narcotic Control Act* created an alternative of a summary conviction and a lesser maximum penalty for marijuana possession (ibid.: 514).

One of the most significant events in the history of Canadian drug policy was the report of the Royal Commission of Inquiry into the Non-Medical Use of Drugs. The Le Dain Commission, as it was later called, was established in 1969. The role of the Commission was to make inquiries into the non-medical use of psychoactive drugs and "to find out the extent to their use, the state of knowledge about each, their effects, and the problems surrounding them" (Giffen, Endicott and Lambert 1991: 518). The Commission was charged with recommending actions that could be taken by the Canadian government. The Commission published four reports: *Interim Report* (1970), *Final Report on Cannabis* (1972), *Treatment* (1972) and the *Final Report* in 1973. The *Final Report on Cannabis* refutes RCMP claims that cannabis turns people into criminals (Nolin and Kenny 2002: 273). This report on cannabis also recommended abolishing simple possession of cannabis as an offence and the *Final Report* recommended the decriminalization of simple possession of all drugs. These recommendations were never implemented in Canada. The Commission also recommended the expansion of methadone maintenance programs and the establishment of a scientific heroin maintenance trial in Canada (Commission of Inquiry into the Non-Medical Use of Drugs 1973).

Following the Le Dain Commission in the early 1970s, many Canadians believed that drug reform would follow (Martel 2006). Yet, external factors were unfolding that would indirectly impact Canadian drug policy. In 1971, U.S. President Richard Nixon coined the term "war on drugs." Nixon's efforts to scale up enforcement included increasing the size of drug enforcement agencies; widespread implementation of policies such as interdiction (stopping and searching people who fit the profile of "drug users" or couriers) on highways, buses, trains; and the saturation of low-income communities of colour with law enforcement, surveillance, undercover operations and raids (Drug Policy Alliance 2012). By the early 1980s, a renewed "war on drugs" emerged in North America led by the Reagan Administration in the U.S. The appearance of crack cocaine in late 1984 and 1985 in impoverished African-American and Latino communities in the U.S. became a rallying cry for Reagan's war on drugs. From 1986 to 1992, media, politicians and moral entrepreneurs portrayed crack as the most contagiously addicting and destructive drug known (Reinarman and Levine 1997). Numerous claims-makers — from media, including newspapers, magazines and television, to then-First Lady Nancy Reagan, promoted fears about crack. Erroneous and hyped claims about this drug helped to shape this renewed war on drugs in the U.S. The U.S. federal government and many states responded with harsh legislation and sentencing practices, including three-strike laws and mandatory minimum sentences that imprisoned disproportionate numbers of persons of colour (Reinarman and Levine 1997). This era was also marked by increased concern about international drug trafficking and its role in supplying drugs to North America. In 1988, Canadian legislators passed amendments to the *Criminal Code of Canada* and the *Narcotic Control Act* to create new offences related to the laundering of proceeds of drug crime and possession of property obtained through drug trafficking (Nolin and Kenny 2002: 285).

In 1987, the Canadian government launched a five-year, $210-million strategy, the National Drug Strategy. This would become the first in a series of national drug strategies. The 1987 strategy acknowledged the need to address both the supply and the demand sides of drug policy and included six components: education and prevention; treatment and rehabilitation; enforcement and control; information and research; international cooperation; and a national focus (aimed at identifying drug demand reduction programs that could serve a national purpose) (Collins 2006: 2). Despite declining levels of use of cannabis and cocaine, by the early 1990s increased resources were directed to drug control efforts in Canada, including the search for small-scale traffickers. During this time, enforcement efforts continued to focus on cannabis. In 1990, 64 percent of drug offences in Canada were for cannabis, the majority for simple possession. Convictions for cocaine rose from 2,793 in 1985 to 6,909 in 1989 and the proportion of federal inmates convicted under the *Narcotic Control Act* rose from 9 percent in 1986 to 14 percent in 1990 (Erickson 1992). Even with some funding going to education, treatment and more publicly funded services, criminal justice control remained primary.

In 1992, the federal government released a second version of its drugs strategy by merging the National Strategy to Reduce Impaired Driving and the National Drug Strategy. In 1998, this strategy was further refined by including four pillars as key strategic priorities: education and prevention; treatment and rehabilitation; harm reduction; and enforcement and control. Funding was significantly reduced in all but the last pillar, and many advocates involved in the field of drug use and abuse policy expressed concerns about the consequences of such financial cutbacks. In 1998, the Canadian Centre on Drug Abuse (CCSA) was created by an act of Parliament. Its purpose, which continues today, is to be the lead agency for the development of research and policy on "drug abuse." The Centre continues to be funded by the federal government.

In 1996, the *Food and Drug Act* and the *Narcotic Control Act* were merged into the *Controlled Drugs and Substances Act* (CDSA), the first major reform of Canada's drug legislation since the 1960s. It added 150 new substances and their precursors to the regulations of the Act. The Act continued the legacy of prohibition despite lesser penalties for cannabis possession. Section 55(1) expanded the powers of the government to make regulations under the act. Section 56 of the Act allowed the Minister of Health to grant exemptions for medical or scientific purposes or in the public interest. Like previous legislation, the schedules of the Act designated controlled substances and their associated penalties (Grayson 2008; Nolin and Kenny 2002: 294–295). The *Controlled Drugs and Substances Act* prohibits possession and trafficking of some drugs, and the import or export of illegal drugs.

This Act defines trafficking as the administering, transferring and selling of illegal substances. As of 2015 recreational use of cannabis remains illegal in Canada. However, the outcome of the federal election in 2015 may bring about legal reform in this area. The federal Liberal party campaigned to legally regulate and tax cannabis; thus promising to end cannabis prohibition in Canada.

The *Controlled Drugs and Substances Act* (1996) outlines the drugs that are illegal and provides the framework for penalties associated with drug crimes. The schedules attached to this legislation govern the severity of the penalties associated with drug crimes. To be clear, Canada's drug laws are harsh, especially in comparison to European nations. Drugs placed in Schedule 1, such as heroin and methamphetamine, carry the most severe penalties, such as incarceration (up to life imprisonment for trafficking and importing).

Provincial and territorial governments are primarily responsible for activities related to prevention, harm reduction and withdrawal management (detox), and drug treatment programs. Exceptions include First Nations peoples living on reserves, inmates in federal prisons and military personnel. Historically, the federal government has contributed to prevention and treatment initiatives with funding from its various drug strategies and through Health Canada. The federal government also funds the RCMP who, along with provincial and municipal police forces, are responsible for the enforcement of Canada's drug laws.

During the late 1990s and early 2000s several significant events occurred in Canada that challenged the historic legacy of drug prohibition. The first of these took place in Vancouver, prompted by a steep rise in heroin overdose and HIV/AIDS and hepatitis C inflections in the 1990s. In 1993, there were 350 deaths due heroin overdose in B.C. (Boyd, Osborn and MacPherson 2009: 72). By 1998, unofficial estimates of the rates of new HIV infections among people who use drugs was 18.5 percent (ibid.: 38). At the same time, the Vancouver Area Network of Drug Users (VANDU) was founded by a group of activists in the downtown eastside (DTES). The DTES had long been home to community-based activism (Boyd, Osborn and MacPherson 2009) and by 2000 was host to numerous political protests organized by and for people who use drugs. Bud Osborn, a founding member of VANDU, was nominated to the Vancouver-Richmond Health Board (ibid.). In 1997, under pressure from Osborn (and other community and health advocates), the Vancouver-Richmond Health Board declared a public health emergency for six health concerns, including hepatitis A, B and C, syphilis, HIV and overdose deaths. After much pressure from activists and health personnel the City of Vancouver also began to recognize the need for a new approach to drug use. Under the leadership of Mayor Philip Owen and Drug Policy Coordinator Donald MacPherson, *A Framework for Action: A Four-Pillar Approach to Drug Problems in Vancouver* was published in 2000. The Framework called for an approach that balanced public health concerns with enforcement issues to address illegal drug use in Vancouver. MacPherson wrote the Framework and drew on the Swiss model to create four pillars for action by a series of partners, including health services and police. These pillars recognized the need to balance the role of law enforcement with increased efforts to provide harm reduction, prevention and treatment services. Over the years numerous successful initiatives of the plan have been completed, including the establishment of Canada's first formally sanctioned safer injection site, Insite (City of Vancouver; Boyd, Osborn and MacPherson 2009).

At the federal level, a special committee of the Canadian Senate was struck in 2001 to examine the scientific literature on cannabis, including reports from twenty-three internationally renowned scientists and testimony from discussion groups and more than two hundred witnesses, from experts to ordinary citizens. In their final report the special committee asks:

> [if it is] appropriate that such considerable resources be funneled into the war against drugs in Canada to the detriment of other important government programs such as the reform of our health care system, education, job creation, and improving the competitiveness of the Canadian economy … The Auditor General's 2001 annual report reveals, over 95% of [Canada's Anti-Drug Strategy] is spent applying the criminal law.

The special committee recommended a legal system of regulated access for cannabis and an amnesty for any person convicted of possession of cannabis under current or past legislation.

On May 17, 2001, the House of Commons created the Special Committee on Non-Medical Use of Drugs based on a motion brought forward by Randy White, M.P. (Langley–Abbotsford) and gave it a very broad mandate to study "the factors underlying or relating to the non-medical use of drugs in Canada" and to bring forward recommendations aimed at reducing "the dimensions of the problem involved in such use" (Jürgens 2002: 9). The Committee issued in November 2002 a report on the Non-Medical Use of Drugs in Canada. The report highlighted a number of important areas in this field, including: the use and harmful use of substances; dependence in Canada; Canada's drug strategy, research and knowledge; public health issues, substance use and public safety; international treaties and legislative reform; and drug policies abroad. In 2003, the federal government announced that it would invest $245 million over the next five years in its drug strategy. The four pillars of the renewed strategy were prevention, treatment, harm reduction and enforcement. By 2004, Canada had moved toward a position somewhat more supportive of harm reduction policies than in previous years (Jürgens 2004: 7–8).

A review of the drug strategy found that approximately three-quarters of the resources had been directed towards enforcement-related efforts, despite a lack of scientific evidence to support this approach and little, if any, evaluation of the impacts of this investment. The authors concluded that, from a scientific perspective, an effective national drug strategy should ensure that federal funds are directed towards cost-effective, evidence-based prevention, treatment and harm reduction services, and that these services should be available to all Canadians (DeBeck, Wood et al. 2006).

In 2004, Canada's federal Liberal government attempted to decriminalize both possession and cultivation of small quantities of cannabis. Though these legislative amendments came to a decided halt with the election of a federal Conservative government in early 2006, they are often touted as evidence of Canada's more "enlightened" approach to drug policy compared to that of the U.S. Despite these seemingly "benign" or more "progressive" efforts, Canada's approach to drug regulation remained firmly prohibitive right up until 2015, employing law enforcement, the courts and social policy to eliminate drug use and production. The election of a majority Liberal federal government in the fall of 2015 may bring about drug policy reform in Canada. As noted earlier, the Liberal Party promised to end cannabis prohibition and supports harm reduction initiatives such as safer injection sites.

THE NATIONAL ANTI-DRUG STRATEGY

In 2006, a Conservative minority government was elected and, in 2007, introduced a new drug policy framework for Canada entitled the National Anti-Drug Strategy (NADS). This new anti-drug strategy unilaterally repositioned the previous strategy, Canada's Drug Strategy, in effect since 1987 and renewed in 1992, 1997 and 2003.[1] The National Anti-Drug Strategy is a "horizontal initiative" comprised of twelve federal departments and agencies, led by the Department of Justice Canada (Department of Justice 2012). In 2007, and subsequent to this time, many groups in Canada have expressed concerns about key features of the NADS.

Note

1. For a historical overview of Canada's Drug Strategy, see <http://www.parl.gc.ca/information/library/PRBpubs/prb0615-e.html>.

4

DRUG USE
IN CANADA

Critical scholars argue that rather than eliminating drug use (and the illicit trade), prohibition of criminalized drugs has inadvertently fuelled the development of the world's largest illegal commodities market, estimated by the U.N. in 2005 at approximately $350 billion a year (Count the Costs 2012a). In addition, harsh drug laws appear to have no impact on the drug trade, drug use and addiction rates (Room and Reuter 2012; Murkin 2014). In fact, the U.S., which has historically adopted harsh prohibitionist policies, has high drug-use rates compared to European nations, such as the Netherlands, which advances a health approach (Room and Reuter 2012; SAMHSA 2012).

CANADIAN CONTEXT

The last national survey was conducted in 2012. The 2012 Canadian Alcohol and Drug Use Monitoring Survey (CADUMS) pegs average use of all illegal substances for individuals 15 years of age and over at 42.3 percent for lifetime use (any use in a respondent's lifetime) and 10.6 percent for past year use (use within the last twelve months). In 2012, for past year use, men were more likely to use illegal drugs than women (men at 14.3 percent and women at 7.1 percent), although women were more likely to report the use of all types of pain relievers (18.2 percent for women and 15.5 percent for men in 2012) (CADUMS 2012).

Overall, cannabis was the most widely used illegal drug with 41.5 percent of Canadians indicating they have used this drug in their lifetime and 10.2 percent in 2012. These figures vary by province with B.C. having the highest rates of lifetime use at 48.7 percent and the highest rates of use for the past year at 13.8 percent. Overall, men are somewhat more likely than women to report having either used cannabis in their lifetime or in the last year.

Data from the 2012 CADUMS on the use of other illegal substances, such as methamphetamines/crystal meth, heroin, cocaine/crack, "ecstasy," "speed" and hallucinogens, are difficult to report because many of the estimates are suppressed due to high sampling variability, meaning that often too few people respond to the question to make the answer meaningful. But data from the 2012 CADUMS survey indicate that in the proceeding year use of cocaine and crack was about 1.1 percent in the general population (CADUMS 2012).

As far as we can determine with current data, the use of drugs like heroin and crack cocaine is mainly concentrated in marginalized populations. Data suggest that since the 1990s, use of stimulants such as crack or methamphetamine among street-involved people who use drugs has increased, primarily due to the low cost and easy availability of these substances. Crack is one of the most commonly used substances by this population (Fischer et al. 2012). Phase 2 of the I-Track study from 2005 to 2008 of people who inject drugs (a repeated study at regular intervals on people who inject drugs monitoring the prevalence of HIV and hepatitis C by the Public Health Agency of Canada conducted in ten cities across Canada) reported that the most commonly injected drugs in the last six months prior to the interview were cocaine (53.1 percent), non-prescribed morphine (14.2 percent), heroin (7.8 percent) and dilaudid or hydromorphone (7.1 percent) (Public Health Agency of Canada 2013: 12). In Phase 3 of the 1-Track study across eleven different sites in Canada from 2010 to 2012 the most commonly injected drugs in the six months

Table 1: Cannabis Use in Canada, 2012

	N	Lifetime Use %	Past Year Use %
Canada	11,090	41.5	10.2
Newfoundland	1,008	38.7	11.0
PEI	1,008	40.9	10.6
Nova Scotia	1,009	42.4	12.1
New Brunswick	1,009	36.4	8.5
Quebec	1,008	40.6	9.0
Ontario	1,011	39.4	9.1
Manitoba	1,009	38.5	13.2
Saskatchewan	1,010	42.5	10.2
Alberta	1,009	44.3	11.4
British Columbia	2,009	48.7	13.8

Source: Adapted from Health Canada 2012: Table 2

prior to the interview were cocaine (64.3 percent), dilaudid or hydromorphone (47.2 percent), oxcycodone (37.7 percent) and heroin (26.7 percent) (Public Health Agency of Canada 2014: 6). A study of crack use in Vancouver demonstrated a large increase in crack use among injection drug users between 1996 and 2005: at baseline, 7.4 percent of participants reported ever using crack and this rate increased to 42.6 percent by the end of the study period (Werb et al. 2010).[1]

NON-MEDICAL USE OF PRESCRIPTION DRUGS

Non-medical use of prescribed opiates is now the fourth most prevalent form of substance use in Canada behind alcohol, tobacco and cannabis (Fischer and Argento 2012). Estimates of exactly how many Canadians use prescription opiates are hard to come by. The most reliable source, a phone survey conducted in Ontario on an annual basis, estimates that 23.9 percent of Ontarians used prescription opiates and 4 percent used these drugs non-medically (that is, without a doctor's prescription) in 2011 (Ialomiteanu et al. 2012). It is difficult to generalize these findings to Canada as a whole because prescribing of opiates varies from province to province (Fischer et al. 2011). The CADUMS study noted above found that 16.9 percent of respondents had used prescription pain relievers in 2012, although the survey cannot reliably estimate how many people used these drugs non-medically (CADUMS 2012). A study conducted in five Canadian cities of people who use drugs indicated that the non-medical use of prescription opiates was more prevalent than the use of heroin in every setting except Vancouver and Montreal (Fischer et al. 2005). Another study observed a relative increase of 24 percent from 2002 to 2005 in the proportion of the street-drug using population who used non-medical prescription opioids only (Popova et al. 2009). A more recent study found that the availability of prescribed opioids among people who use drugs in a Canadian setting increased markedly over a relatively short timeframe (2006 to 2010), despite persistent and high availability of heroin and cocaine (Nosyk et al. 2012). Regardless of the study in question, Canada is second only to the U.S. in dispensing levels of opioid drugs in the world.

YOUTH

Most provinces conduct school-based surveys of youth substance use, although the frequency and the types of questions asked on these surveys can vary from province to province. Notably, nine provinces — B.C., Ontario, Alberta, Manitoba, Quebec and the Student Drug Use Survey in the Atlantic Provinces (New Brunswick, PEI, Nova Scotia and Newfoundland and Labrador) — conduct regular surveys. The Canadian Centre on Substance Use (CCSA) sponsored a re-analysis of data from the 2007–08 round of these surveys to create comparable measures across the country.

Key findings from the 2007–08 school-based surveys include the following:

- Increase in use of alcohol and cannabis between Grade 7 and Grade 12. In Grade 7, depending upon the province, 3 percent to 8 percent report past year cannabis use versus 30 percent to 53 percent among Grade 12 students.
- Alcohol use is almost twice as prevalent as cannabis use (46 to 62 percent of students report alcohol use and 17 percent to 32 percent report use of cannabis in the past year). Consistently, more boys than girls use cannabis, though in some provinces girls report more lifetime alcohol use than boys in Grades 7 through 12.
- Aside from alcohol and cannabis, ecstasy (or what each student assumed was ecstasy) is the most prevalent drug (4 percent to 7 percent lifetime use).
- Use of other substances is not consistently available across the provinces due to survey design issues and low rates of response. Other than alcohol and cannabis, data are not available by gender or by age.
- 2.6 to 4.4 percent of students in some provinces for which data are available reported using inhalants.
- Steroids are used by 1.2 to 1.4 percent of students; lifetime use of heroin is only reported for four provinces and ranges from 0.8 to 1.3 percent of students. Only four provinces provide comparable measures of cocaine and crack use and three of these provinces separate out cocaine from crack. In B.C. 4.4 percent of students have used crack/cocaine. In three other provinces lifetime usage rates vary from 3.3 to 4.2 percent for cocaine and 1.3 to 2.1 percent for crack.
- Use of crystal methamphetamine ranges from 0.9 to 1.5 percent among students.
- The CADUMS data for 2012 found that young people between the ages of 15 and 24 were the most likely age group to use illegal substances, at 21.3 percent (in the year prior to the survey) (CADUMS 2012).
- Substance use among street-involved youth is much higher than among other youth. Surveillance data from seven urban centres across Canada suggests a lifetime prevalence of illicit drug use of 95.3 percent among street-involved youth. Additionally, 22.3 percent of street-involved youth had injected drugs at some time in their life (Hadland et al. 2009).
- Other data sources suggest that non-medical prescription drug use is also becoming an issue for youth. According to the 2009 Ontario Student Drug Use and Health Survey, 22 percent of Ottawa students said they had used a prescription drug non-medically in the past year. Of these, 70

percent said they got the drugs from home and a study of Toronto youth suggests that recreational use of prescribed opioids is on the increase (Pocock 2011).

HARMS OF SUBSTANCE USE

The harms of substance use are related to a number of sociological and individual factors including mental health and health status, levels of poverty, and purity and strength of a substance. Specific drug-related harms include blood-borne viruses, such as HIV or hepatitis C (HCV), skin and respiratory problems and disruption of personal functioning, including troubles with family, friends, co-workers and police, and drug overdose resulting in death or injury.

Sharing used syringes and other drug-use equipment is the main mode of HIV and HCV transmission among people who use drugs. Of the 2,358 new infections reported in Canada in 2010, 16.8 percent were attributed to injection drug use. These figures differ considerably from province to province, between men and women overall and for Aboriginal people compared to other Canadians. In 2010, 30.4 percent of new infections in women versus 13.5 percent of new cases in men were attributed to injection drug use. Cases of HIV attributed to injection drug use among Aboriginal peoples have gone up to more than 50 percent in the period spanning 2001 to 2008 (Public Health Agency of Canada 2010).

Rates of HIV infection related to injection drug use vary by location and population group. In Saskatchewan, for example, results from the 2009 Canadian Alcohol and Drug Use Monitoring Survey suggest that rates of drug and alcohol use in Saskatchewan were lower than the Canadian average for that year (CADUMS 2011). But rates of HIV in Saskatchewan have been rising, and Saskatoon has experienced some of the largest increases in the province. HIV continues to disproportionately affect marginalized populations, including young Aboriginal women and street-involved individuals. According to 2009 data, 77 percent of new cases of HIV diagnosed in the province were among individuals who inject drugs, and of this group, 84 percent were of Aboriginal ancestry (Bell, Dell and Duncan 2011).

The majority of HCV cases in Canada are among people who inject drugs. As of 2009, injection drug use was associated with 61 percent of newly acquired HCV cases with known risk factor information. In B.C., HCV infection related to injection drug use has decreased over the past decade due to increased harm reduction and other prevention measures. Elsewhere in Canada, studies show that people who inject drugs are infected with HCV within one to two years of initiating drug injecting behaviour, leaving a short but important period of time for interventions to prevent the transmission of HCV (Beasley et al. 2012).

HARMS RELATED TO PRESCRIPTION OPIOID USE

Whether people are using prescription opioids medically or non-medically, one of the most significant harms is overdose resulting in either non-fatal injury or death. With only a few provinces actively reporting overdose fatalities, it is difficult to gauge the extent of opioid-related overdose deaths and injuries across Canada (Fischer and Argento 2012). Nor does data exist to allow us to compare jurisdictions or to assess the extent or impact of non-fatal overdose-related injuries (for example, brain injury from lack of oxygen). The lack of data is a disturbing issue in Canada, especially when we look to the U.S. where comprehensive data on overdose is available from the U.S. Centers for Disease Control and Prevention (2013). What we do know is that prescription opioid-related deaths have risen sharply and are estimated to be about 50 percent of annual drug deaths (Fischer and Keates 2012). The annual rate of fatal overdoses for people who inject illegal drugs is estimated to be between 1–3 percent per year (Milloy et al. 2008). Out of 2,330 drug-related deaths in Ontario between 2006 and 2008, 58 percent (1,359) were attributed, either in whole or in part, to opioids (Maladi, Hildebrandt, Lauwers and Koren 2013). A 2015 report by the Municipal Drug Strategy Co-ordinator's Network of Ontario states that the province has "witnessed 13 years of increasing and record-setting opioid overdose fatalities, which now rank as the third leading cause of accidental death" (MDSCNO 2015: 1).

Between 2002 and 2010, there were 1654 fatal overdoses attributed to illegal drugs in B.C., and between 2002 and 2009 there were 2,325 illegal drug-related overdose hospitalizations (Vallance et al. 2012). Opioid-overdose deaths in B.C. in 2012 numbered 256, somewhat fewer than 2011 when there were 294 deaths. The greater number of deaths in 2011 was due in part to an increase in the purity of heroin on the street (BCCDC 2013). There were also 95 opioid-overdose deaths in Quebec in 2011, compared to 51 in 2000 (Carter and Graham 2013).

Overdose is also associated with both the medical and non-medical use of prescription drugs like opioid-based painkillers. Non-medical use of prescribed opioids is now the fourth most prevalent form of substance use in Canada behind alcohol, tobacco and cannabis, and Canada and the U.S. lead all nations in prescription opioid consumption (Fischer and Argento 2012; Fischer, Bibby and Bouchard 2010). In October 2012, the B.C.-based Interior Health Authority released a warning that overdoses in that region from legally prescribed non-methadone opioid use were about twice the B.C. provincial rate; most of these overdoses occurred among people who were prescribed opioids along with other medications.[2] U.S. longitudinal studies have also noted the high risk of overdose when prescribed opioids are used with benzodiazepines and/or alcohol (Calcaterra, Glanz and Binswaner 2012).

GENDER

Feminist scholars have brought our attention to how women's health needs are medicalized. Some (Cooperstock and Hill 1982; Currie and BC Centre of Excellence for Women's Health 2004) have cautioned that women as a group, and First Nations women in particular, are overprescribed benzodiazepines (anti-anxiety medications) and sleeping pills. As researchers suggest, physicians "prescribe benzodiazepines (tran-

What Are Opioids?

Opioids are a class of drugs that share physiological properties. Opioid drugs are primarily used to relieve pain and can produce a sense of euphoria. As the Centre for Mental Health and Addictions in Toronto states:

Some opioids, such as morphine and codeine (also called opiates), occur naturally in opium, a gummy substance collected from the seed pod of the opium poppy, which grows in southern Asia. Semi-synthetic opioids, such as heroin, oxycodone (e.g., OxyContin), hydromorphone (e.g., Dilaudid) or hydrocodone, are made by changing the chemical structure of naturally occurring opioids. Synthetic opioids, such as methadone and meperidine (e.g., Demerol) are made from chemicals without using a naturally occurring opioid as a starting material (Centre for Addiction and Mental Health 2010).

quilizers) and sleeping pills to help women cope with work or family stress, pre-menstrual syndrome, grief and adjustment to life events, such as childbirth and menopause, or for chronic illness and pain. Non-drug treatments for these circumstances and conditions are under-promoted and under-used" (Currie and BC Centre of Excellence for Women's Health 2004). Past-year use of sedatives is higher for women (12.8 percent) than for men (7.5 percent) (CADUMS 2012). In addition, women are prescribed antidepressants twice as often as men (Mintzes 2010: 42). Critics argue that women are prescribed more mood-altering drugs than men, such as selective serotonin reuptake inhibitors (SSRIs) and tranquilizers, to help them cope with "problems that stem from their subordinate status in society" (Boyd 2015: 56). Although many drugs available to Canadians are beneficial and improve health, women (and men) need more than drug solutions (whether legally prescribed or bought on the illegal market) to "poverty, racism, sexism, lack of housing, poor nutrition, environmental pollution, and violence" (Boyd 2015: 56).

Women also visit their doctor and come into contact with the medical professionals more often than men because their health needs and their caretaking roles differ from their male counterparts. Women's higher rate of doctor visits is directly related to reproduction needs (such as menstruation, birth control, pregnancy, birth and menopause) and their role as caretakers of their families' health (Ettore 1992; Ford and Saibal 2010; Mintzes 2010).

In addition, women who inject drugs have twice the number of deaths than men

(Spittal et al. 2002). In a review of coroner case files for illegal drug overdose deaths of individuals in B.C. between 2001 and 2005, it was found that Aboriginal peoples were overrepresented and Aboriginal women were more likely than Aboriginal men to die. The place of death for Aboriginal women was most likely to be the Downtown Eastside (DTES) of Vancouver, an urban neighbourhood characterized by extreme poverty (Miloy et al. 2010). In an ethnographic study of women (46 percent of the women surveyed were Aboriginal) who used crack cocaine in the DTES, the participants described constant physical pain related to violence, chronic illness, past injuries, arthritis and lack of proper health and dental care. Despite the high levels of pain recorded, the women pointed out that there were "significant barriers" to obtaining pain medication (Bungay et al. 2010).

An earlier study conducted by the Vancouver Area Network of Drug Users (VANDU) Women's Care Team also reported similar results for women in the DTES of Vancouver who injected drugs and smoked crack cocaine (VANDU Women's Care Team 2009). At the time of the study, several Downtown Eastside "community health clinics for example, posted signs that it was against 'clinic policy' to prescribe Tylenol 3® or other opiates" (Bungay et al. 2010: 324). Given that we live in a society where legal drug-taking is normalized, it may be surprising to learn that many groups of people have less access to pain medication. However, it is well documented that people who use illegal drugs are under-medicated for pain due to structural barriers and myths about drug-seeking behaviour (Alford, Compton and Samet 2006; Bungay et al. 2010; Compton 1994). Bungay et al. (2010: 328) reveal the "complex nature of women's relationship with [crack cocaine] ... and the significant influence that structural inequities and 'everyday' violence have for this relationship." The researchers note that their "findings suggest that the factors that most contribute to women's suffering are broader than, and serve as precursors to, their drug use and are intricately related to the ever-present racism, sexism and poverty that construct their experiences" (ibid.). These findings suggest that any strategy to address drug use must account for population differences, such as gender and First Nations status, and must be rooted in an examination of the sociological context of substance use.

BENEFITS OF SUBSTANCE USE

There are undoubtedly perceived and sometimes real benefits of psychoactive substance use, even if the substances used are illegal and deemed of no medical or scientific value. Research demonstrates that most drug use is not problematic; it is a social and cultural practice that does not need to be criminalized or medicalized (Reinarman and Granfield 2015). Of course, many psychoactive but illegal substances are also used medicinally or in therapeutic settings (such as LSD, MDMA,

Ayahuasca) to great benefit, including opioids for pain relief, stimulants for ADD and ADHD and cannabis for relief of many symptoms of illness. In fact, the federal government in Canada operates a medical cannabis program for patients who use this drug for therapeutic purposes. Reported anecdotal benefits from non-medical uses of different kinds of substances include pleasure and relaxation, cognitive or creative enhancement, heightened aesthetic appreciation (food, music, art, sex), mystical or spiritual experiences and pain relief. However, the politics of drug research mean that few researchers think about or inquire into benefits of substance use and few have systematically developed an approach for measuring such benefits. Intellectually, this means that most drug research ignores the reasons people choose to take drugs and why they value them. Systematically assessing both the medical and non-medical benefits of substance use might shed more light on why people use drugs and provide information that can help prevent the harms associated with substance use (Tupper 2008).

Examining ethnographic studies and practices conducted around the world, Coomber and South argue that some forms of drug use are positive and enhance cohesiveness and the social health of some groups of people (Coomber and South 2004: 16). The researchers stress that drug use differs in different cultures, settings and historical moments; thus perceiving drug use as only damaging or bad makes invisible the diverse drug-taking practices in Canada and around the globe at different historical moments.

Notes

1. CCENDU reports on Ottawa also suggest increasing crack use. See Pocock 2011.
2. See Carter and Graham 2013.

5

FEDERAL DRUG POLICY: A FAILED DRUG STRATEGY

As we noted in Chapter 1, beginning in 1987, a series of drug strategies outlined the principles of federal policy. By 2003, the Liberal federal government announced an investment of $245 million over the subsequent five years to renew its drug strategy by focusing on four broad areas: enforcement, prevention, treatment and harm reduction. These strategies reflect a long debate about how to address drugs — as a health issue or as a criminal matter. As recently as 2005, this debate culminated in a number of policy decisions that emphasized the health aspects of drug use, including a renewed framework for action on substance use that contained expanded harm reduction, treatment and other supports (Health Canada and the Canadian Centre for Substance Abuse 2007).

However, beginning in 2007, the federal Conservative government initiated the National Anti-Drug Strategy (NADS), a $527.8 million effort to address illegal drug use. This strategy was accompanied by other "tough-on-crime" efforts that expand a punitive approach while doing little to address the root causes of crime. Further amplifying this shift, in 2008 the leadership for the new NADS was removed from Health Canada and relocated within the Department of Justice.

THE NATIONAL ANTI-DRUG STRATEGY

When the new strategy was announced, Tony Clement, Minister of Health in 2007, reportedly stated to the Canadian Press, "In the next few days, we're going to be back in the business of an anti-drug strategy ... In that sense, the party's over" (CBC News 2007). Clement's comments echoed the get-tough-on-drugs stance of the then new Conservative government. The NADS is a "horizontal initiative" comprised of twelve federal departments and agencies, led by the Department of Justice Canada. The initiation of this strategy was informed by antagonism against previous government drug strategies that included policies such as harm reduction. The priority areas of the NADS include preventing illicit drug use, treating illicit drug dependency and combating the production and distribution of illicit drugs. Official government documents give few insights into how these priorities will be implemented although a focus on youth was highlighted in the prevention and treatment priorities.

The NADS continues a long tradition of using law enforcement and criminal justice strategies as the primary means of addressing illegal drug issues. Demand and supply reduction is a central focus of the NADS (Department of Justice 2012). Thus, in keeping with the Conservative Party's primary focus on law and order at that time, it is not that surprising that law enforcement (police, courts and corrections) received the largest percentage of Anti-Drug Strategy funding, and $67.7 million more was allocated above the budget allocation for mandatory minimum penalties enacted in 2012 (Department of Justice 2012). The principles that underscore the NADS have been used to justify an increased range of mandatory minimum sentences for drug and gun crimes; parole review criteria have been abolished or tightened; and reduced credit for time served in pre-trial custody and restricted use of conditional sentences have been eliminated (CIC 2012). A wide variety of evidence suggests these approaches have limited effects in deterring drug demand and supply or increasing overall public safety (Degenhardt al. 2008). And overall tough sentences do not deter people from committing crimes (Elliot 2011; Siren and Applegate 2006). Nor does the 2012 NADS evaluation draw from research findings from other countries that have moved away from law-and-order approaches to health-centred approaches. For example, in 2001 Portugal decriminalized the possession of all drugs for personal use. They moved from a criminal justice to a health approach, setting up social supports and harm reduction and more diverse drug-treatment services (Moreira, Hughes, Storti and Zobel 2011). Rigorous evaluation of the new strategy followed, demonstrating that addiction and drug-use rates did not increase, including youth rates. In addition, there was no increase in drug-related crime, and the prison population decreased significantly (Murkin 2014). In fact, Portugal is not the only county to implement a health approach to illegal drug use; more than twenty-five countries world-wide have eliminated criminal penalties for the personal possession of all or some drugs (Murkin 2014: 2). Yet, the most recent evaluation of the NADS ignores the global shift from punitive drug strategies to more health-centred strategies. The outcome of the 2015 federal election, which resulted in a majority Liberal government win, may begin a process to repeal a number of tough-on-crime laws and funding streams for drug enforcement and prison building that were introduced by the preceding Conservative-led government.

DRUG USE PREVENTION IN THE NADS

The NADS stressed the importance of prevention in achieving the goals of curbing (illegal) drug use. As part of its Prevention Action Plan, the federal National Anti-Drug Strategy (NADS) provided increased funding to the RCMP's Drugs and Organized Crime Awareness Service (DOCAS). Programs developed under DOCAS include the Aboriginal Shield Program, Drug Abuse Resistance Program (DARE), Drug Endangered Children, Deal.org, Drugs and Sport: The Score, E-aware, Organized Crime Awareness, Drug Awareness Officers Training, the Community Education Prevention Continuum and the Racing Against Drugs Program. Other programs receiving funding included the Prevent Alcohol and Risk-Related Trauma Youth Program (P.A.R.T.Y.), Keep Straight, and Building Capacity for Positive Youth Development (Ference, Weicker and Company n.d.). These programs reiterate how dangerous criminalized drugs are, the risk of addiction, and abstinence as the solution. Monies were also allocated to prevention projects funded under the Drug Strategies Community Initiatives Fund, though a complete list of these projects and their outcomes was unavailable (ibid.: 24).

The mass media campaign, comprised of TV, radio, web and print materials, which received $13,889,000 between 2007 and 2010, was not renewed in the second funding period (2012–17) (Ference, Weicker and Company n.d.: 9). No indication was given of the reasons for the elimination of this mass media campaign. However, in 2014 the federal government at that time initiated a new media campaign about marijuana and youth, which we discuss below.

Additionally, as part of the NADS, the Canadian Centre on Substance Abuse (CCSA) prepared a document entitled *A Drug Prevention Strategy for Canada's Youth*. This strategy was one of the recommendations for action in the 2005 *National Framework for Action to Reduce the Harms Associated with Alcohol and Other Drugs and Substances in Canada*. The goals of this strategy include reducing drug use by youth, delaying onset of use and reducing frequency of use. It also identifies three activities it will use to reach these goals, including: development of a Media/ Youth Consortium to help carry forward the anti-drug messages in the NADS; the development of national standards for prevention; and creation of "sustainable partnerships," including a number of working groups to provide advice on the development of national standards and media-youth connections. This strategy promised an impact evaluation of these efforts that will draw on existing data on youth drug use. To date, this evaluation has not been released by the Canadian Centre on Substance Abuse (CCSA 2007).

TREATMENT IN THE THE NADS

One of the initiatives that the NADS continued from earlier federal drug strategies was the Drug Treatment Funding Program (DTFP). This program is managed by Health Canada and provides funding to initiatives across the country focused on system development for drug treatment services. Despite concerns about the overall direction of the NADS, other jurisdictional scans suggest that the DTFP funding has been an important driver of innovation. An example is the "Needs-Based Planning Model" research undertaken at the Centre for Addiction and Mental Health (CAMH) in Toronto. This project is developing methods for estimating the actual population-based need for substance-use services and supports in Canada, an important endeavour given that funding for drug-treatment services has often been driven by political priorities rather than estimations of the actual need for services in the population. The effect of this history of drug treatment is that many regions of Canada are highly underserved. These issues will be discussed in more detail in the next chapter.

Problems with the NADS

This strategy is not national, in that it was not developed in collaboration with, or endorsed by, provinces and territories. More accurately, it is a federal government strategy. And many groups in Canada have expressed concerns about key features of the NADS, including the Canadian Nurses Association and the CAMH in Ontario among others (Canadian Association of Nurses 2011). The CAMH criticized the lack of focus in the NADS on alcohol, prescription drug use issues and harm reduction. A brief prepared by the CAMH on this issue urged the federal government to consider evidence that shows that alcohol, a legally available substance, has significant health and social harms. The brief criticized the federal government for undertaking such a limited definition of substances, one that effectively excluded ones that were currently legally regulated.

The CAMH also drew attention to the abrupt exclusion of harm reduction policies in the NADS. Until 2007, the federal government had included this approach to drug use in its national strategies. The CAMH brief took note of the fact that many provinces include harm reduction in their provincial strategies, yet the Conservative Party-led federal government had eliminated it from the federal approach (Canadian Association of Nurses 2011). The CAMH, like other critics, took note of the renewed emphasis on abstinence and deterrence through the criminal justice system in the NADS. The Canadian Nurses Association also noted:

> Provincial and international policies have increasingly shifted toward harm reduction whereas Canadian federal drug policy appears to be embracing a law enforcement approach in spite of a lack of evidence that such approaches are effective. Such tensions produce a policy schism in which RNs [registered nurses] may be caught between evidence, ethics and policy. (Canadian Association of Nurses 2011: 3)

Other critics also queried the exclusion of harm reduction and noted that federal Conservative politicians assumed that harm reduction is antithetical to the goal of abstinence.

The past Conservative-led federal government's approach to drug policy did not address the broad social determinants of problematic substance use. Therefore, there was little if any coordinated effort to address issues like poverty, homelessness, cultural dislocation and lack of economic opportunity, which tend to affect rates of problematic substance use. For example, the harms of drug use are often exacerbated by homelessness with increased harms associated with the twin problems of substance use and lack of housing (Johnson and Fendrich 2007). Critics have suggested that issues of poverty, homelessness and political disenfranchisement must be addressed to make an impact on the harms of drug use.

Under NADS, law enforcement initiatives received the overwhelming majority of drug strategy funding (70 percent) while prevention (4 percent), treatment (17 percent) and harm reduction (2 percent) combined continue to receive less than a quarter of the overall funding (DeBeck, Wood et al. 2009). In 2012, the Department of Justice released the budget for the next five years of the NADS (2012–13 to 2016–17). Compared to the first five years (2008–09 to 2011–12), the overall budget has decreased almost 12 percent (Treasury Board of Canada). These figures do not account for the myriad of other enforcement activities that go on at the municipal, provincial and federal levels.

Alcohol

CAMH population studies have shown that alcohol is the most widely consumed drug, with 79 percent of adults and 65 percent of students drinking alcohol in the past year (CAMH Population Studies eBulletin 2008; Adlaf and Boak 2007). The level of problematic drinking is concerning. The CAMH monitor reports that about one-third of drinkers exceed the low-risk drinking guidelines and the Ontario Student Drug Use and Health Survey has identified binge drinking among students as a potential public health flag because over one quarter of students had consumed at least five drinks on the same occasion in the past year.

Despite decreases in overall spending, the budget for 2012–17 signals significant changes in the priorities of the NADS. Funding for the Drug Treatment Funding Program (DTFP) and the Drug Strategies Community Initiatives Fund (DSCIF) have been decreased and funding for Crime Prevention Programs has also been eliminated (see DSCIF 2015). Despite promising efforts, funding for the DTFP has decreased from $124.7 in 2007–12 to $80.4 million in 2012–17.[1] The one bright spot is a funding increase to National Native Alcohol and Drug Abuse Program from $36 to $45 million, though it is certainly too early to tell if this funding will be used to create diverse services and whether it will address the scope of issues identified by Aboriginal peoples in Canada.

At the same time, components of the NADS related to the criminal justice system received increased funding, including the RCMP, Correctional Service of Canada, Parole Board of Canada and the Canada Border Security Agency. Overall the RCMP will receive an additional $16 million (for a total of $112.5 million) between 2012 and 2017 for enforcement against marijuana-growing operations and clandestine drug labs. In addition, as mentioned above, $67.7 million has been allocated on top of the budget for mandatory minimum penalties (Department of Justice 2012). These budget increases may shift as the federal government implements its plan to legally regulate cannabis, thus ending cannabis prohibition.

This strategy only accounts for a portion of federal government spending on drug control. Common drug enforcement activities, such as drug interdiction, border services, use of military personnel in international drug control efforts and costs of prison expansion, are not fully included in the NADS. Interdiction, for example, includes efforts to seize drugs, couriers or vessels, between source countries and Canada, including as they enter the country. Accounting for expenditures on interdiction is complicated, since many interdiction efforts serve multiple functions, not just drug control. Nor can policing and corrections costs related to drugs be easily determined. Like drug interdiction, policing and corrections costs are not easily broken down in terms of amount of resources spent on drug enforcement and incarceration due to drug crime. Canadians need more transparency when it comes to the costs and effectiveness of current policies.

The government's own in-house reviews of the NADS suggest other problems. An evaluation of the implementation of the strategy, conducted in 2008, found that there were significant differences between the approach taken by the provinces and the one espoused by the federal government. As the evaluators noted, the "focus on substance abuse in general rather than abuse of illegal drugs, support harm reduction, and take a more holistic approach to substance use issues (for example, many provinces have integrated or are integrating mental health and addictions)" (EDOSPPM 2010). Evaluators also noted other points of discord: Canada's approach at that time did not accord with international developments, including recent calls by some Latin American countries to rethink prohibition as the main means of preventing drug use (see Global Commission on Drug Policy 2011).

A follow-up review of the NADS by the government, released in 2012, pointed out that provinces continue to offer a range of approaches to substance use. Stakeholders surveyed about the NADS noted the lack of coordination between treatment services in Canada. They "rated the need for programming that supports effective treatment and rehabilitation services at 4.9 (n=10), on a scale of 1 to 5, where 1 is no need at all and 5 is a major need" (Department of Justice 2012). Also, due to lack of funding, gaps in treatment services prevail (ibid.: 33). In the 2012 evaluation of the NADS, harm reduction was only briefly mentioned in one sentence in relation to strategies taken up in the Netherlands and Portugal. The 2012 evaluation makes no reference to harm reduction in Canada.

Additionally, the NADS also downplays the importance of robust health promotion programs and does not address the harms associated with legal drugs like alcohol. The NADS also touts a limited approach to prevention. Overall, many current approaches to drug prevention are plagued by a lack of success at eliminating or even curbing drug use among adolescents. Prevention efforts draw on a number of typical approaches, including mass media campaigns and universal classroom-based programs that focus on individual level behavioural change. Anyone younger than 75 in Canada can probably recall participating in some sort of school-based program meant to discourage drug use.

The Drug Abuse Resistance Education (DARE) program is likely one of the most widely implemented drug prevention initiatives, supposedly reaching over 36 million children in forty-nine countries worldwide (Hyshka 2013: 114). In Canada, the DARE program is used by the RCMP and many of its provincial divisions, including B.C. Typically, DARE programs are delivered in schools by police officers and focus on issues like peer pressure, youth deficits in knowledge about drugs and personal and social skills training, all of which are supposed to help youth say no to drugs (RCMP 2013). Evaluations of DARE indicate that there is a lack of evidence demonstrating that these programs have long-term positive effects on levels of drug use (Kilmer et al. 2012). In response to the critiques of DARE, it was revamped in 2001 with components added to its program that enhanced life skills and drew on more constructivist approaches that emphasize interaction and skill development. Yet support for the effectiveness of this revamped approach remains dubious (Hyska 2013: 114). Adding to this is the fact that few other prevention programs have passed the scrutiny of rigorous evaluation (Cuijers 2003). In Canada it is also difficult to track the effects of these prevention programs on drug use especially given that there are no overall strategies that identify goals against which effects could be measured; and there is no way to know if the programs currently in use are weak or poorly implemented or both (Kilmer et al. 2012: 45).

To date, no long-term assessment of these NADS-funded programs has been conducted. There is also no comprehensive accounting for the content of these programs, nor has the federal government or the RCMP publicly released any information on their effectiveness. The methods used for the CCSA evaluation and its results will be keenly important to assessing the effectiveness of the NADS. Additionally, the need for national standards for prevention programs is particularly acute given the number of community-based and other organizations that offer drug prevention programs to young people. It is, however, beyond the scope of this book to evaluate either the content or the effectiveness of the CCSA standards. There are, however, excellent resources that point to the best practices in prevention as described below.

The other mainstay of drug prevention programs is the "public service message" conveyed through a number of mediums, including TV, radio, newspapers and, more recently, the internet. A mass media campaign directed toward youth was part of the NADS funding for 2007–12. It generated a website — "Drugs Not for Me" — and series of PSAs featuring youth and the supposed effects of drug use shown on TV, in print media and as trailers in movie theatres. One short video depicted a handsome blonde male youth (around age 14) in a youthful party situation. In the video he is offered a toke of marijuana from some multi-racial friends. He quickly flashes forward to series of consequences of using marijuana, including fighting with his parents, using harder drugs, getting in trouble with teachers and falling asleep in the classroom. Based on these images he decides against trying marijuana. The video manages to very quickly emphasize common myths about marijuana use: that it is a gateway to hard drug use and that even one toke can lead to excessive personal consequences. The depiction of his friends as racialized youth is disturbing given that some groups of racialized youth have long been stereotyped as drug users with devastating consequences.

The other companion video in this series depicts a young white girl (around age 15) in her suburban bedroom. In the video she does not leave her room but is shown using drugs, likely a stimulant. As the video unrolls, her physical appearance degrades and she is finally shown cutting off her own hair in front of a mirror. The videos are meant to illustrate the supposedly gendered consequences of drug use — undermining of personal success at school for boys and the destruction of physical appearance for girls. These videos are another entry in a long line of similar attempts to curb drug use using simplistic messaging and slogans. Studies of similar mass media campaigns show little if any positive long-term effects on levels of drug use. What is more worrisome is that these campaigns are expensive to produce and disseminate with little to show for them. In fact, a meta-analysis of studies of these programs suggested that while they may have little effect on adolescent drug use, "anti-drug PSAs may nevertheless contribute to support for abstinence and enforcement-based policy response to illicit drug use" (Werb et al. 2011: 838).

Ignoring studies that suggesting that anti-drug ads are ineffective, the past Conservative-led government launched a new campaign on marijuana in November 2014. Critics argue that the $7.5 million taxpayer-funded Conservative-led government anti-drug campaign by Health Canada is in direct response to the Liberal Party of Canada's support for legally regulating marijuana (Curry 2014; McGregor 2014). The past federal government posted an anti-marijuana ad on YouTube to alert parents and youth about the dangers of the drug. They also advertised in other media formats, such as radio, newspapers and TV. In addition, attack ads were directed at Liberal leader Justin Trudeau and his support for legally regulating marijuana. The YouTube clip and ads claim that marijuana is three hundred to four hundred times stronger than it was thirty years ago, that the drug harms teen's brains and that marijuana can damage a teen for life. All of these claims are unsubstantiated. In fact, when Health Canada asked professional physician groups (the Canadian Medical Association, the College of Family Physicians of Canada and the Royal College of Physicians and Surgeons of Canada) to endorse the campaign against marijuana, they said no (McGregor 2014). In fact, the physician groups sent out a media statement: "We did not, and do not, support or endorse any political messaging or political advertising on this issue" and the spokesperson for the Royal College stated that the anti-marijuana campaign "has now become a political debate" that they do not endorse (ibid.).

Prevention-Promising Practices in Health Promotion

A substantial research base points toward more effective models that have been proven to reduce health-related and community concerns attributable to drug use and reduce the unintended negative effects of drug policies (Wood et al. 2012: 19). There is little evidence to support the use of prevention initiatives that simply use scare tactics or simplistic messages about the hazards of drug use. But there is no magic bullet or one program that can eradicate the harms of substance use. Programs that mobilize community-wide efforts (Kilmer et al. 2012) and programs that are part of larger health promotion activities show promise particularly when these programs support the development of young people's social and emotional learning skills (Durlak et al. 2011). These programs do not focus directly on substance use; rather, reduced substance use is one of the benefits of improved decision making skills (Kilmer et al. 2012: 23).

Successful programs also draw on well-established principles of health promotion (health promotion is the process of enabling people to increase control over and to improve their health) (World Health Organization 1986). Health promotion recognizes that good health and healthy decision making are a result of healthy environments. It focuses on both universal and tailored strategies. Universal strategies address large-scale inequities in supports for health like adequate income and housing, access to information and supportive environments. One example is programs that provide support to parents before, during and after the birth of children. Evidence suggests these programs can contribute to healthy child development and appear to help reduce behavioural problems in children as they grow up (Toumbourou et al. 2007). At the level of school programs, newer initiatives informed by this evidence embed substance education in larger health promotion efforts that help students learn critical skills needed to make healthy decisions. Prevention programs in schools also appear to be more successful when they include a number of strategies and occur over a number of years (ibid.). These programs contrast significantly with prevention efforts focused solely on the "notion that drug use is the product of an individual's susceptibility to peer pressure" (Hyska 2013: 113). Peer networks are an important component of adolescent development and can influence substance use. But the direction of the relationship is unclear. It may be that adolescents select friends based on mutual interests, including drug use. In fact, simplistic notions of peer pressure overlook the "agency of adolescents to select their own peers and choose or abstain from drugs" (ibid.: 112). Research by Tim Rhodes on adolescent substance use suggests it is affected by complex social networks and is more a part of an active set of choices in keeping with social contexts and group norms (Rhodes 2009).

A growing body of research argues "there is essentially no relationship between the punitiveness of a country's drug laws and its rates of drug use. Instead, drug use tends to rise and fall in line with broader cultural, social or economic trends" (Murkin 2014: 2). Thus, strategies to prevent injuries and other harms are useful, as are recognizing the cultural, economic and social factors that shape drug use. In the light of these findings, the approach to prevention supported by the NADS is potentially quite limited. Though the CCSA has established standards that could positively reorient prevention approaches, overall efforts are hampered by the vision of the NADS that still conceptualizes prevention as a matter simply of reduced drug use. The NADS does not look beyond to the social conditions that shape substance use; nor does the strategy measure effectiveness of its programming in terms of overall attitudes and behaviours toward all substances, including alcohol.

> **Social Context**
>
> Social context can seem like a vague concept but it is a complex phenomena affected by government policies and laws; social network norms and values; economic policies and practices of the private sector; spatial issues such as urbanity and relative levels of housing; ideas and practices about gender and race; and meanings associated with drug use.

Note

1   See also *Development of Needs-Based Planning Models for Substance Use Services and Supports in Canada.* <http://needsbasedplanningmodels.wordpress.com/>.

6

THE "WAR ON DRUGS": CRIMINALIZING DRUG USE

In Canada, the use of particular drugs is regulated and controlled by the federal *Controlled Drugs and Substances Act* (CDSA), which includes possession, trafficking, importing and exporting and production-related offences. The seriousness of penalties included in the CDSA is related to the *perceived* levels of harm caused by each drug. The CDSA does not recognize that drugs such as alcohol and tobacco are at least as harmful as some illegal drugs.

As we illustrated in Chapter 2, historically, concerns about public safety have been linked to illegal drug use or drug dealing. In Canada, as in many nations around the world, the response to these concerns has been to increase the scope of laws, the severity of punishments and the scale of policing.

CRIMES RATES AND DRUG CRIME

In Canada, although law agents and government officials claim that drug policy and funds are directed at stopping high level production and selling of criminalized substances, drug statistics over time demonstrate that it is youth and poor and marginalized users who are most vulnerable to arrest, not high-level traffickers. In addition, rather than arrests for trafficking and production, drug possession makes up the majority of arrests in Canada. In 2013, 71 percent of all drug offences were for possession, and cannabis possession made up the majority of these arrests (54 percent) (Cotter, Greenland and Karam 2015: 3, 5). Bacchi's framework for policy analysis provides an "opportunity to question taken-for-granted assumptions that lodge in government" and medical policies related to the problem of illegal drugs. She claims that law-and-order discourse makes "drug use a matter of illegal behaviour" and people who use illegal drugs are "marked as addicts" (Bacchi 2009: 92). In Canada, people who use illegal drugs are also marked as criminals and subject to discrimination and punishment. Compared to the U.S., where drug crime has been a main driver of incarceration, Canada can seem like a more compassionate place when it comes to the regulation of drugs. But Canada has a record of increasing numbers of drug crimes and high levels of incarceration due to drug convictions. Although there has been a steady decrease in the crime rate in Canada — for example, in 2013, the crime rate was at its lowest since 1969 — the number of drug offences has been increasing since the early 1990s with a slight decrease of 2 percent in 2013 from the year before (Boyce, Cotter and Perreault 2014; Brennan 2012). In fact, from 1998 to 2011 the drug offence rate increased 39.5 percent (Public Safety Canada 2012: 1). In 2013, the police reported 109,057 drug offences. Seventy-one percent of all drug offences were for possession. Cannabis possession increased by 1 percent from the year before (Boyce, Cotter and Perreault 2014). In addition, 67 percent of the total drug offences were for cannabis, primarily for possession (Cotter, Greenland and Karam 2015: Table 1).

Similar to previous years, in 2013, B.C. reported the highest rate of drug offences among the provinces. While B.C. also had the highest rate for cannabis offences, Saskatchewan reported the highest rate of cocaine offences (Boyce Cotter, and Perreault 2014: Table 6). Keep in mind that "rates" measure police-reported offences per 100,000 population. Thus, due to its larger population, more people in B.C. are arrested for drug offences than in Saskatchewan.

Increases or decreases in police-reported drug crime do not necessarily represent real changes in actual occurrences of crime. Police- reported crime statistics in Canada are compiled using the Uniform Crime Reporting (UCR) Survey, which collects information on all criminal incidents reported to, and substantiated by, Canadian police services. These data are based on a nationally approved set of common crime categories and definitions that have been developed in cooperation with the Canadian Association of Chiefs of Police. Data provided by the UCR reflects crime that comes to the attention of police.

The data in the UCR are made up of crimes known to the police; however, many crimes are unknown to the police. In addition, official crime statistics (and many crime surveys) disproportionately capture street crime and low-level crime rather than white collar or corporate crime. The focus on property crime and street crime (including drug offences) is directly related to legislation, the criminal code, selective police enforcement and priorities and profiling. Thus, crime statistics and data can be influenced by policing priorities that allocate time and resources to the detection of certain categories of crime (Brennan 2012: 11). The increase in police-reported drug offences may also be related to policy practices, resources, enforcement priorities and targeting of particular offenders or offences (Boyce, Cotter and Perreault 2014).

Crime rates are also shaped by the size of youth populations (historically, crime rates are higher for youth and crime rates increase when baby boom generations become young adults) in specific eras, police profiling, new laws and shifting police-enforcement practices, technological developments, political pressures and societal "intolerance for specific forms of behaviour" (Balfour and Comack 2006: 63). The increase in drug offences over the last thirty years does not reflect a rise in drug-use rates in Canada; thus, we can assume that the rise in drug arrests in Canada is largely do to other factors.

Given the steady increase in the percentage of Canadians who favour decriminalization or drug reform in relation to cannabis possession — in 2012, 66 percent of Canadians and 75 percent of British Columbians surveyed favoured the decriminalization of cannabis (Angus Reid 2012; 2011) — societal intolerance may not be at play in relation to rising drug arrests (the largest category of arrests is for possession of cannabis). Rather, the steady increase in drug offences is more probably linked to increased law-enforcement focus on this particular criminal activity, increases in resources for police enforcement, police targeting of drug offenders and specific urban and rural areas, vocal claims-makers and political pressure.

Renewed focus by the past Conservative-led government of Prime Minister Stephen Harper also shaped drug arrest rates. However, it would be a mistake to assume that all federal Conservative politicians are in favour of tough drug laws or that all federal Liberal and New Democratic Party politicians favour drug reform. However, over the last thirty years, the Conservative Party of Canada has taken on a law-and-order and tough-on-crime stance that includes drug offences and, with the enactment of the *Safe Streets and Communities Act* in 2012, harsher drug laws. Critics have long argued that since the 1980s the renewed "war on drugs" is fuelled by the conservative response to perceived liberalism and loss of power in the 1960s and 1970s (Willis 1992). In Canada, since 2007, the Conservative-led government of Canada renewed the "war on drugs." However, signalling a shift in policy, in 2015 the Liberal-led federal government pledged to end cannabis prohibition.

Youth crime also fell in 2013, continuing a downward trend that has been apparent for a number of years (Boyce, Cotter and Perreault 2014). These declines are explained by the enactment of the *Youth Criminal Justice Act* in 2003, which provided clear guidelines for the use of extrajudicial measures (that is, informal sanctions) (Brennan 2012: 21). Regardless, in 2013, roughly 17,000 youth were arrested for a drug violation. Eighty-one percent of the total arrests were for possession of cannabis (Boyce, Cotter and Perreault 2014).

Prisons in Canada

When a person is convicted of a crime in Canada, the judge imposes a sentence or punishment for breaking the law. The penalty ranges. A judge could impose a fine, probation, community service or imprisonment. Imprisonment is most often reserved for society's most heinous crimes. Even though Canada's crime rate has been falling, prison populations are rising. Between 2003 and 2013, the total prison population in Canada increased by 16.5 percent (an increase of almost 2,100 prisoners) and visible minority prisoners increased by 75 percent in that ten-year period (Sapers 2013).

About 55 percent of people incarcerated in federal prisons have problems with substance use (ibid.). Despite this clear need for in-prison treatment, prison-based substance use programming is also in decline; the Correctional Service of Canada budget for these programs fell from $11 million in 2008–09 to $9 million in 2010–11 (CIC 2012: 16). In addition, health care is the most common area of complaint received by the Office of the Correctional Investigator in Canada by people incarcerated in federal prisons (Public Safety Canada 2012: 31). Though Canada's rate of incarceration in 2013–14 was 118 per 100,000 people, a middle rate compared to many other nations in the world (for example, the U.S. at 707 and Iceland at 45), mandatory minimum sentences have the potential to push rates of incarceration higher in Canada (Correctional Services Program 2015). In fact, in 2013–14 although provincial/territorial incarceration rates fell by 3 percent from the previous year, the federal incarceration rate increased by 3 percent during the same period (Correctional Services Program 2015).

Programs and other services inside prison that help inmates transition to life after prison are also either in decline or plagued by lack of available resources. For instance, the safer tattooing initiative in prisons was cancelled in 2006 despite the effectiveness of such programs in curbing the spread of HIV and HCV (Harris 2009). This program recognized that tattooing takes place inside prison walls and that sharing of used equipment could potentially result in HIV and HCV infections. The Correctional Service of Canada (CSC) evaluated the program and found positive results, including an enhanced level of knowledge and awareness amongst staff and inmates regarding blood-borne infectious disease prevention practices. The evaluation also found that the initiative had the potential to reduce exposure to health risks and enhance the safety of staff members, inmates and the general public. The initiative also provided additional employment opportunities for inmates in the institution, and work skills that are transferable to the community (Correctional Service of Canada 2009). The passage of the *Safe Streets and Communities Act* in

2012 follows on these and other moves by the federal government that make prisons less safe and reduce the discretion of the judicial system in developing appropriate sentences for individuals convicted of drug crimes.

Canada's federal prison system is severely overcrowded, leading to increasing volatility behind bars. In the two-year period between March 2010 and March 2012, the federal in-custody population increased by almost 1,000 inmates or 6.8 percent, which is the equivalent of two large male medium-security institutions. As of April 1, 2012, more than 17 percent of people in Canada's prisons are double-bunked (meaning that two people are incarcerated in a cell that was built for only one occupant) (ibid.: 3). This increase occurred even before the imposition of mandatory minimum sentences, which will stress Canada's incarceration system even further. It is important to remember that in 2012, the year mandatory minimum drug sentences were enacted, already 26.7 percent of female federal offenders and 15.7 percent of male offenders were serving a sentence for a drug crime (Public Safety Canada 2012: 61).

To accommodate increases in Canada's prison population, the federal government planned to add 2,700 cells to thirty existing facilities at a cost of $630 million. By 2013, the government closed three federal facilities as part of budget reduction plan (Kingston Penitentiary and the Regional Treatment Centre in Ontario, and Leclerc Institution in Quebec). These closures affected one thousand people, who were relocated, including 140 people residing at the Ontario Regional Treatment Centre, a stand-alone facility at Kingston Penitentiary. The government argued that the closure of the three federal institutions and the transfer of prisoners to other facilities would save over one million dollars a year, yet there is little evidence of these savings. Rather, critics of the government's prison closures and transfers point to the social and personal cost of overcrowding, double-bunking and elimination of effective prison programs in Canada's (Sapers 2013, 2014).

Prisons, Race and Gender in Canada

The racial composition of prison populations in Canada is a stark reminder that prison sentencing is racially motivated. In addition, the increasing numbers of women in prison suggest the increased meting out of harsh sentences for low-level drug crimes. The number of Black prisoners increased by almost 90 percent between 2002 and 2013 (Sapers 2013). Over the last thirty years the number of women charged with a criminal offence has also risen in Canada and the increase is also reflected in the women's prison population (Mahoney 2011). Although Aboriginal people (including Metis and Inuit) make up 4.3 percent of the total Canadian population, Aboriginal women make up over 34 percent of all federally incarcerated women in Canada compared to 21.5 percent of Aboriginal men, an increase of 85.7 percent over the last ten years (Statistics Canada 2013: 4, 9; Office of the Correctional Investigator 2012: 4; Public Safety Canada 2012: 51; Public Safety Canada 2012: 53). Almost 27 percent of women compared to 16 percent of men were serving time in federal prison for a Schedule II drug offence in 2012 (Public Safety Canada 2012: 61).

In 2012, the Office of the Correctional Investigator noted that the overrepresentation of Aboriginal people in prison is worse in many provincial prisons, especially in the Prairie Provinces (CIC 2012: 11). In B.C., 47 percent of the women in provincial prisons in 2013 were racialized women; of these, 38 percent were Aboriginal women (BC Corrections 2014). In addition, 50 percent of the total number of women serving time in a B.C. provincial prison in 2013 were sentenced for a drug offence compared to 31 percent of men (ibid.).

Section 81 of the CCRA was intended to give CSC the capacity to enter into agreements with Aboriginal communities for the care and custody of offenders who would otherwise be held in a CSC facility. Section 84 was to enhance the information provided to the Parole Board of Canada and to enable Aboriginal communities to propose conditions for offenders wanting to be released into their communities.

The over-representation of Aboriginal and racialized peoples in Canadian prisons, and the higher percentage of women serving prison time for drug offences than men, are disproportionate to their drug-arrest rates, their drug-use rates and their involvement in the illegal drug trade. In fact, only 18 percent of people accused of a drug offence in 2013 were women and drug-use rates for women are much lower than men and most often women are not major players in the drug trade (Cotter, Greenland and Karam 2015: 16). Aboriginal drug use rates are not higher than rates for Caucasian people. However, women's involvement in the drug trade mirrors their social status in Canada; they are often at the lowest echelons of the drug trade, engaged in importing or exporting drugs, selling small amounts of illegal drugs on the street to support themselves and their families, or to support their own drug use (Boyd 2006). In 2013, drug offences for importing and exporting drugs had the highest proportion of women accused (29 percent) (Cotter, Greenland and Karam 2015; 16).

Most criminalized drugs enter Canada hidden in planes, boats, trucks and other transport vehicles that hold much larger quantities than what can be found on (or in) an individual body or a suitcase. There is a growing body of research about women's involvement as drug couriers (or drug mules) in the drug trade (importing or exporting drugs). The research demonstrates that women drug couriers are most often poor, first-time offenders and that their decision to carry drugs is economic. They are most often paid a flat fee and they do not share in any drug trade profits (Boyd 2006; Office of the Sentencing Council 2011). Women drug couriers are also poorly paid (given the risk) and the most "disposable of workers" (Boyd 2006; Sudbury 2005: 175).

In Canada (and the U.S. and U.K.) the majority of women sentenced to prison for drug importation and exportation are foreign nationals; poor, racialized women whose choices are framed by global and national political and economic concerns and Western demand for specific substances (Boyd 2006: 145). In 2011–12, 53 percent of Black women in federal prison were incarcerated for a Schedule II drug offence (Office of the Correctional Investigator 2014). Some of these same conditions shape the experience of poor, racialized men. Police profiling and harsher sentencing of both Black and Aboriginal peoples are systemic practices in Canada (Wortley 2004; CIC 2012; Sapers 2014). The Office of the Correctional Investigator also claims that the disproportionate rates of incarceration for Aboriginal and Black peoples reflect gaps in Canada's "social fabric and raise concerns about social inclusion, participation and equality of opportunity" (Sapers 2013). The Office of the Correctional Investigator also argues that Aboriginal over-representation in prison is "systemic and race-related" and exacerbated by the Canadian criminal justice system and colonial history (Sapers 2013).

Safe Streets and Communities Act and the Social Construction of Safety

With the introduction of the NADS in 2007, the Conservative-led government at that time signalled its intention to "get tough" on drugs. This approach means more public spending on law enforcement and more severe penalties. In 2012, Canada's federal government passed and enacted the *Safe Streets and Communities Act* (SSCA). The SSCA is an omnibus law that introduces a wide variety of changes, including amendments to currently existing laws and the enactment of new laws. The law ends house arrest for property and other serious crimes, focuses on detaining supposedly violent young offenders, requires the Crown to consider seeking adult sentences for youth convicted of violent crimes, eliminates pardons for serious crimes, adds additional criteria for the transfer of Canadian offenders back to Canada, allows Canadians to sue organizations that supposedly support terrorism and protects foreign nationals from exploitation by making it more difficult for them to enter the country (Department of Justice 2012).

Among the vast array of changes is the introduction of mandatory minimum sentences for some drug crimes, including production, trafficking, importing and exporting. Mandatory minimum sentences reduce the discretion used by justice officials through the application of predefined minimum sentences for some crimes. These changes apply to drugs listed in both Schedule I (heroin, cocaine, methamphetamine) and Schedule II (marijuana) of the *Controlled Drugs and Substances Act*. These changes also increase the maximum penalty for the production of marijuana from seven to fourteen years and add more drugs to Schedule I, including amphetamine-type drugs, which will result in higher maximum penalties for activities involving these drugs (Department of Justice 2012). The SSCA was touted as an effort to extend greater protection to the most vulnerable members of society, enhance the ability of the justice system to hold offenders accountable and "improve the safety and security of all Canadians" (Department of Justice 2012).

Throughout the federal government materials on the SSCA, notions of safety and security are wielded in support of increased criminalization and decreased judicial and criminal justice discretion. "Tough on crime" approaches, such as mandatory minimum sentences, are often touted as efforts to attack the "big players" in underground drug markets rather than focusing on individuals who possess drugs for personal use. When the past Conservative-led government announced the NADS in 2007, Stephen Harper's speech sharply delineated between drug users and drug sellers and producers. As he said:

> Our government recognizes that we also have to find new ways to prevent people from becoming enslaved by drugs. And we need to find new ways to free them from drugs when they get hooked. That's what the new National Anti-Drug Strategy I'm unveiling today is all about. Our message is clear: drugs are dangerous and destructive. If drugs do get a hold of you — there's help to get you off them. And if you sell or produce drugs — you'll pay with jail time. (Office of the Prime Minister 2007)

This approach by the past federal government ignores research noted above that found that dealers who are often drug users are more likely to be caught up in police efforts against drug crime.

The passage of the SSCA followed a protracted media campaign by law enforcement in Canada to depict Canada's court system as too lenient on offenders despite the harshness of its treatment of drug offenders (Boyd and Carter 2014: 68). The imposition of mandatory minimum sentences for some instances of cultivating marijuana is the also the logical extension of a protracted media-based drug scare about the impacts of marijuana-growing operations, which extended from the late 1990s to the present day. During this period newspaper reports carried extensive coverage of the public safety and other dangers of these operations

---

What Is a Mandatory Minimum Sentence?

Mandatory minimum sentence approaches can take several forms, including: laws that specify minimum prison sentences for some crimes; incremental penalties imposed on convicted persons based on particular criteria (that is, so-called aggravating factors such as using a weapon in the commission of a crime); or three-strikes laws that require minimum and usually lengthy prison sentences for anyone convicted of a designated crime who has previously been twice convicted of a similar crime (Tonry 2009: 66).

by drawing on police-based spokespeople. These stories continually reiterated the notion that marijuana-growing operations bring other crime, undesirable people and dangers such as house fires to otherwise supposedly innocent residential homeowners and neighbourhoods (Boyd and Carter 2014: 186).

The SSCA was passed into law despite extensive opposition. In particular, criticism of this legislation focused on the approach to crime highlighted by these changes — a reactive approach that focuses on punishment after the fact, instead of a proactive approach that focuses on key issues like early learning and development, overall health promotion and community and economic development as a means to lower crime.[1] The Canadian Bar Association, for example, warned that mandatory minimum sentences subvert important aspects of Canada's sentencing regime, including principles of proportionality and individualization and judges' discretion to impose a just sentence after hearing all the facts in the individual case. Before the SSCA, judges could weigh each case and assess aggravating factors, such as violence, presence of weapons and proximity of a crime to children, to determine a sentence. Judges could also determine the likelihood of an offender committing further crimes and mete out a sentence appropriate to these issues (Canadian Bar Association 2009). As we pointed out previously, without mandatory minimum sentences, sentencing practices in Canada were already discriminatory. Critics of the new law have pointed out that these new sentencing provisions are unlikely to be meted out fairly. Two cases below are illustrative of how some women come into conflict with the law for transporting drugs.[2] The lenient sentence that they both received was heralded as a breakthrough at the time. If the women had been arrested and sentenced today, the judge would have had to abide by the mandatory minimum sentences implemented in 2012. Thus, both women would have spent years in prison.

In Canada, even before the enactment of mandatory minimum sentences for some drug offences, drug couriers are typically sentenced harshly. But two different Canadian cases in 2004 had a different outcome (*R. v. Hamilton* 2004; see Boyd 2006). In both cases, women were arrested at Toronto's Person International Airport after returning from visits to Jamaica. Marsha Hamilton was arrested in 2000, and Donna Mason in 2001. The trial judge sought to place the participation of both of these women as drug couriers against a backdrop of race, gender, poverty and inequality. His analysis of the cases speaks to the social conditions that shape women's conflict with the law.

Marsha Hamilton is a Black woman with a Grade 9 education. At the time of her arrest she was unemployed and living in Canada, with family in Jamaica. She was 28 years old and a single parent with three children under the age of 8. She had made a trip home to Jamaica and, in preparation for returning to Canada, had swallowed ninety-three pellets of cocaine with an estimated $69,000 street value.

She almost died on the trip because the pellets leaked cocaine into her body. Marsha had no prior arrests or police record, and she stated that she had committed the crime for financial reasons.

Donna Mason is a Black woman with a Grade 12 education. At the time of her arrest she was 33 years old and living in Canada. She had three children whom she solely supported on a limited income. Prior to the birth of her third child, she had worked full-time at a Wendy's restaurant for $8 an hour, supplemented by welfare assistance. She was also the choir leader at her church. Before returning to Canada from Jamaica she had swallowed under one kilogram of cocaine pellets. She had no prior arrest or police record, and she also said that financial hardship was the main reason she committed the crime.

Both women pleaded guilty to importing cocaine, in an amount of under one kilogram, from Jamaica. Both were Black women of limited economic means. Both had dependent children. Both were first-time offenders. Their "profile" is similar to that of other women in prison for drug importation in Canada, Britain and the U.S. In 2003, both women were sentenced by Justice Hill of Ontario's Superior Court of Justice. Their cases are groundbreaking because both women were given conditional sentences and not sent to prison. Hamilton was sentenced to twenty months; Mason to twenty-four months less a day.

The defence in each of these cases highlighted the role of the judiciary, and specifically the sentencing judge, in addressing injustices against Aboriginal peoples in Canada — injustices recognized in *R. v. Gladue* (1999). The defence argued that Black women should be granted similar consideration when the evidence presented at the trial suggests a history similar to that of Aboriginal women — of poverty, discrimination and overrepresentation in the criminal justice system (*R. v. Hamilton* 2003). Judge Hill's decision was significant for its recognition of systemic factors in the imposition of conditional sentences. Nevertheless, it did little to challenge Canada's drug laws, nor did it recognize the criminal justice system as a site of conflict and oppression. In addition, it did not entirely dispel well-worn myths about Black women and crime. Yet, even with the limitations of the case, today the outcome and the issues addressed in court would not have prevailed because mandatory minimum sentencing allows no room for recognition of systemic factors in the imposition of sentencing.

Mandatory minimum sentences and three-strike laws were implemented extensively in the U.S. between the mid-1970s and 2006. As the U.S. experience shows, the brunt of mandatory minimum sentences was borne by people who are drug dependent and those facing economic challenges, and not those involved in the higher levels of drug selling and production. Moreover, although rates of drug use and selling are comparable across racial and ethnic lines, Blacks and Latinos are far more likely to be criminalized for drug law violations than whites (U.S.

Department of Health and Human Services, Substance Abuse & Mental Health Services Administration 2012; Human Rights Watch 2008). In addition, individuals who sell drugs at the street level are more often than not involved in tasks such as carrying drugs and steering buyers towards dealers; real profiteers in the drug market distance themselves from visible drug-trafficking activities and are rarely captured by law-enforcement efforts (Chu 2012). One of the effects of mandatory minimum sentencing laws in the U.S. is to give the country the distinction of having by far the highest rates of incarceration in the world, the largest proportion of which is attributable to drug offences. Despite high rates of incarceration, data supplied by the U.S. government shows that it has one of the highest levels of drug use and a vast and increasing supply of illegal drugs (SAMHSA Office of Applied Studies 2012).

The imposition of mandatory minimum sentences also flies in the face of evidence of their ineffectiveness. The potential deterrent effects of these laws are often touted as the key reason for their implementation. Studies of mandatory sentencing laws in the U.S. and Australia, however, have found no convincing evidence that the imposition of these laws deters crime (Tonry 2009). Most of the reviews of the effects of these penalties were conducted well before the imposition of the SSCA. In fact, the 1987 Canadian Sentencing Commission report, a 1993 report of the Committee on Justice of the Canadian Parliament and the 2002 Department of Justice review all concluded that the effects of these laws on deterrence was negligible. The 2002 Department of Justice report concluded that mandatory minimum sentences are "least effective in relation to drug offences" and that "drug consumption and drug related crime seem to be unaffected, in any measurable way, by severe mandatory minimum sentences" (Gabor and Crutcher 2002: 31). Putting people in prison does not reduce levels of harmful drug use or the supply of drugs. Instead, the effects of mandatory minimum sentences include increases in the prison population in already overcrowded prisons, increases in the costs to the criminal justice system and a number of well-documented consequences on already marginalized populations (Canadian Bar Association 2009; Mallea 2010). In Canada, as was the case in the U.S., mandatory minimum sentences have the potential to increase the numbers of people in prison, thus exposing more people for longer periods of time to increased potential for violence and an environment characterized by mental, emotional and physical degradation (Iftene and Manson 2012).

Incarceration is costly and the introduction of mandatory minimum sentences only serves to increase these costs. Even very cautious estimates suggest that changes associated with the *Safe Streets and Communities Act*, including the imposition of mandatory minimum sentences, will cost the Canadian federal government about $8 million and the provinces another $137 million annually. In fact, as noted above, in 2012 the federal government budgeted $67.7 million above the NADS budget for mandatory minimum penalties (Department of Justice 2012). These facts fly in the face of the federal government's claim that these changes would not cost anything (Yalkin and Kirk 2012). A study by the Quebec Institute for Socio-economic Research and Information suggests that the costs for the provinces will be much higher due to increases in the prison population, as much as $1,676 million (Institute de recherché et d'informations socio-economiques 2011). Already annual expenditures on federal corrections have increased to $2.375 billion in 2010–11, a 43.9 percent increase since 2005–06. The annual average cost of keeping a federal inmate behind bars has increased from $88,000 in 2005–06 to over $114,364 in 2010–11. The annual cost of incarcerating women in federal prison is much higher, costing $214,614 (Public Safety Canada 2012: 25). This is due to the fact that there are fewer women's prisons and a much smaller female prison population. The daily cost of federal imprisonment increased to $313 from $255 in 2006–07 (Public Safety Canada 2012: 25). In contrast, the daily average cost to keep an offender in the community is $80.82, or $29,499 per year (CIC 2012). Given these soaring costs, Canada's Correctional Investigator, Howard Sapers, has suggested that "at a time of wide-spread budgetary restraint, it seems prudent to use prison sparingly, and as the last resort it was intended to be" (ibid.).

A 2013 report by the B.C. Provincial Health Officer warns that changes to sentencing and other justice practices brought about by the enactment of the *Safe Streets and Communities Act* will be extremely impactful on Aboriginal peoples. These changes will put Aboriginal people at greater risk for incarceration and the resulting consequences of incarceration, including lack of access to culturally safe services that support healing and reintegration (Office of the Provincial Health Officer (B.C.) 2013). This report also notes that the SSCA appears to conflict with other federal programs aimed at reducing prison time, specifically section 718.2(e) of the Criminal Code, which requires sentencing judges to consider all options other than incarceration (ibid.: 43).

An October 2012 report by the Correctional Investigator of Canada entitled, *Spirit Matters: Aboriginal People and the Corrections and Conditional Release Act* echoed these concerns (CIC 2012). This report speaks to the lack of resolve on the part of the Correctional Service of Canada (CSC) to meet the commitments set out in the *Corrections and Conditional Release Act*. Sections 81 and 84 of this Act were meant to help mitigate the over-representation of Aboriginal peoples in federal prison and to provide a healing path based on cultural and spiritual practices. Healing lodges were originally conceptualized by the Native Women's Association as a way to "connect Aboriginal women to their communities and traditions as *the* method of providing correctional services for Aboriginal women." (ibid.: 52). "Section 81 of the CCRA was intended to give CSC the capacity to enter into agreements with Aboriginal communities for the care and custody of offenders who would otherwise be held in a CSC facility ... Section 84 was to enhance the information provided to the Parole Board of Canada and to enable Aboriginal communities to propose conditions for offenders wanting to be released into their communities" (Office of the Provincial Health Officer (B.C.) 2013: 4). Included among these require-ments was the establishment of healing lodges that emphasize Aboriginal beliefs and traditions and focus on preparation for release (Office of the Provincial Health Officer (B.C.) 2013). Although the original intent of the healing lodge has never been fully realized, eight healing lodges are now operating, four operated by CSC and their staff, and four operated by CSC and community partner organizations.

The report found that in B.C., Ontario, Atlantic Canada and the North there were no section 81 healing lodge spaces for Aboriginal Women (Office of the Provincial Health Officer (B.C. 2013). In addition, because healing lodges limit intake to minimum-security offenders, 90 percent of Aboriginal offenders were excluded from being considered for a transfer to a healing lodge. The report concludes with a critique of the lack of action by the Correctional Service of Canada: "Consistent with expressions of Aboriginal self–determination, sections 81 and 84 capture the promise to redefine the relationship between Aboriginal people and the federal government. Control over more aspects of release planning for Aboriginal offend-ers and greater access to more culturally-appropriate services and programming were original hopes when the CCRA was proclaimed in November 1992" (ibid.: 33). The report concludes by calling on the CSC to ensure that the provisions of the Act are implemented in good faith.

The implications for Canadian drug policy are clear: rising rates of incarcera-tion of Aboriginal peoples, higher rates of substance-use problems combined with a lack of commitment to social structural change and alternative healing paths means more federally and provincially sentenced Aboriginal peoples will not receive the services they need. In fact, recognizing the high financial and social costs of mandatory minimum sentences, as well as their widespread failure, the states of New York, Michigan, Massachusetts and Connecticut have repealed these sentences for non-violent drug crimes, with other U.S. jurisdictions set to follow. New York in particular repealed all of what were called the Rockefeller Drug Laws (Wood et al. 2012: 37; Tonry 2009: 69). In August 2013, U.S. Attorney General Eric Holder announced the softening of the application of minimum sentencing laws on federal offenders.

Does the "War on Drugs" Work?

As we noted in the beginning of this book, Bacchi's work suggests that policy con-structs as much as it reflects the nature of a problem. When it comes to drug use, the major institutional claims-makers in Canada, such as the RCMP, shape drug use as primarily an issue of drug supply with a smaller nod to the issue of prevention.

For this reason, extensive public monies and effort is put into curbing the drug supply without regard for how these efforts, in fact, produce the very problems they seek to alleviate. Perhaps the most stunning display of unimaginative thinking when it comes to solving current drug problems is the refusal by governments to consider the failure of the overarching policy framework that not only creates much of the drug crime in Canada but also constrains our ability to address many drug-related health harms. Far from eliminating drug use and the illicit trade, prohibition (making some drugs illegal) has inadvertently fuelled the development of the world's largest illegal commodities market, estimated by the U.N. in 2005 at approximately $350 billion a year. Just as with alcohol prohibition in the early twentieth century, the profits flow untaxed into the hands of unregulated, sometimes violent, criminal profiteers (Count the Costs 2012a). Banning drugs and relying on enforcement-based supply-side approaches to discourage their use has not stemmed the increase in drug use or the increase in drug supply. Despite Canada's significant investment in drug control efforts, drugs are cheaper and more available than ever (Werb et al. 2010). There is a growing consensus among international experts that drug prohibition has failed to deliver its intended outcomes and has been counter-productive (London School of Economics 2014; Global Commission on Drug Policy 2011, 2014).

A growing body of evidence has a suggested that rather than protecting public health and safety, the current overarching policy framework of prohibition not only constrains our ability to address many drug-related health harms, but produces other harms, listed below.

Increases in violence
Because of the lack of formal regulation used in the legitimate economy, violence can be the default regulatory mechanism in the illicit drug trade. It occurs through enforcing payment of debts, through rival criminals and organizations fighting to protect or expand their market share and profits and through conflict with drug law enforcers. In Canada, gang violence sometimes results from turf wars over control of illegal drug markets. A "get tough" approach to crime assumes that more enforcement will eliminate the problem of gang violence. But as a comprehensive review by the International Center for Science in Drug Policy states: "Contrary to the conventional wisdom that increasing drug law enforcement will reduce violence, the existing evidence strongly suggests that drug prohibition likely contributes to drug market violence and higher homicide rates" (Werb et al. 2010: 91). Indeed, the demand for drugs means that as soon as one dealer is removed others are there to take their place. The Global Commission on Drug Policy supports these findings:

Vast expenditures on criminalization and repressive measures directed at producers, traffickers and consumers of illegal drugs have clearly failed to effectively curtail supply or consumption. Apparent victories in eliminating one source or trafficking organization are negated almost instantly by the emergence of other sources and traffickers. Repressive efforts directed at consumers impede public health measures to reduce HIV/AIDS, overdose fatalities and other harmful consequences of drug use. Government expenditures on futile supply reduction strategies and incarceration displace more cost-effective and evidence-based investments in demand and harm reduction. (Global Commission on Drug Policy 2011: 2)

The creation of unregulated drug markets

Drug policies that prohibit some substances actually eliminate age restrictions by abandoning controls to an unregulated market. In addition, when we prohibit rather than regulate substances, it becomes impossible to control the purity and strength of drugs. Illegally produced and supplied drugs are of unknown strength and purity, increasing the risk of overdose, poisoning and infection (Health Officers' Council of B.C. 2011). When people buy on the illegal market, they have no way to determine the quality of the drugs they purchase (all legal drugs are regulated for quality). For example, heroin bought on the street varies in strength. Hypothetically, heroin could be 100 percent unadulterated; however, this is unlikely and most often heroin bought on the illegal market ranges in purity and strength. However, because the drug trade is unregulated, buyers have no way to ascertain the purity or strength of the heroin they purchase. One day's purchase could be 10 percent pure, another day's purchase can be 30 percent pure. Thus, users are vulnerable to drug overdose. Also, on the illegal market, other substances are added to increase weight and volume, hence more profit. Sometimes these substances are benign, other times not.

In 2015, B.C. saw a rise in drug overdoses from fentanyl, a strong narcotic (CBC 2015c). The drug fentanyl was being sold on the street as heroin. However, fentanyl is a much stronger narcotic than heroin, leading to a spike in drug overdoses (ibid.). The illegal drug ecstasy (MDMA) is a synthetic drug used recreationally most often by young adults. The amount of MDMA in each pill (or batch produced) on the illegal market may vary drastically, and sometimes other substances are added, leading to unexpected harms (CCSA 2015). Thus, rather than reducing the supply of drugs, prohibition also abdicates the responsibility for regulating drug markets to organized crime groups, and increases the risk of harm to people who use criminalized drugs.

Substance displacement

As the United Nations Office on Drugs and Crime reports, if the use of one drug is controlled by reducing supply, suppliers and users may move on to another drug with similar psychoactive effects, but less stringent controls (Count the Costs 2012b). For example, studies of the effects of banning mephedrone (a cathinone analogue) in the U.K. suggest that people who used this drug before the ban either continued their use, or switched back to prohibited substances like ecstasy and cocaine, both of which are unregulated and thus of unknown purity and strength (Van Hout and Brennan 2012; Winstock, Mitcheson and Marsden 2010).

Market displacement

Studies suggest that geographically specific enforcement practices tend to displace drug markets to other locations rather than eliminate them (Kerr, Small and Wood 2005). This is due to the fact that "drug supply networks are generally not limited to a few central 'kingpins,' but rather include numerous diverse enterprises, and therefore removing the entire supply network is beyond the resources and scope of even the most well-supplied enforcement agency" (ibid.: 215). In addition, the supply network is made up of small, diverse and fluid groups of people rather than "cartels" or kingpins (Tickner and Cepeda 2012). Many people who sell drugs, especially street-level sellers, are unorganized and have no established ties to organized crime (Dorn and South 1993). Yet, they are most vulnerable to arrest and quickly replaced by other sellers (Dorn and South 1993; Kerr, Small and Wood 2005). These findings raise serious concerns about the capacity of law-enforcement strategies to eliminate drug supply.

The neglect of medical applications

The complete prohibition of some substances curtails their potential medical uses and benefits, as well as research into potential beneficial applications of controlled substances. An example is the use of pharmaceutical-grade heroin to treat individuals for whom other treatments have not worked. As we note in Chapter 9, the findings of a Canadian trial of heroin-assisted treatment — the North American Opiate Medication Initiative (NAOMI) study conducted in Vancouver and in Montreal — were positive; participants' physical and psychological health improved. Yet the continued prohibition of prescribed heroin hinders the use of this drug in treatment settings. Indeed the implementation of medical cannabis programs in Canada has been repeatedly thwarted by the prohibited status of this drug despite evidence that shows it has beneficial effects for many patients (Grindspoon 1998). As we discuss elsewhere in this book, Canada has a federal medical marijuana program, yet the past Conservative-led government changed the policies regulating medical marijuana use and production, eliminating both personal and designated growers, although a Charter challenge regarding these policy changes will be heard at the Supreme Court.

An inability to limit use

Comparisons between states or regions show no clear correlation between levels of drug use and the toughness of laws and penalties (Count the Costs 2012a; Degenhardt, Chiu, et al. 2008), nor do studies tracking the effects of relaxation in policy show that drug use increases — for example if new laws decriminalizing possession are introduced (Hughes and Stevens 2010). For instance, as noted earlier, when Portugal decriminalized possession of all drugs for personal use, drug use and addiction rates did not rise (Moreira et al. 2011; Murkin 2014). In short, any deterrence is at best marginal compared to the wider social, cultural and economic factors that drive up levels of drug use. A study at the B.C.-based International Centre for Science in Drug Policy culled from two decades (1990 to 2010) of government databases on illegal drug supply and found the supply of major illegal drugs has (with a few exceptions) increased. Regardless of harsh federal and state drug laws, with the exception of powder cocaine, the purity and/or potency of illegal drugs in the U.S. has generally increased. Their findings also confirm that the price of illegal drugs has generally decreased (Werb et al. 2013). These findings once again throw into question the effectiveness of current government-level drug policies that emphasize supply reduction at the expense of other goals. These deficiencies are aptly illustrated by the World Drug Report, an annual publication of the United Nations Office on Drugs and Crime that relies on reports of police drug seizures (that is, the size and estimates of drugs found in raids) along with police-based estimates of crop size (for cannabis and coca) to evaluate the effectiveness of drug policies. The larger the seizure, the more enforcement officials assert the effectiveness of their approaches. But the findings described above suggest that no matter how hard we try to apply supply-side drug enforcement, drugs are still widely available, cheap and increasingly potent.

An increase in the negative effects of drug use

The reality is that making some drugs illegal does not stop people from using substances as is evident from the United Nations data demonstrating increasing levels of drug use over the past three decades (United Nations Office on Drugs and Crime 2013). Criminalization of substance use further stigmatizes people who use drugs, making it more difficult to engage people in health care and other services. Criminalization also increases marginalization and encourages high-risk behaviours among people who use drugs, such as injecting in unhygienic environments, poly-drug use and binging. Evidence from other countries suggests the stigma and fear of arrest deter people from seeking treatment and it is more effective to divert users into treatment without harming their future prospects with a criminal record for drug use (Room and Reuter 2012).

Trying to manage drug use through incarceration diverts law enforcement away from efforts to improve community safety with crime prevention programs. Funding prisons and police also takes away precious resources from services like adequate housing and family income, and robust educational programs, all of which have the potential to address the root causes of crime (Canadian Council on Social Development 2014). None of these strategies were at the forefront of the approach taken by Canada's Conservative-led federal government from 2007 to 2015. Yet, readers should keep in mind that in Canada, the U.S. and the U.K., drug possession charges (the majority being for cannabis) make up the bulk of drug arrests (Boyd 2015). Even though federal governments have chosen to criminalize this activity, critical drug researchers argue that marijuana users are not "criminals" and past theories about the causes of criminality are not relevant due to the fact that marijuana use is not only prevalent in Western countries, it is a normalized youth practice (Boyd and Carter 2014; Manning 2007).

Despite the well-documented failures of prohibition, Canada pursued a strictly prohibitionist approach to many drugs and in fact, scaled-up this approach from 2007 to 2015. The election of a Liberal majority government in 2015 may bring about promised drug policy reform.

Cannabis as a Case in Point

In the lead up to the 2015 federal election, Liberal Party leader, Justin Trudeau, promised to legalize, regulate and tax cannabis. The Liberals won a majority government in the election and in his throne speech in December 2015, Prime Minister Trudeau reaffirmed that he would create a legal regulatory framework for cannabis following consultation with all levels of government, experts in public health and substance use, and policing (Bronskill 2015). However, as this book goes to press, Canada's cannabis laws remain unchanged.

In Canada, next to alcohol and tobacco, cannabis is the most often used drug. Young people in Canada use cannabis extensively (depending upon the province, 30 percent to 53 percent of Grade 12 students reported using cannabis during their lifetime) (Canadian Centre on Substance Abuse 2011). In fact, a report from UNICEF suggests that Canada has the highest rate of youth cannabis use among developed countries, but one of the lowest rates of tobacco use (UNICEF 2013). Heavy use, including using more than once daily, can have negative impacts on lung health, cognition and mental health. Yet, the overall public health impacts of cannabis use are low compared with other illicit drugs, such as opioids, or with alcohol. The risk of overdose is very low, as is the risk of cannabis-related accidents (Fischer, Rehm and Hall 2009; Room, Fischer et al. 2008). In addition, death due to cannabis overdose is "difficult, if not impossible" (Deganhart and Hall 2012: 62). A review of the harms of various substances published in the medical journal *The Lancet* found that alcohol was the most potentially harmful drug over even heroin and cocaine. Of the twenty drugs assessed by this study cannabis was ranked at eight in terms of harmfulness behind most major illegal substances (Nutt, King and Phillips 2010). The researchers called on drug specialists to meet and score each of the twenty drugs on "16 criteria, nine related to the harms that a drug produces in the individual and seven to the harms to others" (ibid.: 1558). The criteria included measuring drug-specific mortality (such as risk of overdose), drug-specific damage to physical health, crime, impact on family and community and economic costs (ibid.: 1560).

Cannabis-control policies, whether harsh or liberal, appear to have little or no impact on the prevalence of its consumption and production (Potter et al. 2015; Room, Fischer et al. 2008). Police reports tell us that Canada has a robust (underground) cannabis industry. The RCMP and police agencies regularly report the amount of marijuana seized in drug busts, including kilograms of marijuana and marijuana plants (Boyd and Carter 2014). However, police drug seizures only tell us part of the story. Although researchers provide estimates, due to the fact it is a hidden economy, no one can accurately state how large marijuana growing is in Canada. However, one study suggests that retail expenditures in Canada on cannabis are as high as $4.6 billion annually (Kilmer and Pacula 2009: 94). The most recent estimates of the size of the underground cannabis economy in Quebec peg it at three hundred tonnes in 2002; in B.C. estimates of the size of the economy suggest it could reach as high as $7 billion annually (Easton 2004). However, a 2012 study estimated that annual retail expenditures on cannabis by British Columbians was $407 million and daily users accounted for the bulk of the cannabis revenue, with a median estimated expenditure of approximately $357 million (Werb et al. 2012: 1). The authors conclude that given the size of the cannabis industry in B.C., it would be worthwhile to legally regulate the activity, and benefit from taxing the sale of it (ibid.). Clearly, cannabis is a popular drug, but the potential financial benefits of a regulated and taxable product like cannabis (for recreational use) were completely lost to past federal and provincial treasuries (Werb et al. 2012). In 2013, Uruguay became the first nation to repeal cannabis prohibition. In addition, four U.S. states and the District of Columbia have also repealed cannabis prohibition. In Uruguay, these states and the District of Columbia, cannabis is now legally regulated (both production and sale) by the state and taxed. In Chapter 7 we discuss more fully what legal regulation is and how it might be applied to different drugs currently criminalized.

One of the arguments put forward for legally regulating cannabis relates to the sizeable costs of criminalizing cannabis, including policing, courts and corrections borne by governments and Canadian taxpayers. In 2013, for example, there were 58,965 incidents reported to police involving possession of cannabis for the whole of Canada. Police-reported incidents of cannabis possession are far higher than any other illegal drug. The rate of 168 per 100,000 population far exceeds the rate of 22 for cocaine possession and a rate of 32 for all other illegal drugs combined. Indeed, the rate of cannabis possession arrests in Canada have more than doubled since 1991 (Cotter, Greenland and Karam 2015: 7). Between 2012 and 2013, drug offences decreased by 2 percent; however, cannabis possession offences increased by 1 percent (Boyce, Cotter and Perreault 2014: 20, 33). In fact, even with a decrease of 2 percent, drug arrests remain higher than ten years ago (ibid.).

A study in B.C. suggests that charges for possession of cannabis in the province doubled between 2005 and 2011 despite low public support for the imposition of a criminal conviction for this conduct. This study also found that charges for cannabis possession vary considerably between police departments and between municipal police and RCMP detachments (N. Boyd 2013). The RCMP are responsible for an overwhelming majority of the charges in B.C. Due to the RCMP's "investment" in drug crime, in 2013 (for the fourth consecutive year), Kelowna, B.C. reported the highest rates of possession charges in Canada — 80 percent of all drug offences were for possession. Seventy percent of the total possession charges in Kelowna were for cannabis. Kelowna has a rate of 707 possession offences per 1000,000 population, almost double the rate of Vancouver (Cotter, Greenland and Karam 2015: 12). It is conservatively estimated that it costs about $10 million annually in B.C. alone to enforce criminal prohibition against cannabis possession (N. Boyd 2013). Given the relatively low impact cannabis has on public health compared to other drugs, and the significant limitations placed on people with criminal convictions (employment and travel restrictions), research suggests that our current policies likely do more to undermine collective respect for the law and law enforcement than they do to protect public health (N. Boyd 2013).

If the goals of our current laws are to reduce cannabis production and consumption, clearly these laws are not effective. Even though, as shown earlier, there is high use among young people, there are no regulatory controls, such as

---

Motion Passed by

Union of British Columbia Municipalities in 2012

WHEREAS marijuana prohibition is a failed policy which has cost millions of dollars in police, court, jail and social costs; AND WHEREAS the decriminalization and regulation of marijuana would provide tax revenues:

THEREFORE BE IT RESOLVED that UBCM call on the appropriate government to decriminalize marijuana and research the regulation and taxation of marijuana. (Union of BC Municipalities 2012)

age restrictions, on cannabis as there are on tobacco. Nor can purchasers reliably determine the dose (that is, the level of THC) or the origin of this substance. When it comes to tobacco use, a regulatory system that includes age restrictions on purchase, prohibiting lifestyle marketing and focusing on clean air initiatives has been effective in making Canada safer and healthier. Recognizing the unique challenges presented by cannabis policies, and the potential of a public health regulatory framework to control the use and availability of this drug, in 2012 the Union of British Columbia municipalities endorsed a motion to encourage the B.C. provincial government to support the decriminalization and regulation of cannabis.

Polls also suggest that a majority of Canadians (57 percent) support the legalization and regulation marijuana. In B.C., 77 percent of respondents to a poll indicated support for cannabis law reform (Angus Reid 2012). They are not alone. In an effort to stem the damage that underground drug markets create, leaders in Central and South America have called for changes to the way cannabis is regulated. In 2011, the Global Commission on Drug Policy encouraged governments to experiment with the regulation of cannabis with goals of safeguarding health and safety of all citizens (Global Commission on Drug Policy 2011).

The Curious Case of Canada's Marijuana for Medical Purposes

Although marijuana for recreational use is illegal in Canada, the federal government has operated the Medical Marihuana [sic] Access Program since 2001, prompted by court rulings that upheld the right to access cannabis for serious and chronic medical conditions (Belle-Isle and Hathaway 2007). That program underwent a major overhaul and the federal government established new regulations for the program, passing them in 2013 (Government of Canada 2012a). Thus, the old program, the Medical Marihuana Access Program was replaced by the Marihuana for Medical Purposes Regulations (MMPR) on April 1, 2013. The MMPR program requires patients to obtain a prescription-like document from a physician or nurse practitioner, rather than applying for an "Authorization to Possess" through Health Canada. The elimination of the very cumbersome application process and the addition of nurse practitioners as authorized health care prescribers are welcome moves. But in Canada too few physicians currently know enough about the benefits and risks of cannabis for medical purposes to make sound medical judgments and recommend it to their patients, nor are enough physicians sufficiently aware of the appropriate use of cannabis for medical purposes (Canadian Medical Association 2012). More education of physicians is needed to ensure that patients will have adequate access to the program. In the meantime, Health Canada must take proactive steps to establish fair and timely access to the program.

The new MMPR eliminates the Personal Use Production Licences (PUPL) and Designated Licences, which allowed people or a designated person to grow their own cannabis. This is of concern for several reasons. Many people choose to produce their own supply because current prices of available cannabis are prohibitive (Lucas 2012). Producing their own cannabis also enables patients to select the strain(s) that work best for them and to grow them without an undue financial burden (Health Canada 2013). The elimination of the PUPL responds to concerns expressed by law enforcement and vocal claims-makers about the cultivation of medical cannabis in residential homes (Boyd and Carter 2014). Rather than eliminating this option, the MMPR could have addressed these concerns through routine inspections and certification of home gardens. Health Canada's decision to centralize the cultivation of cannabis for medical purposes in the hands of licensed corporate producers has increased the costs substantially because patients have to turn to a limited number of commercial producers (Government of Canada 2012a). The MMPR requires that cannabis production be located in indoor sites away from residential homes, that access to these operations be restricted with the use of visual monitoring systems and intrusion-detection equipment and that personnel hold a valid security clearance issued by the federal Minister of Health. These requirements mean that producers will need to heavily capitalize just to start an operation. As of 2015, there are twenty-seven corporate producers approved by Health Canada although more than one thousand have applied (Health Canada 2015; Lupick 2015: 14). In addition, the security requirements alone are so extensive that small growers find that they cannot afford them, thus eliminating them from participating legally in the market (Lupick 2015).

The new regulations also exclude currently existing medical cannabis dispensaries in the supply and distribution system. These dispensaries are not legal; however, they have long played a key role in disseminating information about cannabis and they offer a range of cannabis strains, products and services, such as peer counselling and referrals to other services. The Health Canada-licensed medical marijuana corporate producers can only sell dried marijuana via mail order. No other cannabis products, such as tinctures, creams and edibles, can be produced or sold. Medical marijuana patients are not allowed to buy on the premises. Including medical cannabis dispensaries in the distribution system would have addressed some of the barriers to access to cannabis for medical purposes that Canadians currently experience. In response to the high cost of marijuana from licensed producers and the lack of cannabis edibles and other services, medical marijuana users continue to turn to illegal medical marijuana dispensaries in cities throughout Canada. Since the new medical marijuana policy came into effect the number of illegal dispensaries has increased. In Vancouver alone, it is estimated that there were about twenty illegal dispensaries before 2012 (Woo 2015). That number increased to one hundred in 2015 (CBC 2015b; Lepard 2015). In April 2015, the City of Vancouver responded to the rapid growth of unregulated illegal medical marijuana dispensaries. The City of Vancouver proposed new regulations to control the dispensaries. For example, the proposed regulations make clear that dispensaries cannot be established near schools or community centres, a licensing fee of $30,000 will be charged and the operator must obtain a development permit, among other requirements (CBC 2015a; Woo 2015). However, the federal government responded one day after the City's proposals were released. Then federal Health Minister Rona Ambrose warned the Mayor of Vancouver not to regulate the dispensaries because they are illegal and it would "encourage drug use and addiction" (Woo 2015). She also noted that regulating the dispensaries would send a "dangerous message to youth" (ibid.). In response to the Health Minister's warning, City Councillor Kerry Lang reported that the City drafted the regulations to "keep marijuana away from children" and to regulate the growing number of dispensaries (ibid.). He also made clear that the City has been researching what is going on in Colorado and other places that voted to legally regulate cannabis (CBC 2015a). Following these events, the B.C. Health Minister, Terry Lake, made public that the provincial Liberal-led government supports the City of Vancouver's proposed marijuana dispensary regulations. On April 24, 2015, the Federal Minister of Health at that time, Rona Ambrose, commented to the media that: "marijuana is not medicine" (CBC News 2015a). Her public comment makes clear the previous federal government's view on medical marijuana and the federal MMPR. However, on June 24, 2014, Vancouver city councillors voted in favour of the new regulations to license medical marijuana dispensaries. They are the first city in Canada to do so. In response to a complaint, the Vancouver Police Department (VPD) released a report on marijuana dispensaries in September 2015. The VPD argues that:

> Using the criminal law to close marihuana dispensaries is generally ineffective, raises concerns about proportionality, and is a significant drain on valuable police resources that is difficult to justify in the absence of overt public safety concerns …. Bylaw enforcement, however, is an effective tool to shut down a business that isn't compliant with municipal bylaws. (VPD 2015)

This statement reveals the high level of discord between federal, municipal and provincial approaches to marijuana.

In fact, on Health Canada's website for the MMPR, they added a disclaimer in a bolded box. It states:

> Dried marijuana is not an approved drug or medicine in Canada. The Government of Canada does not endorse the use of marijuana, but the courts have required reasonable access to a legal source of marijuana when authorized by a physician. (Health Canada 2015)

By blaming the courts for the continuance of, though greatly reorganized, federal medical marijuana program, the Conservative-led government at that time condoned it publicly. However, the government's policy changes have not gone unnoticed. Prior to the policy changes, medical marijuana scholars and advocates presented research and evidence to the government about the benefits of the plant for medicinal purposes and the need to keep intact personal and designated grower options. The Conservative-led federal government at that time failed to listen and eliminated personal and designated growers. Following these events, a Charter challenge was initiated by four plaintiffs. The issue before the Supreme Court is whether the new medical marijuana policy (MMPR) put into place in 2014 by the federal government violates section 7 of the *Canadian Charter of Rights and Freedoms*. It is being argued that the elimination of personal and designated growers infringe on the plaintiffs' liberty and security of the person. This case and others related to cannabis will be impacted once the Liberal-led federal government implements its legal regulatory framework for cannabis.

Alternatives to Prohibition

In this book we argue that drug use is a health, not criminal, matter and should be treated as such. We also note that not all drug use is problematic and cultural and social factors shape drug use. Prohibition does not deliver on its intended goals, but it does result in the marginalization of whole groups of people and in some cases their deaths. It is time to consider an approach that helps to contain the negative effects of drug use, provides a variety of treatment modalities and harm reduction services and avoids criminalizing those who choose to use drugs.

New models for addressing drug-related problems are also emerging across the globe. In fact, since 2012 the international consensus on prohibition seems to be coming apart. Countries are beginning to experiment with approaches that show more promise for achieving the health and safety goals for their communities. At least twenty-five jurisdictions around the world are currently deploying some form decriminalization of drugs (Rosmarin and Eastwood 2012). Portugal, Uruguay, Guatemala, Colombia and the Czech Republic, as well as some U.S. states, are among the jurisdictions experimenting with either decriminalization or legal regulation of some drugs. Portugal decriminalized all illegal drugs in 2001. The Czech Republic has ventured down this same road. The Czech Republic decided to decriminalize all drugs in 2010 after undertaking a cost-benefit analysis of their policies that found that, despite drug prohibition: penalization of drug use had not affected the availability of illegal drugs; increases in the levels of drug use had occurred; and the social costs of illicit drugs had increased considerably. After decriminalization and similar to Portugal, drug use has not increased significantly but the social harms of drug use have declined. In Portugal, decriminalization has had the effect of decreasing the number of people injecting drugs, decreasing the number of people using drugs problematically and decreasing trends of drug use among 15- to 24-year-olds (ibid.). These decreases in drug use were achieved by rejecting law-and-order approaches. Portugal decided to shift their drug policy in 2001. They adopted a health approach by increasing social supports, harm reduction and diverse drug treatment services (Moreira et al. 2011; Murkin 2014).

In 2014 Uruguay legislators voted to create a legally regulated and state-controlled regime for cannabis. Uruguay is the first nation to end cannabis prohibition. In November 2012, the U.S. states of Washington and Colorado voted to create regulated markets for cannabis for adults and legislation to do the same has been introduced in eight other state legislatures. In 2014, Alaska, Oregon and the District of Columbia followed suit. These events follow on a long history of decriminalization of cannabis, including the Dutch coffee shop model (which allows for the legal sale of small amounts of cannabis in select coffee shops in the Netherlands) and the decriminalization of cannabis in several Australian and U.S. states.

Canada has contributed some of the best thinking in the world when it comes to offering alternatives to prohibition. Since 1998, the Health Officers Council of British Columbia has created a series of discussion papers that recommend an end to prohibition and its replacement with a regulated market for all substances based on the principles of public health (Health Officers Council of British Columbia 2011). The latest of these papers, published in 2011, describes how public health-oriented regulation of alcohol, tobacco and prescription and illegal substances can better reduce the harms that result both from substance use and substance regulation, compared to current approaches.

A model for legalizing and regulating cannabis draws on a public health approach that includes price controls through taxation, restriction of advertising and promotion, controls on age of purchaser, driving restrictions, limited hours of sale, labelling that contains information on potency and health effects, plain packaging and licensing guidelines for producers of cannabis. Similar approaches could be taken to cannabis to balance the need to limit use but avoid re-creating an illegal market for contraband (Emont, Choi, et al. 1993; Levy, Chaloupka and Gitchell 2004; Lewit et al. 1997; Room, Babor and Rehm 2005).

Taxation has been shown to decrease levels of alcohol and tobacco use, and similar strategies could be applied to cannabis. For example, Stockwell et al. (2007: 6) outline three approaches for using alcohol taxation strategies to reduce harm: 1. taxing the alcohol content of drinks; 2. linking tax rates to the cost of living; and 3. raising small additional taxes to fund treatment and prevention programs. The researchers also explain that there is "strong evidence from other countries for the effectiveness of such tax changes" (ibid.). A relevant example is Australia, where the sale of low-alcohol beverages (rather than high-alcohol beverages) increased due to their taxation changes:

> With the major success of low to mid-strength beers (2.5% to 3.8% alcohol by volume), after tax incentives to encourage the production of these products were introduced in the late 1980s.... The market share of these beverages in terms of value reached 40% of the total Australian beer market by the late 1990s. These products are also widely used at large-scale sporting venues as a way of reducing problems with alcohol-related violence. (ibid.)

Figure 1 illustrates the relationship between drug control and its supply and demand. When a drug is fully prohibited it ends up being controlled by underground organizations. When a drug is legalized and promoted without regard for public health impacts, there are similar consequences for supply and demand. From the perspective of public health, the ideal mode of regulation sits in the middle: where a substance is available in a regulated market with appropriate age and other controls and appropriate programs that address the harms and benefits of its use.

Figure 1: The relationship between drug policy and supply and demand

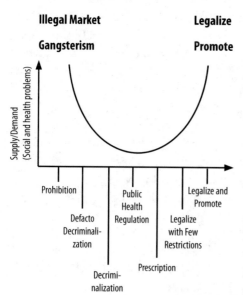

Source: Adapted from: Health Officer's Council of British Columbia 2011

This model draws on the kinds of evidence presented in this chapter and focuses on the prevention of illness, injury and mortality. It is not suggested or advocated that a completely free drug market be established; careful thought must be put into all aspects of a regulatory model for drugs. It also recognizes that changing how we control substances requires a robust governmental response to provide adequate health care and other supports. In particular, a public health approach proposes that the supply chain for drugs would be under comprehensive societal control in order to maximize control over availability and accessibility and reduce consumer demand (Health Officers Council of British Columbia 2011).

Drug prohibitionist approaches have been shown to be ineffective at reducing drug use and promoting pubic safety in other places around the world. In fact, drug prohibition and increasingly punitive policies have been demonstrated to create harms that undermine public safety and human rights (Count the Costs 2012a; Global Commission on Drug Policy 2011; Room and Reuter 2012). Internationally, drug reform efforts are moving forward. However, Canada and other nations are signatories on a number of United Nations drug control treaties that espouse punitive prohibitionist policies.

Waterloo Crime Prevention Council

The Waterloo Region Crime Prevention Council (WRCPC) has been a model for crime prevention through social development since 1995. The Council's mission is to prevent and reduce crime, fear of crime and victimization — and always in partnership with community, including those most affected by program/policy design and delivery. The WRCPC facilitated the Waterloo Region Harm Reduction Network in 2005 and later, the Ontario Network of Municipal Drug Strategy Coordinators. The WRCPC established the "KW Drug Users Group" as a safe place for people who use illicit drugs to meet and talk with each other about important issues. At any level, change always starts with dialogue. In the absence of interest from any sector, the WRCPC undertook primary research on the extent and typology of accidental drug overdoses, the third cause of accidental death in Ontario. They subsequently facilitated the establishment of Preventing Overdose Waterloo Wellington, a unique peer and service-provider effort to train citizens and providers in overdose prevention and intervention. In 2012, the WRCPC published *Between Life and Death: Barriers to Calling 9-1-1 During an Overdose Emergency*, a report unique in Canada, which demonstrates a clear reluctance of overdose witnesses to call 9-1-1, primarily out of fear of police attendance.

Notes

1. See for example: Canadian Bar Association; Collaborating Centre for Prison Health and Education, Vancouver; Assembly of First Nations; B.C. Representative for Children and Youth; St. Leonard's Society of Canada; John Howard Society; Elizabeth Fry Society.
2. The two drug courier cases described below are an excerpt from Boyd 2006.

7

THE INTERNATIONAL DRUG CONTROL SYSTEM

As in Canada, policies and laws that prohibit and punish the use of certain substances have been the mainstay of the international approach (Barrett et al. 2008). The current United Nations drug control system is based on international treaties, including the 1961 Single Convention on Narcotic Drugs, the 1971 U.N. Convention on Psychotropic Drugs and the 1988 Convention Against Illicit Traffic in Narcotic Drugs and Psychotropic Substances. The 1961 Single Convention on Narcotic Drugs, one of three United Nations drug-control conventions, limits the "production, manufacture, export, import, distribution of, trade in, use and possession" of cannabis "exclusively to medical and scientific purposes" (Article 4) (United Nations 1961). The 1988 U.N. Convention Against Illicit Traffic in Narcotic Drugs and Psychotropic Substances obliges signatory states to make cannabis offences a criminal matter in domestic laws (United Nations 1988). Together these conventions underscore the international system of controls on many drugs. The management and enforcement of the treaties is done by several international agencies. The Commission on Narcotic Drugs governs drug issues and operates under the U.N. Economic and Social Council. The U.N. Office on Drugs and Crime (UNODC) is the U.N. agency that operates as a secretariat for the Commission. The International Narcotics Control Board (INCB) is comprised of thirteen experts elected by the U.N. Economic and Social Council. The Board oversees the operation of the international treaties and management of access to medicines controlled by the treaties (such as morphine) and often publishes its own interpretation of the treaties (Room and Reuter 2012). In its annual reports it has often chastised Canada for the existence of Vancouver's supervised injection site and for Canada's medical marijuana access program (INCB 2014).

This drug-control system requires member states to take measures to prevent the non-medical use of a wide range of drugs through restrictions on production and supply and by suppressing demand for drugs. Canada participates in international forums and agencies that monitor the implementation of these treaties, including the Commission on Narcotic Drugs and the International Narcotics Control Board (INCB).

International drug control bodies involved in shaping drug policy like the INCB have historically emphasized law enforcement and operate in isolation from the U.N. agencies that deal with the health and social consequences of drug markets, such as the World Health Organization (WHO), World Bank, UNAIDS, United Nations Development Programme (UNDP) and the U.N. bodies that focus on human rights issues. The INCB, for example, operates as a guardian of drug prohibition and chastises member states for policy developments it considers to be inconsistent with the international treaties. For example, in 2014 the INCB lauded the Canadian government for putting forth a new bill to make it near impossible for other safer injection sites to open in Canada. The *Respect for Communities Act* was passed in 2015 (we discuss the Act and safer injection sites more fully in Chapter 9); however, when the 2014 INCB report was released the Act was still under deliberation. The INCB refers to these life-saving harm-reduction initiatives as "drug injection rooms" and "drug consumption rooms." The INCB states that they look forward to working with governments who have permitted these facilities and they remind them once again "that such facilities could be inconsistent with the provisions of the international drug control conventions" (INCB 2014: 54). In fact, in the INCB 2012 report, they chastised the Canadian Supreme Court for ruling in favour of Insite, Vancouver's first supervised injection facility. The INCB takes the position that supervised injection facilities contravene the international drug control conventions, as noted above, despite their excellent record of preventing the harms of drug use, especially drug overdose deaths (INCB 2012).

In 2012, the INCB also voiced its concern about the outcome of referenda in Washington and Colorado that effectively legalized the simple possession, production and sale of cannabis by adults (INCB 2012). In 2014, the INCB reiterated these concerns, reprimanding Alaska, Oregon and the District of Columbia for following suit. They also made clear, once again, that they are opposed to the establishment of legal medical marijuana programs and claim that cannabis has "no scientifically proven medical value" (INCB 2014: 53). The INCB advances prohibitionist policies in their reports, stressing "the importance of drug demand reduction as an indispensable element of such an approach" (INCB 2014: 4).

These comments reflect INCB support for harsh policing and its tendency to use its reports as a mechanism to criticize states that deviate from repressive and supply-oriented international drug policies. While criticizing innovative and effective public health programs, the INCB overlooks the most heinous and repressive of drug policy developments around the globe, including human rights abuses. Drug control cannot operate in isolation from international law, including human rights law; nor can it be unconnected from the concerns of public health or medical ethics (Csete 2012).

CHANGE IS IN THE WIND

But despite these international bodies, the current system of drug control is under considerable pressure to change. Some national governments have begun to chart their own paths when it comes to drug control. Some countries do not suppress socially and culturally embedded uses of controlled drugs like cannabis, opium and coca leaf chewing. Other governments have introduced pragmatic measures based on public health that focus on reducing the harms associated with drugs (such as needle syringe programs). And a number of governments have introduced de-penalization or decriminalization of some or all drugs to move away from the mass incarceration of people who use drugs (International Drug Policy Consortium 2012). As we discuss above, 2012 was a monumental year for drug policy reform around the world. Cannabis legalization is now a reality in the U.S. with the passing of voter initiatives in Colorado and Washington State, followed by two other states (Alaska and Oregon) and the District of Columbia in 2014. In 2014, Uruguay became the first nation in the world to end cannabis prohibition. Sitting politicians are beginning to speak out and call for dialogue on alternative approaches. Leaders throughout Latin America have begun to openly denounce the war on drugs and table reforms. The Organization of American States has begun a formal review process of the hemisphere's drug policies. There is an emerging consensus that the global war on drugs has been a catastrophic failure. Nowhere has this been made more evident than with the situation in Mexico. Although the war on drugs in Mexico has been waged for almost fifty years, scholars note that since the North American Free Trade Agreement (NAFTA) was signed with the U.S. and Canada in 1994, violence has escalated. Free trade and increased pressure from the U.S. to enact harsher drug laws and neoliberal economic policies have led to increased poverty, violence and destabilization.

When newly elected President Peña Nieto took office in 2012, Mexico had already witnessed the deaths of over sixty thousand people stemming from drug war-related violence (Steinberg 2013: 1). The current epidemic of violence was unleashed when his predecessor, former President Felipe Calderón, stepped up the war on drugs by employing the army; thus creating a "climate of violence, lawlessness, and fear" (ibid.). The war on drugs claimed the lives of 64,000 people from the end of 2006 to the end of 2012 (ibid.; Zedillo 2012: 12). As in all wars, the victims are not confined to drug traffickers, police or even cartel members; rather, innocent children, students, women and journalists have suffered. Journalists and human rights groups have noted "the rise of femicide" in Mexico. Femicide refers to the killing of women. In addition, the number of

---

Mexican Poet and Activist: Javier Sicilia

In 2012 Javier Sicilia, one of Mexico's most well-known poets, launched a grassroots movement to end the War on Drugs. In an open letter to Mexico's "politicians and criminals" he referred to the cruelty and "senselessness of the cartels" and the "complicity of the Mexican elite" in the ongoing War on Drugs. The Movement for Peace with Justice and Dignity has organized street events, dialogues and caravans travelling throughout Mexico and the U.S. On October 28, 2013, the Canadian Drug Policy Coalition invited Javier Sicilia and Teresa Carmona from the Movement for Peace with Justice and Dignity to join in a community dialogue in Vancouver. Both have lost children in the drug-war-driven violence that continues unabated in Mexico. "Both have chosen to forge their tragedies into opportunities to become agents of the changes so urgently needed in Mexico as well as in North America" (Farooqt and Guy 2012; CDPC 2013).

---

women imprisoned for drug and organized crime offences has also increased. Mares (2011) claims that the increase in women in the drug trade is due to economic deprivation. This increase is also reflected in prison rates. Since 2007 the number of women in Mexican prisons has increased by 400 percent (Mares 2011). About 60 percent of the total prison population in Mexico is serving time for a drug offence, oftentimes for possession of small amounts of marijuana.

A number of scholars note how the harms of drug prohibition are revealed when examining Mexico and the U.S. The U.S. is the "world's largest consumer of drugs" and Mexico is "the U.S.'s largest supplier" of illegal drugs (Zedillo 2012: 9). Yet, Mexico bears the brunt of the U.S.'s demand for drugs — corrupt politicians and cartel-like organizations, violence and instability. The continued demand for drugs by U.S. citizens is in opposition to U.S. federal government policy. Mexico's close proximity to the U.S. and their shared border has not brought peace or prosperity and U.S. economic aid is often linked to harsh drug enforcement and neoliberal policies (Boyd 2015: 283). Yet, this situation may change in the future as more and more Latin American countries and leaders condemn drug prohibition and propose new directions.

THE GLOBAL COMMISSION ON DRUG POLICY
AND THE VIENNA DECLARATION

One of the key events that helped turn the tide was the release of the first report of the Global Commission on Drug Policy in June 2011. The nineteen-member panel — including current and former heads of state and former United Nations Secretary General, Kofi Annan, and Canada's Louise Arbour, among others — criticized global prohibition and recommended that policies be based on evidence of what works to protect the health and safety of citizens. The Global Commission called on countries to end the criminalization, marginalization and stigmatization of people who use drugs but who do no harm to others and called for wide-ranging changes in drug policies. Some of these recommendations include: experiment with models of legal regulation of drugs to undermine the power of organized crime; make available a variety of approaches to health, harm-reduction and treatment services; abolish abusive practices associated with treatment, such as forced detention; invest in effective prevention activities that avoid simplistic "just say no" messages and "zero tolerance" policies in favour of educational efforts grounded in credible information and programs that focus on social skills and peer influences; focus repressive actions on violent criminal organizations to undermine their power and reach while prioritizing the reduction of violence and intimidation; and replace drug policies and strategies driven by ideology and political convenience with fiscally responsible policies and strategies grounded in science, health, security and human rights (Global Commission on Drug Policy 2011).

In 2010 the International AIDS Conference endorsed the Vienna Declaration. The Declaration affirms the body of research that demonstrates that the criminalization of drugs and enforcement efforts at the international and national level are costly and ineffective when it comes to curbing substance use. The Declaration also outlined the unintended consequences of drug law enforcement and the criminalization of people who use drugs, including rising rates of HIV, the undermining of public health approaches to substance use and human rights abuses among others. The Vienna Declaration has been endorsed by thousands of people and organizations, including the Canadian Public Health Association and the Urban Public Health Association, which represents the medical health officers of Canada's eighteen largest cities (Vienna Declaration 2010).

CANADA ON AN INTERNATIONAL STAGE

Meanwhile, Canada's federal government, once a leader in the field of drug policy, fell behind from 2006 to 2015 and embraced punitive policies, such as mandatory minimums for drug offences, which have already proven to be ineffective in curbing drug use and detrimental to society at large. Despite evidence to the contrary, at that time Canada continued to address the harms of its large underground drug economy by expanding a "war on drugs" approach that other countries are beginning to question. Since October 2015, the federal government, under the leadership of Prime Minister Justin Trudeau, plans to adopt a less punitive approach.

Canada possesses a wealth of public health expertise, drug researchers, scientists and activists to help lead the country toward a more humane and just drug policy. Unfortunately this expertise was not translated into national policy under former Prime Minister Stephen Harper's leadership. Despite signs of progress in other countries, Canada's approach to drug policy took significant steps backwards after 2006. Before that time, the Canadian government participated in the growing movement towards reforming drug policy to incorporate a public health approach. To this end, in the past, Canada attempted to decriminalize minor cannabis possession and supported some innovative harm reduction and treatment programs for injection drug users, including supervised consumption services and heroin-assisted treatment. Three federally funded reports — the 1973 Le Dain Commission, the Report of the Senate Special Committee on Illegal Drugs and the House of Commons Special Committee on Illegal Drugs report — have all recommended various versions of drug policy reform (Le Dain 1973; Nolin and Kenny 2002; Tornsey 2002). But since 2006, Canada has ceased to be a leader in innovative drug policies on an international stage.

In 2013, Canada expressed its opposition to Bolivia's reservation to the 1961 Single Convention on Narcotic Drugs. In 2011, Bolivia proposed an amendment to Article 49, deleting the obligation that "coca leaf chewing must be abolished." The coca leaf has been chewed and brewed for tea for centuries in the Andean region and produces a mild stimulant effect similar to caffeine. Without any objections, Bolivia's request would have been approved automatically. When its attempt to amend the Single Convention failed in 2011, Bolivia left the Convention with the intent to rejoin with a new reservation designed to align its international obligations with its constitution, which protects Indigenous rights, including the right to chew coca leaves (Blickman 2013). Coca chewing is part of traditional and Indigenous practice in Bolivia and has many important social and health benefits. With the support of 169 countries, Bolivia re-entered the Convention in 2013 with the reservation in place, though the exportation of coca internationally remains prohibited. Only fifteen countries objected to Bolivia's reservation, including Canada (Transnational Institute, Drug Law Reform 2012). Bolivia's actions are part of a rising tide of efforts to assert unique national perspectives on the regulation of drugs and to affirm respect for traditional Indigenous use of these substances.

Canada also opposed the U.N. resolution to hold a special session on drug policy globally, now scheduled for 2016. The United Nations General Assembly Special Session (UNGASS) will take place in New York. The resolution was co-sponsored by ninety-five countries, including countries in Latin America and the Caribbean and in the European Union, as well as Japan, China, Australia and the United States (Drug Policy Alliance 2012). This resolution was initially brought forward by the leaders of Mexico, Colombia and Guatemala, three countries suffering some of the worst harms of global drug policies that focus on enforcement to the exclusion of human rights and health concerns. Support for this resolution was an acknowledgement of a deepening crisis in the hemisphere. Canada's refusal to support this resolution signals its approach: to keep to the status quo and to refuse to acknowledge that a vigorous discussion about the harms of drug prohibition is taking place around the globe.

CANADA'S INCREASING INVOLVEMENT IN THE WAR ON DRUGS

Canada has also scaled up its involvement in drug enforcement around the world. Since 2006, the Canadian Forces have joined with other countries in an unprecedented increase in military involvement in drug interdiction in Latin America. Canada, for example, participates in ongoing counter-narcotics missions in the Caribbean Sea and the eastern Pacific. Canadian warships and aircraft have acted as eyes and ears for the U.S.-led Joint Interagency Task Force–South to prevent transport of drugs and money by air and sea between South America, Central America, the Caribbean islands and North America (Forget 2011). Canadian military aircraft and warships have been involved in interdiction efforts in the Caribbean Sea, including assisting the U.S. Coastguard to board vessels and seize illegal drugs. Canadian military aircraft have been involved in surveillance sorties in the region (Government of Canada 2012b).

These moves signal a renewed emphasis on a repressive approach both at home and internationally (Hyshka et al. 2012). The rationale for the Canadian military's involvement in the war on drugs is built on a series of faulty premises. Firstly – military might and securitization can defeat drug cartels. One need only look to Mexico, which saw an explosion in violence after President Calderón declared war on the drug cartels in 2006, to see how woefully dangerous an idea this is. Secondly, regardless of the Canadian military's interdiction efforts, the supply of illegal drugs to Canadian consumers has remained the same. As with all attempts over the last forty-plus years to control the flow of narcotics into Canada, as long as a demand exists, the supply will continue. No counter-narcotic activity, no matter how costly or logistically sophisticated, has ever managed to halt the flow of drugs across Canadian borders.

Canada's involvement in the "war on drugs" internationally may cease due to political shifts at the federal level. However, the scaling up of the war on drugs in and outside of Canada's borders from 2006 to 2015 reminds us that policy making is political, although not static.

8

SERVICES AND SUPPORTS FOR PEOPLE WHO USE DRUGS

This chapter examines questions about policy making that affect the availability of services and supports for people who use drugs. International conventions, the *Controlled Drugs and Substances Act*, the National Anti-drug Strategy and provincial and municipal initiatives shape drug treatment and services in Canada. Drug policy decisions act as an overarching framework that shapes how governments plan, organize and deliver services and how public monies will be spent on these services. For example, if drug use is considered a law-and-order issue, the majority of federal funding will go to law enforcement and there may be little allocated for drug treatment and related services. Today, the availability of services to address substance-use problems is important to many Canadians. Yet, how substance use is framed also determines what treatment will look like and what other supportive services will be established. As Bacchi (2009: x) makes clear, policy is a cultural product that constitutes and gives "shape to 'problems.'" Prohibitionist policies continue to shape how we understand the problem of addiction and drug use and, thus, the services we establish. At the core of drug treatment and the services we provide is a contradiction inherent in drug policy in Canada — illegal drug use continues to be constructed as both a criminal and a health issue. In addition, further complicating the issue is the fact that most drug use is unproblematic. Only a small percentage of people become addicted to drugs and/or have a problematic relationship with them; thus, how we talk about drugs is important. Assuming that all drug use fits narrowly into a criminal or medical framework is faulty. Assuming everyone who uses drugs needs treatment is faulty.

In Chapter 3 we discussed how people who used drugs from the 1920s to the 1950s were seen primarily as criminals, rather than as individuals who might benefit from publicly funded drug treatment services. At that time, abstinence was advanced as the only cure for addiction; however, it was believed that criminal addicts were incurable. Law enforcement and prominent doctors stressed that even when "criminal addicts" achieved abstinence they remained criminals and a threat to society because their criminality preceded their addiction; thus, there was no need to provide publicly funded treatment or drug maintenance programs (Boyd 2014). For poor and working-class people addicted to narcotics, abstinence was often achieved in a prison cell following arrest with little medical oversight (Carstairs 2006).

As we noted, publicly funded drug treatment and drug substitution therapies, such as methadone maintenance, were not available to Canadians until the late 1950s and 1960s, and access to treatment was quite limited. In fact, doctors could be arrested for prescribing narcotics to people for maintenance purposes right up until the 1950s (Giffen, Endicott and Lambert 1991: 343). The Division of Narcotic Control maintained primary control of drug policy. The Division firmly purported that drug use was primarily a criminal matter and they vocally rejected alternative frameworks that might necessitate publicly funded drug treatment and drug mainte-nance programs. In fact, the Minister of Health in the late 1920s publicly endorsed Canada's drug laws and the arrest of doctors who might prescribe to people "for the gratification of the appetite" rather than for a medical condition (ibid.). The Division of Narcotic Control had little opposition as they increased surveillance, maintaining comprehensive files from 1928 to the early 1970s on those individuals they labelled "addicts," "traffickers" and "doctors" to better regulate their activities (Carstairs 2006). Thus, right up until the late 1950s, the "problem" of illegal drugs and addiction was constituted by the Canadian government and law enforcement as a criminal matter requiring harsh drug laws and punishment.

In the late 1940s and 1950s, psychiatrists began to advance new theories about addiction; they argued that people addicted to illegal drugs were suffering from a psychiatric disorder. Yet the criminal addict model endured. People addicted to drugs were considered to be doubly deviant, both criminal and pathological. Rather than offer public treatment, in the 1950s a small number of prison programs were established in Canada to treat prisoners. Psychiatrists worked side-by-side with law enforcement and prison administrations, and abstinence was the goal for prisoners (Boyd 2014).

As we noted in Chapter 3, in the 1950s and early 1960s some doctors and other concerned Canadians began to rally towards a shift in drug policy in Canada. They sought to frame illegal drug use as a health issue rather than a criminal one. Slowly, over time, publicly funded drug treatment was established in Canada. Yet, debates continue about the nature of drug use and addiction and, stemming from that, what services to provide. For example, if illegal drug use is problematized as primarily a criminal matter, then harsh drug laws, punishment and abstinence are considered the appropriate response to the "problem." However, if illegal drug use, or heroin use and addiction, are understood as health issues, then the establishment of drug treatment and methadone maintenance programs may be seen as appropriate responses. If a strict abstinence model is adopted, people who cannot achieve abstinence may be punished or discriminated against for failing to control their drug use. Or, if drug prohibition and other social factors are seen as contributing to individual and social harms related to drug use, then another response may be advanced, such as the repeal of some drug laws and the setting up of diverse services, not just abstinence-based ones, along with legal regulation of currently criminalized drugs. Further, if addiction is seen as solely a health issue, social and economic factors may be ignored, and the majority of drug users whose drug use is recreational and unproblematic may be ignored as well. SNAP, an independent group in Vancouver, made up of people who were participants in two heroin-assisted treatment (HAT) clinical trials in the DTES, advocate for less restrictive and medicalized HAT programs and drug treatment services (Boyd and SNAP 2013). SNAP and other critics argue that health initiatives are not necessarily benign; thus, attention must be paid to how drug services are constructed.

In this chapter we discuss drug treatment in Canada and how services are funded and organized. Human rights, health professionals and drug users argue that access to services for drug dependence is also an essential element of human rights. Governments have a responsibility to ensure that all people can access services that will help them attain the highest possible level of physical and mental health. Canada is a signatory of several international covenants, such as the Universal Declaration of Human Rights, International Covenant of Economic, Social and Cultural Rights and the Covenant on the Rights of People with Disabilities. These international covenants provide a framework for understanding the concept of health and access to health care and treatment as a human right. In addition, the *Canadian Charter of Rights and Freedoms* guarantees that individuals will not be "subjected to any cruel and unusual treatment or punishment," nor will they be discriminated against based on "mental or physical disability" (*Canadian Charter of Rights and Freedoms* 1982: sections 12, 15(1)). Furthermore, section 7 of the Charter guarantees that "everyone has the right to life, liberty and security of the person and the right not to be deprived thereof except in accordance with the principles of fundamental justice." These sections of the Charter, along with health care defined as a protected core of provincial power, have served to establish diverse drug treatment services as a human right.

Although not all Canadians agree on what drug treatment is or should be, drug treatment may not always lead to abstinence; however, research and practice demonstrates that treatment can dramatically improve the mental and physical health of people who use drugs. Treatment for drug dependence shares three of the principal conditions identified in international law as necessary for the full realization of the right to health: it is an important element of controlling epidemic illnesses because of its role in reducing the risk of HIV/AIDS and hepatitis C; it provides a health service to those who are ill; and treatment for parents and pregnant women can contribute to improved health and the development of young children (Csete and Pearshouse 2007). People who use criminalized drugs in Canada have also demanded that their health and human rights be upheld. The Vancouver Network of Drug Users (VANDU), a drug-user union, have been fighting for the human and health rights of their members since 1997. In 2005, the Canadian HIV/AIDS Legal Network published *"Nothing About Us Without Us" — Greater, Meaningful Involvement of People Who Use Illegal Drugs: A Public Health, Ethical, and Human Rights Imperative*. The report includes a manifesto by people who use criminalized drugs, upholding their human and health rights, especially in relation to their involvement in drug programs and services, and the prevention of HIV/AIDS and other disease that impact them and their families. VANDU and the report highlight how illegal drug users are discriminated against and denied access to health care and effective drug treatment services in Canada (Canadian HIV/AIDS Legal Network 2005; VANDU Women Care Team 2009). VANDU and other advocates advance harm reduction services as vital to their members' health and security. Programs such as needle exchange, heroin-assisted treatment and diverse, non-abstinent-based treatment are advocated for. In Chapter 9 we discuss more fully harm reduction philosophy and services in Canada.

ORGANIZATION OF SERVICES IN CANADA

Most services that address drug use problems are planned, organized and delivered by provincial ministries responsible for health services or by regionalized health care authorities or networks. In fact, under the Canadian Constitution, health service delivery is the jurisdiction of the provinces and territories, each of which is responsible for the enactment of laws and policies related to health and the delivery of health services. The provinces and territories receive funding for substance-use services from their respective ministries of health. These services are delivered either by (centralized) provincial health authorities or by (regionalized) regional health authorities. Many provinces strive to provide a range of services that run the gamut from education, harm reduction, prevention, screening, early intervention and withdrawal management (detox) to day treatment, residential treatment and supportive recovery services. Generally, more intensive and specialized drug treatment services are offered in more populated, urban areas (B.C. Mental Health and Substance Use Project 2007; Centre for Addiction and Mental Health 2011). In addition, some private services are available, such as residential drug treatment services. These services are not always publicly funded. The actual structure of substance-use services across Canada varies widely, for a number of reasons: health system regionalization, geographic differences and differing political priorities related to substance use, including shifts in drug use (Pirie and National Treatment Indicators Working Group 2015). In 2014, across the provinces and territories there were eighty-seven heath authorities responsible for service provision in Canada. Individual health authorities and other jurisdictions have developed their own systems of services and supports, with little emphasis on consistency and co-ordination within or between jurisdictions.

Policy statements from many provinces suggest planning for a more integrated system is underway. Despite these positive indications, the system of drug treatment and detoxification services is still a collection of clinics, hospitals, community agencies and private service providers developed over time in response to local pressures, political advocacy and availability of funding and without a great deal of systematic attention to the actual needs for services (Rush 2012). What this means is that people who seek help with their substance use often must navigate a complicated and sometimes labyrinthine system of services characterized by long wait times, lack of coordination and questionable accessibility.

The development of these services has also been hindered by long-standing moralistic attitudes about substance use described at the beginning of this chapter and in Chapter 2. Traditionally, outside of methadone maintenance programs and needle exchanges, drug treatment established in Canada is abstinence based: the goal of treatment is abstinence. As we pointed out in Chapter 2, historically, drug treatment was seen as a more humane and scientific approach to substance use than simply putting people in prison for using drugs. Drug treatment, however, is only one part of an effective continuum of services for people who use drugs, a topic we will return to later in this and the following chapter. Drug treatment can also vary in quality, approach and availability, each of which is affected by the overall importance placed on these services by governments.

Historically, many abstinence-based approaches to drug treatment have been based on assumptions about "addiction" and the people who use drugs. The moral model of drug use that we discussed in Chapter 2 has also shaped how drug treatment has been designed. The moral model of drug use assumes that people who are "addicts" cannot be trusted to effectively run their own lives or to even trust their own thoughts. Lying and other forms of deceit are seen as common. Drug treatment programs are then designed for therapists to take control of clients' lives because they cannot be trusted to do it on their own. "Rehab" programs then require that clients observe strictly defined rules and infringement of these rules can be harshly enforced through threats of being dismissed from treatment. Hollywood movies and newspaper articles promote this view of "addiction" and tout the benefits of treatment programs that browbeat people into admitting their problems and acting according to strictly imposed program rules. Confrontation is promoted as a way to break down an "addict's" distorted thinking. One such example of this way of viewing drug treatment was published in the *Toronto Star* newspaper in November 2013. This article describes what the infamous mayor of Toronto Rob Ford could expect if he were to submit himself to drug treatment. The practices described in the article reflect an older view of treatment and one that is often depicted in the above noted Hollywood movies (Coyle 2013).

Some contemporary therapeutic approaches to substance use draw on different psychological principles that understand clients as complex individuals capable of thinking for themselves. Practitioners work with clients instead of imposing a certain way of thinking; the guiding principles of treatment are dignity and respect. The role of the therapist is to encourage clients' autonomy to enable clients to take control of their lives, follow their own values, to explore how clients make sense of the world and to assist them to make decisions about the direction of their own lives. In this approach confrontation is discouraged because of research that shows it is not effective and can in fact do harm to clients who are already traumatized (White and Miller 2007). Yet, these programs, although based on a different philosophy than the moral model, are primarily abstinence-based too. Contemporary drug treatment services often provide a twelve-step program, which refers to steps developed by Alcoholics Anonymous (AA) and Narcotics Anonymous (NA), premised on the disease model of addiction and abstinence as the treatment. Rarely do drug treatment providers in Canada draw from a critical addiction model (as described in Chapter 2), especially in residential drug treatment.

There is no one place in Canada where we can turn to find out about the services and supports available to people with substance-use issues. Nor is there one source that can tell us what these services are, where they are available and who we should contact if we want to seek help. There is also no clear set of boundaries that demarcate what these services are or should look like. In addition, there are no national or international standards for drug services to draw from. However, we do know that most Canadians use publicly funded non-residential drug services rather than residential drug treatment. In addition, alcohol is the most common substance used by people seeking drug treatment and services. Further, men account for the majority of people using both residential and non-residential drug services (Pirie and National Treatment Indicators Working Group 2015: 47, 50).

WHAT ARE WE DOING WELL?

Canada possesses a wealth of expertise when it comes to putting our commitments into action. Many highly skilled, committed and passionate people work very hard to create policy and provide care and services. These include the many peer groups, professionals in health care and justice, educators and community-based organizations committed to helping people address problematic substance use and challenging the heavy burden of discrimination. Community-based agencies in particular often lead when it comes to putting innovative policy initiatives into action. And sometimes they provide this leadership while under intense public scrutiny and in communities resistant to change.

A bright spot is the number of provinces that have made public commitments to improve their system of supports for people who use drugs. Virtually all provinces and territories have a strategic plan to address substance use either in existence or under development. Several of these plans stress the integration of mental health and substance-use services and the importance of integrating substance-use services into primary care services, such as family doctors and community clinics. These plans also underline the importance of accessibility, with emphasis on seamless access to services and reduced wait times for underserviced populations. Some of these plans also stress the need for more health promotion and prevention of the harms of substance use, most notably through early intervention programs, along with training for people working in these systems, provision of more services to caregivers, attention to the needs of people living in rural and remote areas and collaboration between service providers, especially for people with complex needs (Centre for Addiction and Mental Health 2011). These strategies almost universally emphasize the importance of evidence-based and best practice models of policy development and service delivery.

Another bright spot is the existence of the recommendations of the National Treatment Strategy Working Group. Their report, *A Systems Approach to Substance Use in Canada: Recommendations for a National Treatment Strategy*, lays out a set of principles to guide the development of treatment systems, a set of strategic areas that require action, including building increased capacity using a tiered model that emphasizes that not everyone needs the same level of services, and supports a continuum of services and supports. The National Treatment Strategy (NTS) was developed by a pan-Canadian group of experts in the field of substance-use treatment. Several provinces draw on the NTS model as an organizing tool for the distribution of their services (National Treatment Strategy Working Group 2008).

The NTS model of services is arranged in tiers to indicate that care is to be provided in a "stepped" manner. Figure 2 illustrates these concepts. This diagram represents the tiers according to the acuity, chronicity and complexity of substance-use problems. Each tier includes a cluster of services and supports that offer similar levels of access or require similar eligibility criteria and address problems of similar severity, requiring comparable levels of specialization.

Tiers 1 and 2 are meant to be accessible to the widest range of people by using low eligibility criteria. These tiers include a range of health care services and supports that should be offered as locally as possible. Services and supports in the upper tiers focus on the needs of a smaller but potentially more severely affected group of people. These services are more costly, have formal admission requirements and can be offered regionally instead of in communities. Pathways through the tiers are supposed to operate either sequentially or simultaneously and should be tailored to the needs of the client (National Treatment Strategy Working Group 2008: 15). Services occur either along a continuum or in a stepped-care model, recognizing that service-level intensity increases to meet the client's needs. The NTS also stresses the importance of increased research capacity about treatment, the importance of reducing discrimination against people who use drugs and the need to measure and monitor system performance. The principles of this report lay out a model for a person-centred approach through services and supports that put consent to treatment at the heart of effective programs (ibid.). The report also acknowledges the important role that leadership must play in moving its recommendations forward, including the involvement of people who use drugs.

Figure 2: Dimensional Description of the Five Tiers

	Eligibility	Nature of Problems	Share of Population	In Need Cost per Person	Degree of Specialization and Intensity	Degree of Integration with Community Lilfe
	Limited	Severe	Smallest	Highest	Highest	Lowest
Tier 5	↑	↑	↑	↑	↑	↑
Tier 4						
Tier 3		Moderate				
Tier 2						
Tier 1	↓	↓	↓	↓	↓	↓
	Open	At Risk	Biggest	Lowest	Lowest	Highest

Source: CCSA 2008: 14

SOCIAL AND CULTURAL FACTORS THAT SHAPE ACCESS AND SYSTEMS OF TREATMENT SERVICES

Discrimination

Discrimination against people who use drugs is one of the main obstacles to reducing substance-related harm. In earlier chapters and above we discussed how ideas about addiction and drug use have emerged in Canada. Moralistic and discriminatory attitudes and policies continue to shape individuals' encounters with services. Discriminatory attitudes and behaviours by health care providers can be barriers to accessible, respectful and equitable care (Bungay et al. 2010; Henderson, Stacey and Dohan 2008; Pauly, MacKinnon and Varcoe 2009; VANDU Women Care Team 2009). People who use drugs report unmet treatment and harm reduction service needs and can be under-medicated or denied medication because they are labelled as "drug-seeking."

Lack of Participation

People who use drugs have set up groups across Canada, such as VANDU, SOLID and the Toronto Drug User's Union, have received support and endorsement from a number of agencies and organizations. People who use drugs have advanced their self-organization to promote the health and human rights of people in their communities and to reduce stigma and drug-related harm. They also advance an end to punitive drug policies and drug prohibition. But their involvement as recognized stakeholders in planning and implementing services and supports, and in helping services evolve to be more person-centred, is still insufficient. These organizations argue that they must be involved in helping to set the direction of Canadian drug policy.

Underfunded Services

Despite several well thought-out provincial strategic plans that guide a comprehensive system of services, many jurisdictions still lack a full continuum of services. While some services are well resourced, others still operate continuously in "survival mode" and do not have the resources to serve all those who need assistance. And availability and access to services is often still chaotic and confusing for people who use drugs and for their families (Pocock 2011). Wait times for drug treatment can be long and can also vary significantly from jurisdiction to jurisdiction. Long wait times have been shown to discourage people from seeking treatment. In Canada, publicly available information on wait times is scarce (National Treatment Strategy Working Group 2008; Rush et al. 2012).

Privately Run Services

In most jurisdictions, treatment services are still provided by a mix of private and public providers and the cost of private treatment is a barrier to service for many individuals. For example, one private drug treatment centre on Vancouver Island, B.C., costs over $450 a day for residential treatment and upon admission a $15,000 fee is required (Edgewood 2015). Thus, treatment at this centre is out of reach for patients who cannot afford it. In Canada, private treatment providers are not subject to mandatory accreditation requirements and many Canadians are unaware that drug treatment services are a mix of public and private service providers.

Lack of Service Bridging

One of the most acute difficulties reported by key informants was the issue of bridging between services. In times of transition between services, the risks of gaps in service where people may "fall between the cracks" are significant. This can happen when youth transfer to adult services, when persons with concurrent disorders transfer between mental health and addictions services, when people transition from withdrawal management to drug treatment, when patients are discharged from inpatient treatment programs to community-based or outpatient services and when people are released from jail or prison. This is especially challenging for people whose housing is unstable or non-existent. Without a safe place to stay, chances of relapse are higher. In addition, the lack of after-care services is a challenge for many people exiting drug treatment services (Rush et al. 2012).

Neglect of Gender-Based Needs

Scholars and practitioners in Canada have illuminated the role that gender relations play in shaping problematic substance use. The B.C. Centre for Excellence in Women's Health has helped to foreground issues like the over-prescription of benzodiazepines to women and they have articulated a set of principles for gendering initiatives like the National Framework for Action to Reduce the Harms Associated with Alcohol and Other Drugs and Substances in Canada (Health Canada and the Canadian Centre on Substance Abuse 2007, see also Poole, Uruhart and Talbot 2010). Yet gender-based needs are often either completely ignored or underplayed when planning and delivering services and supports. In addition, conventional drug treatment is most often resistant to addressing gender and the classed and "racialized power differentials" that shape the lives of women who enter drug treatment (Campbell and Ettorre 2011: 1).

Lack of Access to Services

Many groups, such as First Nations and Métis, have been under- or not served by existing systems for generations. There are also few services for LGBT (lesbian, gay, bisexual and transgender) people in Canada. Lack of access to services can result in a higher burden of illness and greater risk for substance-use problems. Young people also experience difficulties accessing appropriate drug treatment, particularly when they are homeless (Hadland et al. 2009). In addition, available services and their chosen modalities of treatment are not always appropriate. Twelve-step programs, for example, though immensely valuable for some, may not be appropriate for others.

Geography

There are significant differences in the availability of treatment services depending upon geographic location. This is most acutely the case for rural and remote areas, though there can be significant differences between the services offered in medium-sized cities as compared to large metropolitan areas, even within the same jurisdiction.

Making a lasting difference depends on addressing all needs. Throughout Canada, key informants repeatedly stressed that the system of supports lacks the tools to address key issues that increase the harms of problematic substance use, including poverty, homelessness, discrimination and lack of consistent and quality community supports like childcare.

Lack of Transparency

In many cases, the funding mechanisms used in regionalized health care systems lack transparency. For example, it is unclear to many frontline service providers how provincial ministries of health allocate funding, and then how monies are spent at the regional level. Indeed, health care spending on substance use is insufficiently accountable to the people most affected by the issues. More than this, as our discussion of the NADS reveals, at least at the federal level, the majority of funding still goes to enforcement activities.

No Challenges to Prohibition

No province explicitly challenges the reality of drug prohibition. Though the legal context for substance use is not a provincial responsibility, provinces and territories must routinely shoulder the costs of prohibition either through criminal justice costs or through health and social harms of substance use, which are exacerbated by the lack of regulation of substances. In addition, as discussed more fully in Chapters 3 and 5, the legal framework for substances in Canada constrains the ability of provinces and local jurisdictions to respond to substance use in innovative ways.

THE INTEGRATION OF MENTAL HEALTH
AND SUBSTANCE-USE SERVICES

Most provinces have produced policy statements that support the integration of mental health and substance-use services (CCSA 2012). The impetus for this integration has been driven by evidence that many people who experience problematic substance use may also experience mental health challenges and that two independent systems of services cannot effectively or efficiently meet people's needs. Over the years, it has become apparent that people can be bounced from one system of services to another without a holistic approach to their needs. This lack of coordination is most acutely felt at the service level when mental health services do not accept clients who use drugs, including clients on methadone, while some addiction services do not accept clients on certain types of prescription medications, including antipsychotic drugs. These policies add to the already frustrating process of accessing limited services.

Integration has been driven by a number of factors. Service providers and policy makers have also recognized that approximately 20 percent of people who have mental health issues experience problematic substance use. The overlap between mental health and substance-use issues is higher in some sub-populations, including incarcerated individuals and young men diagnosed with personality disorders (Rush and Nadeau 2011). However, the construction and compounding of mental health and addiction and the integration of mental health and substance-use services are problematic because "it assumes that most people who use illegal drugs have mental health problems. However, this is not the case for many people who use drugs" (Boyd, Boyd and Kerr 2015; see also Keane 2002; Manning 2007; Moore 2008; Reinarman and Granfield 2015). In an analysis of Vancouver Police Department reports, focused primarily in the DTES, mental illness and addiction is linked with dangerousness; thus requiring increased "police surveillance and control" (Boyd, Boyd and Kerr 2015). Boyd et al. argue that this construction of the so-called problem "contrasts with the need, for example, for increased funding to social services, broad social and structural interventions, or an analysis of systemic injustice" (ibid.)

It is beyond the scope of this book to comprehensively examine the integration of mental health and addictions. There are several excellent reports, literature reviews and papers on this issue (Boyd, Boyd and Kerr 2015; Rush, Fogg et al. 2008). We can, however, raise some important questions about this integration from the perspective of a comprehensive and socially just approach to substance use. But it is important to think and act comprehensively when it comes to complex and intertwined issues like substance use and mental health. People should be able to easily access services that can address the full spectrum of their needs. The integration of mental health and substance-use services, however, suffer from two interrelated challenges: 1) the need to continue to provide comprehensive services to individuals who do not experience mental health challenges; and 2) the need to acknowledge that substance-use issues overlap and are shaped by other key structural factors, such as neoliberalism, poverty, gender violence, colonialism, trauma, racism and drug policy itself. This latter point is important because the majority of people who experience challenges with substance use do not have co-occurring disorders (Rush, Fogg et al. 2008: 12).

While it is very important to have services that can address this important overlap, systems must protect already existing services that address the needs of people who experience problematic substance use and its related issues. Indeed, many people accessing services for their substance use have experienced trauma. This trauma is not a mental illness, but often the lived effects of systemic issues like colonialism and residential schools, discrimination and violence, including systemic forms of violence like violence against women in intimate relationships and violence against Indigenous women. Services do not have the capacity to effectively counter the impact of ongoing structural violence; yet it is beneficial to be able to acknowledge and deal with the complexity of people's lives without necessarily medicalizing substance-use issues. Most importantly, services must be offered in a way that recognizes the need for physical and emotional safety and choice and control over how interventions will be applied. Trauma-informed approaches are similar to harm-reduction-oriented approaches in that they focus on safety and engagement (Canadian Network of Substance Abuse and Allied Professionals N.D.; see also Poole and Greaves 2012).

The underlying social context of substance use, including lack of adequate housing, poverty, the history of and ongoing colonialism and issues such as discrimination in its many forms, shape how people experience their substance use (Nova Scotia 2012). These are urgent issues that need a thorough and integrated public policy response.

INFORMATION ABOUT DRUG TREATMENT SERVICES

Effective service planning relies on good information that can assess what services people need and how clients utilize services. Until now data that would allow comparisons between jurisdictions (provinces, regions, municipalities) has been unavailable. Though the Canadian Centre on Substance Abuse (CCSA) has initiated the process of gathering national data on treatment programs, one report released in 2012 and another in 2015 suggest that the availability of comparable data from all provinces and territories is uneven at best and work remains on developing comparable data collection systems in each of the provinces (Beasley et al. 2012; Pirie and National Treatment Indicators Working Group 2015). The

Table 2: Withdrawal Management and Treatment Episodes 2009–10

Juris-diction	Residential Withdrawal Management		Non-Residential Withdrawal Management		Residential Treatment		Non-Residential Treatment	
	N	%	N	%	N	%	N	%
AB	11,402	24.1	N/A	N/A	5,273	11.1	30,712	64.8
NB	3,194	35.	35	0	351	3.8	5,580	61.2
NS	4,063	28.8	28.8	407	1,107	7.9	8,516	60.4
ON	41,462	31.2	31.2	1881	10,535	7.9	79,005	59.5
PEI	920	28.4	28.4	772	84	2.6	1,467	45.2
SK	3,733	20.2	20.2	0	1,918	10.4	12,822	69.4
CSC*	0	0	0	0	0	0	2,719	100

* Correctional Service of Canada

Source: CCSA 2012; Canadian HIV/AIDS Legal Network

first CCSA report focuses on publicly funded specialized services; data is available on treatment episodes, usage of services by treatment type, gender, age and use of public opioid substitution by age. The report does not measure community-based, non-specialized and private service providers. Nor can it assess the gap between the need for services and the existing capacity of treatment programs. And to date comparable data is not available on service wait times. The intention of the National Treatment Indicators Working Group is to build on this first step in subsequent annual reports by continuing to improve the scope and quality of the data collected. Table 2 shows one portion of the data in the CCSA report — in this case, individual episodes (not persons) of withdrawal management and drug treatment in comparable jurisdictions.

DRUG TREATMENT COURTS

Drug treatment courts are promoted as a way to reduce drug use and prevent crime. Since 1998, drug treatment courts have been set up in Toronto, Edmonton, Vancouver, Winnipeg, Ottawa and Regina. Drug treatment courts (DTCs) are often touted as the solution to a cycle of drug addiction and crime. But are they? That's the question the Canadian HIV/AIDS Legal Network (CHALN) sought to answer in a 2011 review of the operations of six federally funded drug treatment courts in Canada (Allard, Lyons and Elliot 2011). The report does not dismiss DTCs but raises some important questions about how they operate and their effectiveness. They argue that the DTCs use quasi-coercive and punishing methods more akin to the criminal justice system. Applicants to a drug treatment court program must plead guilty to a crime, submit to a mandatory urine screening, attend abstinence-based treatment and meet with the judge in court on a regular basis.

A 2015 Open Society report raises serious questions about the reliability of the information on drug treatment courts (Csete and Tomasini-Joshi 2015). Because of the lack of follow-up research on the experiences of participants, and the low retention rates in many DTC programs, it is difficult to conclude at this stage whether or not drug treatment courts result in decreased drug use and/or recidivism.

A Canadian HIV/AIDS Legal Network report noted that women are less likely to apply to DTCs and less likely to graduate at comparable levels to men, partly due to a lack of gender-specific programming and program flexibility that accommodates parenting responsibilities (Allard, Lyons and Elliot 2011). Indigenous women and men are also less likely to complete drug treatment court programs due in part to the lack of Indigenous-specific treatment services. The report also questions how voluntary one's entry to treatment is when prison is the alternative and access to other treatment is limited. Critics also question the practice of sending drug treatment court participants back to prison when they violate their drug treatment agreement, such as relapsing. The medical model advocates that addiction is permanent and progressive. It also recognizes that relapse is a component of the disease. Thus critics question how sending people to prison for a disease they have little control over is therapeutic. In addition, drug treatment courts may also violate human rights, specifically, the right to health outlined in Article 12 of the International Covenant on Civil and Political Rights because participants can be denied access to a health service if they do not follow the rules of a DTC program (ibid. 2012).

FIRST NATIONS, MÉTIS AND INUIT COMMUNITIES

Data on the non-medical use of prescription drugs and the health, social and economic impacts among Canada's First Nations population are very limited, but concerns about the use of these drugs have risen in recent years. Data on prescription drug use suggest that 18.4 percent of Inuit youth aged 12 to 17, 11 percent of Aboriginal youth and 8.9 percent of Métis youth living in urban Canada, compared to 5.6 percent of non-Aboriginal youth, report using prescription drugs for non-medical purposes (Canadian Medical Association 2012). In early 2012 Cat Lake First Nation in Ontario was the latest First Nations community to declare a state of emergency to federal and provincial officials due to the widespread use of prescription drugs. The non-medical use of prescription drugs has been linked with the impoverished health status of First Nations across Canada (Dell et al. 2012).

First Nations, Métis and Inuit communities face severe deficiencies in funding for substance-use services. Funding issues combined with health issues, such as higher rates of HIV infection and tuberculosis compared to other Canadians, reflects the colonial history of Canadian society. Racism and other forms of legal and social discrimination are key issues that affect the health of First Nations, Métis and Inuit peoples. Systemic racism has resulted in policies of assimilation, residential school, lost culture and language and over-representation in the justice system, all of which affect the health and well-being of communities and contribute to lower social and economic status, crowded living conditions and high rates of substance use (Health Canada and the National Native Addictions Partnership Foundation 2011; Redding and Wien 2009). Compounding this is the institutional racism enshrined in federal, provincial and municipal policies, police, RCMP, criminal justice and other professional practices, such as health care and social work, and at the societal level, violence against First Nations women (Royal Commission on Aboriginal Peoples 1996).[1]

Failure to keep agreements made with First Nations, Métis and Inuit groups, along with jurisdictional conflicts between the provinces and the federal government, have also plagued the development of services for First Nations, Métis and Inuit peoples. The history of colonialism combined with the numerous authorities involved in the provision of health care have resulted in a complex policy context and a great deal of diversity of services between geographic areas as well as conflicts between the federal and provincial governments over who should pay for services (National Collaborating Centre for Aboriginal Health 2011). Other challenges facing First Nations, Métis and Inuit communities include differences in access to services between Status and non-Status First Nations, and between on-reserve and urban First Nations people, limited access to provincial detoxification services, lack of culturally appropriate services, lack of coordination of care between services and lack of adequate training for service providers (Health Canada and the National Native Addictions Partnership Foundation 2011). Providing culturally appropriate services includes a range of initiatives, such as engaging with elders and Aboriginal communities, recognizing diverse First Nations knowledges, cultural and spiritual practices, art and languages and developing First Nations-initiated and run treatment and services.

In 2011, a report entitled *Honouring Our Strengths: A Renewed Framework to Address Substance Use Issues Among First Nations People in Canada* was released. This framework for action was developed by a comprehensive community-based review of substance-use-related issues and services driven by the Assembly of First Nations, the National Native Alcohol and Drug Abuse Program (NNADAP) and Health Canada's First Nations and Inuit Health Branch. This framework clearly articulates culturally based values and principles that should drive a renewal of

Tribal Journeys:
West Coast of British Columbia

Tribal Journeys has become a movement embraced by international coast First Nations communities. For two weeks each summer, canoe families of all ages from up and down the coast make a drug-and-alcohol-free journey to a host community. The journey has profound therapeutic value and promotes a healthy lifestyle, not just during the journey, but also in the months leading up to it. Spiritual, emotional, social, physical, cultural and mental challenges are supported by elders and knowledge keepers such as canoe builders, skippers and traditional food gatherers, cooks and paddlers. Team meetings allow people to speak about their emotions during the trip. Skipper meetings recognize the skills of those who know the water and embrace the longing of others to learn. In each First Nations community the visitors are fed as they rest overnight. The success of these tribal journeys is based on a strong cultural foundation that embraces both the past and the modern world. Family involvement allows for intergenerational healing and relationship building that span decades. Families and friends celebrate in sobriety, a practice that stresses strong ancestral processes (Minister of Health 2011: 24).

substance-use services for First Nations people on reserves. This strategy offers a comprehensive vision for the design, delivery and evaluation of services required to meet the needs of First Nations peoples. This strategy shows promise, but there is no guarantee that the work put into its development will translate into concrete, lasting federal support for effective programs despite budget increases to the NNADAP. However, the report highlights a number of diverse Aboriginal programs throughout Canada, such as the Tribal Journeys on the west coast of Canada.

Another promising sign is a recent strategic plan, B.C. First Nations and Aboriginal People's Mental Wellness and Substance Use. The plan clearly acknowledges the colonial history of Canada and its impact on First Nations, Métis and Inuit peoples, especially when it comes to understanding the context of substance use. The plan also offers the following analysis of the role that cultural safety can play in fostering change:

> First Nations and Aboriginal people need a range of culturally safe services and supports that respect their customs, values and beliefs. Cultural safety in health care is about empowering individuals, families and communities to take charge of their own health and well-being. It is important to note that achieving cultural safety requires that health institutions and service providers respect the diversity between and amongst First Nations and Aboriginal people and their worldviews. Currently there is an abundance of evidence to show that First Nations and Aboriginal people do not

receive the same quality of health services or report health outcomes on par with other Canadians. (First Nations Health Authority, BC Ministry of Health, Health Canada 2013)

This strategic plan recognizes that healing and reconciliation between Indigenous and non-Indigenous Canadians is necessary to further the wellness of all (ibid.). But like the NNADAP plan, the promise of these words can only be fulfilled by meaningful follow through on the part of governments.

Yet, the medicalization of healing and wellness has some critics. First Nations scholar Dion Million reflects on how identified social problems such as "drug addiction" have become medicalized and constructed as primarily linked to colonial trauma for Aboriginal peoples. She examines how an ethos of trauma and healing has emerged (with its emphasis on self-regulation) at the same time that self-determination and political power for First Nations peoples is denied. She asks how healing can come about when the ongoing destruction of "racism, gender violence, political powerlessness, and the continuing breakdown" of Aboriginal networks, communities and families continues unabated in these neoliberal times (Million 2013: 19). Million also notes that Aboriginal healing and health programs are rarely adequately funded or given form by real transfers of power to Canadian Aboriginal governments. Thus, adopting "culturally appropriate" services is only one part of the picture. Million asks that we examine the structural factors that shape First Nations peoples' lives today, including neoliberal economic policies, inequality and gendered violence against First Nations women, which she argues is an enduring feature of colonial power relations in Canada (ibid.: 7).

Million (2013) also writes about the Canoe Way, which is the larger Indigenous practice that the Tribal Journeys, described above, participates in. She notes that although the Canoe Way is often referred to as a healing practice, it is much more. Million (2013: 168) argues that it is "not ever imagined so instrumentally." Rather it is an alternative Indigenous practice and space that challenges neoliberalism and colonial power relations.

RACISM IN HEALTH CARE: WHAT WILL IT TAKE FOR CANADA TO CHANGE?

As the discussion above indicated, state, legal and social policies that discriminate against First Nations, Métis and Inuit peoples in Canada can permeate health care settings. Racism can impact health in several ways. Racist treatment and policies are not only added stressors, but lead to mistreatment in education, employment and health care settings. Discriminatory policies, attitudes and practices result in discrimination against Aboriginal peoples and misinformation about Aboriginal peoples and about Canadian history, as well as a lack of trust between Aboriginal peoples and non-Aboriginal Canadians. In a 2012 report by the Health Council of Canada on the health care experience of urban Aboriginal Canadians, many Aboriginal respondents reported that they had been treated with contempt and judgment and their health concerns were downplayed or ignored due to racist stereotypes. This was especially true when it came to stereotypes about substance use. The authors note that they heard many stories, such as:

> doctors who would not prescribe painkillers to Aboriginal people (even when they were in severe pain) because of a mistaken and racist belief that Aboriginal people are at high risk of becoming addicted, or a similarly racist assumption that they may already be engaging in prescription drug abuse. (Health Canada 2012: 8)

They also heard accounts of "Aboriginal people who went to emergency departments with various ailments (one suffering from a diabetic coma, another from an injury) who were assumed to be under the influence of drugs or alcohol and not given proper assessments as a result" (ibid.: 9).

Another person recounted an experience at an emergency ward:

An Aboriginal man who was beaten and bloodied was brought to an emergency department, where he was not allowed to lie on a bed. When a physician asked why the patient was not lying down, the nurse explained that the man was dirty, and would just return to the street after leaving the hospital to engage in the same risky behaviours that had landed him in emergency. In fact, the patient was employed, owned a home, and had been attacked on his way home from work. (Health Canada 2012: 9)

Case Study
Organizing for Change:
People Who Use Drugs

People who use drugs have been organizing in cities and regions in Canada for a number of years. Groups are active in Vancouver (VANDU), Victoria (SOLID), Toronto (TODUU), Ottawa (DUAL) and in Quebec (ADDICQ). Two groups — the BC/Yukon Association of Drug War Survivors and AAWARE in Alberta — operate at the regional level. The Canadian Association of People Who Use Drugs operates at a national level. Though most organizations of people who use drugs remain small and have minimal funding and budgets, they have had key impacts on drug policy. The Vancouver Area Network of Drug Users, for example, emerged in 1998 to play a key role in mobilizing community support for change in response to over 1,000 overdose deaths and high rates of HIV infection among people who injected drugs.

Racist attitudes not only support practices and policies that result in discrimination against Aboriginal peoples, but also create a lack of trust between Aboriginal and non-Aboriginal Canadians. When accessing health care, people are often at their most vulnerable. Racist treatment can drive people away from services and thus exacerbate the harms of problematic substance use (Health Council of Canada 2012).

The report makes recommendations directed at all levels of the health care system, including enhancing the cultural competency of workers and organizations and creating opportunities for partnerships and collaborations that will enhance cultural safety for First Nations, Inuit and Métis peoples (Health Canada and the National Native Addictions Partnership Foundation 2011: 54). These attitudes and discriminatory practices have been well documented by researchers, Aboriginal organizations and others in Canada over the years.[2]

The lack of consistency and coordination between health authorities across Canada has resulted in fragmentation and inconsistency, rather than an integrated system of services and supports (National Treatment Strategy Working Group 2008).

Note

1   See also Trevethan and Rastin 2004.

2   See, for example, *The Royal Commission on Aboriginal Peoples 1996*. Excerpts available at <http://www.aadnc-aandc.gc.ca/eng/1100100014597/110010001463 7#chp6>. For an excellent analysis of the intersections of sexism and racism in the representations violence against Indigenous women in Canadian media, see Culhane 2003. For more discussion of this issue, see de Leeuw, Greenwood and Cameron 2010.

9

HARM REDUCTION SERVICES IN CANADA

arm reduction initiatives and programs are an integral part of drug services in Canada. However, harm reduction philosophy and practices differ from conventional models of drug treatment and addiction. Since the 1990s, harm reduction has been considered a key pillar of any strategy to address the harms of problematic substance use. Advocates claim that reducing the harm of drug use to individuals, families and communities should be the fundamental goal of drug policy and the standard against which all drug policies should be evaluated. Harm reduction offers many benefits and we argue in this chapter that the scale-up of harm reduction services is urgently needed in Canada.

WHAT IS HARM REDUCTION?

"Harm Reduction" refers to policies, programs and practices that aim primarily to reduce the adverse health, social and economic consequences of the use of legal and illegal psychoactive drugs without necessarily reducing drug consumption. Harm reduction benefits people who use drugs, their families and the community. (International Harm Reduction Association 2010)

Harm reduction programs are aimed at reducing the risks and harms associated with substance use. These programs vary from place to place but may include some or all of the following services: education about safer drug use and safer sex; distribution of new supplies for injection and inhalation; condom distribution; safer consumption services and/or facilities; programs to prevent and treat overdose; and methadone and other opioid substitution therapies.

Harm reduction approaches to substance use tend to go against the disease or abstinence model of addiction, which insists that the only way to recover is to maintain total abstinence from drugs and alcohol; in this view, harm reduction is perceived as giving people permission to use drugs. Additionally in this view, the "addict" is seen as suffering from the disease of addiction and morally compromised — unable to tell the truth to themselves and others, and thus cannot be trusted (Collins and Marlatt 2012). Their lives are seen as chaotic and undisciplined. By virtue of having an addiction the person must be in denial and/or immature and/or narcissistic. This leads to the belief that people who use drugs are prone to lying and self-deceit. By virtue of having these supposed characteristics, people who use drugs are deemed to be incapable of effective self-care.

In contrast, harm reduction involves a pragmatic, non-judgemental approach to the provision of health services that respects the dignity of people who use drugs and values their human rights. Harm reduction provides skills in self-care (and care for others), lowers personal risk, encourages access to treatment, supports reintegration, limits the spread of disease, improves environments and reduces public expenses. It also saves lives. People who use drugs were responsible for initiating some of the first harm reduction programs in the 1970s. These were guerrilla groups organized to address the transmission of hepatitis C. With the arrival of HIV/AIDS, harm reduction programs began to appear in frontline services. These programs were underscored by a strong philosophical belief that people who use drugs are key participants and allies in their own individual and collective health. As a result, harm reduction programs are often very committed to including people who use drugs in the planning and implementation of services (Marlatt, Larimer and Witkiewitz 2012: 25; Friedman et al. 2007).

Harm reduction services are supported by international human rights conventions (Csete and Pearshouse 2007). As we noted in Chapter 2, the provisions of the International Covenant on Economic, Social and Cultural Rights supports the right to health and puts the responsibility on governments to provide the necessary services to help people achieve the highest possible health outcomes. Access to harm reduction services was further supported because they are life-saving services that prevent the transmission of blood-borne pathogens; thus a legitimate and necessary health service that supports this right to health.

Harm reduction is both an approach to service delivery and a philosophy of care. Both abstinence-based and harm reduction approaches are part of an integrated continuum of care. Where the abstinence-based approaches discussed earlier in this book generally require people to completely stop using all non-prescribed drugs and methadone to access drug treatment and to be in a "state of readiness," harm reduction services do not require people to stop using drugs, but meet people "where they are" in terms of their drug use. Exemplary harm reduction services have minimal requirements for involvement and are points of entry to other health and social services. Ideally, harm reduction services are culturally appropriate and implemented in a variety of contexts that maximize people's positive contact with these services (Rachlis et al. 2009). Harm reduction is not the only approach to substance use, but it is a major means of preventing the transmission of disease and overdose, connecting people to services, opening a pathway to change and preserving the dignity of all Canadians. Harm reduction services have key secondary benefits, such as increased access to health services, housing referrals, drug treatment, counselling, education and testing for HIV and HCV (Marlatt et al. 2012).

Harm reduction services first began in Canada around 1989 with the opening of needle- and syringe-exchange programs for people who use drugs, as a way to reduce the risk of transmitting HIV through the use of used needles. The programs were influenced by similar earlier initiatives in Europe offered in a variety of settings, including through outreach workers on the street, mobile vans, evening and weekend hours and fixed-site programs (meaning programs located at fixed geographic sites, such as health clinics).

VANCOUVER AND THE FOUR PILLARS APPROACH

One of the first regions in the country to implement harm reduction into municipal approaches was the City of Vancouver. In the 1990s the availability of high-grade heroin and cheap cocaine, combined with poverty and marginalization in Vancouver's DTES, precipitated a public health crisis marked by escalating rates of HIV infection and overdose deaths. A report by Coroner Vince Cain in 1994 responded to this emergency by calling for an overhaul of drug treatment and a reorientation that would see drug use as a health not a criminal matter. Though Cain's report did not immediately galvanize leaders, it signalled the beginning of a growing movement of people who wanted to change the way things were done in Vancouver. These changes were driven by a combination of efforts: a grassroots social movement comprised of people who use drugs, the initiation of a formal declaration of a public health emergency by the local health authority and the growing awareness that change was needed by leaders, including then-Mayor Philip Owen (Boyd, MacPherson and Osborn 2009). In 2000, to complement the efforts of other partners, the City of Vancouver released a drug strategy: *A Framework for Action: A Four Pillar Approach to Drug Problems in Vancouver*. The strategy called

Case Study
The Toronto Drug Strategy and the
Dignity of People who Use Drugs

In 2005, the City of Toronto developed a drug strategy encompassing prevention, harm reduction, treatment and enforcement. The Toronto Drug Strategy (TDS) is a multifaceted effort to address the harms of substance use drawing on health and other policy approaches. Like other municipal drug strategies in Vancouver, Thunder Bay and the Waterloo Region, the TDS does not shy away from the importance of harm reduction services as part of a full continuum of care for people who use drugs. The TDS also centres the rights and dignity of people who use drugs in its vision statement and principles and draws attention to the role that discrimination plays in undermining health.

In 2010, the TDS conducted focus groups to hear directly from people who use alcohol and/or other drugs about their experiences of stigma and discrimination. The purpose of the research was to identify types and sources of stigma and discrimination experienced by people who use alcohol and/or other drugs, document the impact of these experiences and identify strategies to help reduce their negative impacts. Six focus groups were held at a range of community-based agencies across Toronto, with a total of sixty participants. People who were homeless and/or otherwise living in poverty were the main focus of this study as they represent the most marginalized group of people who use drugs in our society. Key findings of this study included the following:

1. Families are the most significant source of discrimination, with the most negative impacts. People are facing multiple forms of discrimination at the same time (for example, related to their substance use, poverty, race, gender and age), and the compounded effect intensifies the severity of the stigma and discrimination.
2. Discrimination creates barriers to accessing services people need to stabilize their lives, and discrimination stops people from seeking help due to fear of how they will be treated.
3. Peer support is an important coping strategy for people affected by stigma and discrimination, and people need to be better informed of their rights to access services and language about substance use needs to be more neutral and less judgemental.

Recommendations for action in this report to help reduce stigma and discrimination related to substance use include the following: training and education for health and social service workers; storytelling and peer initiatives; support and education for family members; and promoting expanded delivery of health services in community-based settings (Toronto Drug Strategy 2010).

for a comprehensive approach to address the dire circumstances in Vancouver and challenged the status quo by calling for new and innovative interventions, such as supervised injection sites and heroin-assisted treatment programs. The strategy included health and enforcement and had as its two main goals public health and public order (MacPherson, Mulla and Richardson 2006).

The Four Pillars approach drew on a model developed by the Swiss in the 1980s to address the problems Swiss communities were experiencing with open drug scenes, homelessness, high rates of drug overdose deaths and HIV infection among drug users. Up until that time, services for street-involved people, many of whom were homeless, relied primarily on a system of high-threshold treatment services. These high-threshold services often required individuals to stop using substances before entry into treatment services, or created administrative barriers for people seeking substitution treatment, such as methadone, and other health or medical services. Consequently few people at the street level were able to access these services. The results of that approach left thousands of individuals out in the cold, effectively without services of any kind, as few were able to navigate the "system of care." The problems the Swiss were having in the 1980s mirrored the experience of Vancouver in the 1990s and beyond.

One of the key innovations borrowed from the Swiss experience and only partially implemented through the Four Pillars approach was to put a strong emphasis on outreach and harm reduction initiatives to engage people using drugs and bring them into low-threshold services — services that were specially created and immediately accessible to people. These services provided an exit from the street and an entry into health, social services, supportive housing and employment services. These innovations were complemented by innovations in substitution treatment and the hoped-for introduction of heroin-assisted treatment (HAT) for long-term heroin users, through a clinical trial. These services were meant to operate as entry points into a larger system of care and provide people with options beyond what existed at the time. A combination of efforts by the people who use drugs, the health authority, the City and the Vancouver Police Department put in place an expanded treatment system, more harm reduction services, including a needle exchange/distribution program and a supervised injection site.

Harm reduction strategies are not limited to Vancouver; in fact, many other regions have adopted harm reduction as integral to their drug strategy, including Toronto, Thunder Bay, Waterloo and Peterborough. Other municipalities, such as Victoria, offer some harm reduction initiatives; however, they have been unable to establish a more integrated strategy. For example, for a number of years they did not have a permanent fixed site for needle exchange. In contrast, in 2005, the City of Toronto put into effect a drug strategy that encompasses harm reduction.

CANADA'S RECORD ON HARM REDUCTION

In Canada, the provinces are responsible for the provision of health care services. But provincial commitments to harm reduction are mixed and in some cases absent. Some provinces include harm reduction in their overall mental health and substance-use strategies and some do not. Some provinces, such as Saskatchewan and Manitoba, include harm reduction only in HIV strategies (Saskatchewan Ministry of Health 2010). B.C. and Quebec include strong commitments to harm reduction in their strategic documents. On the other hand, Ontario and Nova Scotia's strategies on mental health and substance use do not mention harm reduction, though it is part of Ontario's public health standards and receives a brief mention in Nova Scotia public health standards. Harm reduction is also a key component of the 2012 Ontario document entitled *The Way Forward: Stewardship for Prescription Narcotics in Ontario,* prepared as an advisory report for the Minister of Health. Alberta's strategy on mental health and addictions notes that harm reduction will be offered to people with "complex needs" (Albert Health 2011; B.C. Ministry of Health 2010; Nova Scotia 2011, 2012; Ontario 2011; Ontario Expert Group on Narcotic Addiction 2012). In 2015, under the leadership of the NDP government in Alberta, there was a debate in the Legislature on harm reduction: "Be it resolved that the Legislative Assembly urge the government to review how best to integrate harm reduction policies throughout Alberta's public health care and human services systems with the goal of amending and incorporating these policies in related legislation and regulations" (Taylor 2015). In addition, the provincial Minister of Health created a new board to govern Alberta Health Services. The board includes at least one professional who works in and advocates for harm reduction services.

HARM REDUCTION IN ACTION

The following sections provide examples of successful harm reduction programs throughout Canada. We also discuss opposition to effective harm reduction initiatives. In addition, we highlight resistance by drug users and service providers to not only establish innovative harm reduction services, but to keep the successful programs that already exist.

Harm Reduction for Crack Cocaine Use

Crack cocaine use remains prevalent in Canada, although, as noted in Chapter 4, only a small percentage of Canadians use it. The B.C. Centre for Disease Control, for example, reports that the prevalence of local crack cocaine smoking has been rising amongst injection drug users. Crack smoking is independently associated with HIV and HCV status and linked to outbreaks of tuberculosis and streptococcus pneumonia. Harm reduction for crack use remains a neglected issue even in comparison to other underfunded harm reduction services (B.C. Centre for Disease Control 2012).

Given the prevalence of harms associated with crack cocaine use and the lack of a widely deliverable treatment option, there is an urgent need for health-oriented interventions, such as harm reduction programs that deliver safer crack use programs that include safer smoking supplies such as alcohol swabs, glass stems, mouth pieces, push sticks and screens and filters. A study on the distribution of safer crack use kits (each kit included the supplies listed above along with an instructional sheet explaining how to use the equipment) in Winnipeg also shows that this harm reduction service is cost effective over both the short and long run. Average costs of kits were fifty-nine cents while the costs of treating one patient with HCV over one year is $10,000 ($100,000 over a lifetime). As this study notes, preventing "only one case of HCV or HIV infection annually with the use of safer crack use kits can translate into a very cost effective harm reduction program" (Bracke et al. 2012: 9). Safer crack use supplies have also been found to help reduce unsafe smoking practices that can lead to HIV/HCV infection, including pipe sharing and use of broken supplies, and to engage marginalized individuals in health care services (Leonard 2010; Leonard et al. 2007; Isvins et al. 2001; Johnson et al. 2008; Boyd, Johnson and Moffat 2008).

More importantly, people who use crack are on the blunt end of many discriminatory practices and are often extremely marginalized. The distribution of safer crack use kits offers an important means of engaging a marginalized population in order to provide education and to refer people to health, treatment and other services (Fischer et al. 2012). A review of the safer crack use kit distribution in Winnipeg found that relationships of trust were developed between people who smoke crack and service providers through outreach and supply distribution (Bracke et al. 2012).

The availability of safer crack use supplies varies greatly across the country. A study suggests that a substantial proportion of people who smoke crack have difficulty accessing crack pipes in a setting where pipes are available at no cost, but are limited in quantity (Ti et al. 2012). Some programs in Newfoundland, New Brunswick, Ontario, Quebec, Manitoba, Alberta and B.C. provide safer crack supplies on a routine basis. B.C.'s Harm Reduction Supply Program makes three sizes of mouthpieces and push sticks available but pipes are not available. Vancouver Coastal Health completed a pilot project to distribute safer crack use kits, including glass pipes, in Vancouver (Vancouver Coastal Health 2013). They found that distributing the safer crack kits "reduced the number of injuries users experienced and clients shared their supplies less, which is important to reduce the potential risk of disease transmission" (Vancouver Coastal Health 2015). Other programs throughout the country offer safer crack supplies as their budgets permit, though often the distribution of these supplies is done quietly because of public opposition. In fact, opposition to the distribution of safer crack supplies has resulted in the closure of programs in Ottawa, Calgary and Nanaimo, though the project in Ottawa was reinstated (CBC 2011).

Mothering, Pregnancy and Drug Use

Since the 1950s, pregnant women and mothers suspected of using drugs have been demonized. They are often constructed as failed mothers and a risk to the developing fetus. It is assumed that their quest for drugs supersedes their concerns for their pregnancy and their fitness to parent is called into question. Historically, illegal drug use during pregnancy and alleged drug use while parenting resulted in child apprehension in Canada, especially for poor and First Nations women (Boyd 2015). Due to fears of child apprehension, many women avoided antenatal care during their pregnancy. Responding to these problematic practices, Sheway offers an alternative. Sheway is a Pregnancy Outreach Program (P.O.P.) located in Vancouver's DTES. The program provides non-judgemental health and social service supports to pregnant women and women with infants under eighteen months who are dealing with drug and alcohol issues. The focus of the program is to help women have healthy pregnancies and positive early parenting experiences. Sheway is connected to Fir Square, which opened its doors in 2003. Fir Square is a maternity unit at B.C. Women's Hospital, and it offers a harm reduction approach for women unable to practice abstinence during pregnancy. Fir Square has eleven beds mixed between antepartum and postpartum care for women who want to stabilize or withdraw from drug use during pregnancy. At Fir Square, infants room with their mother after birth and supportive housing is available for some of the women and their children when they leave the hospital.

Another successful harm reduction program is the Jean Tweed Centre in Toronto. It provides counsellors at multiple sites to offer support services to women and children and connect mothers with local resources. The Healthy, Empowered and Resilient Pregnancy (H.E.R) program operates in conjunction with Streetworks in Edmonton. H.E.R. provides harm reduction, outreach and peer support to mostly First Nations women and some of the hardest-to-reach women. Other harm reduction programs with a focus on pregnancy include Herway Home in Victoria and the Mothering Project in Winnipeg. These harm reduction programs, similar to Sheway and Fir Square, offer non-judgemental services and support to women and their children. These programs recognize that drugs are only one factor shaping pregnancy and mothering, and that social, health and economic supports are just as important in relation to positive pregnancy outcomes, infant development and parenting (Boyd 2015).

Safer Consumption Services in Canada

Supervised injection sites have been an established practice for decades in European cites. Since 2003, Vancouver has had a rigorously evaluated and highly successful stand-alone supervised injection site (SIS) in the DTES that provides a safe, clean space for adults to inject drugs (Milloy et al. 2008; Small et al. 2009). Twelve injection booths, clean injecting equipment and health and social supports are provided for each client. The vast amount of evidence from the reviews conducted of Vancouver's SIS — Insite — suggest that this unique service has several beneficial outcomes. Since Insite opened, it has been used by the people it was intended to serve, which includes hundreds of clients a day (ibid.). And it is being used by people who might ordinarily inject drugs in public. Significantly, not one drug overdose death has occurred on site (ibid.). This service has also reduced risk behaviours by reducing the sharing of needles and providing education on safer injecting practices. Insite has also promoted entry into treatment for drug dependency and has improved public order. In addition to reducing overdose deaths, it provides safety for women who inject drugs, and it does not lead to increased drug use or increased crime (Urban Health Research Institute n.d.).

Vancouver is also the site of the Dr. Peter Centre, a combined day and residential program for people living with HIV/AIDS. The Dr. Peter Centre is a multiservice site located on the west side of Vancouver offering low-threshold access to care, including counselling, illness prevention, advocacy and referral services. Recognizing the needs of its many clients who use drugs, the Centre added to its harm reduction programs by integrating supervised injection services into its health services beginning in 2001. However, it took until January 2016 (and a federal election) for the Dr. Peter Centre to be granted formal approval for its supervised injection services by the federal government. The Centre has been instrumental in establishing supervised injection as a legitimate aspect of nursing practice because of its intent to provide care, prevent the transmission of illness and prevent death and injury from overdose (Wood, Zettel and Stewart 2003).

Given the relationship in Canada between injection drug use and HIV and HCV infections, scale-up of these services is urgently needed. But opposition from the federal government has stalled the implementation of these beneficial services. In 2007, the federal government refused to grant a continuation of the legal exemption to Insite (section 56 of the *Controlled Drugs and Substances Act*). Proponents of the site, including the PHS (Portland Hotel) Community Services Society, VANDU and Vancouver Coastal Health, challenged this refusal all the way to Canada's Supreme Court. In 2011, that Court ruled in favour of the exemption and ordered the federal Minister of Health to grant a continuation of the exemption.

In the light of this court decision, other Canadian cities are considering the establishment of similar services. Each new site will be required to submit an application for an exemption to the *Controlled Drugs and Substances Act* to the federal Minister of Health. These applications are time consuming to prepare and there is no guarantee that the federal government will look favourably on these applications. In fact, there is every indication that the Conservative-led government at that time planned to make sure that other supervised injection sites would not open. Due to their efforts, the criteria for establishing a supervised injection site became much more difficult. The Conservative-led federal government enacted Bill C-2, the *Respect for Communities Act* in June 2015. The Act effectively bans siss by creating a more rigorous set of hoops for health care providers and administrators to jump though should they decide to apply for a CDSA exemption. The new requirements are so "onerous, that in practice, it likely will block proposed new facilities from opening" (MacPherson and Klassen 2015).

To date, Health Canada has not issued clear criteria for how it will assess these applications. MacPherson and Klassen (2015) explain that Health Canada authorities have the power to approve or reject each proposal "at their own discretion and on their own timetable." Provincial governments have also been tight-lipped about whether or not they support establishing these important health services in their jurisdictions.

Notable exceptions are the B.C. Ministry of Health and the Quebec Ministry of Health. The B.C. Ministry has signalled its support of these services by revising and reissuing its "Guidance Document for Supervised Injection Services" while the Quebec Ministry of Health has drafted a similar document (B.C. Ministry of Health 2012). Written for health care professionals, these documents provide advice to health authorities and other organizations that plan to submit an application for supervised injection services in their local areas. The City of Montreal plans to open a supervised injection site soon. Montreal's Mayor Denis Coderre asserts that the city will proceed to set up a site regardless of Ottawa's opposition. The City of Montreal has consulted with local police and the site has been approved by city council and the Quebec government (CTV News 2015). It is too soon to know whether or not the *Respect for Communities Act* will be repealed or modified; however, in response to a questionnaire about drug policy from the Canadian Drug Policy Coalition and other organizations prior to the federal election in the fall of 2015, the Liberal Party of Canada responded:

> Our party believes that safe injection sites are an integral party of a broader, evidence-based national drug policy that promotes public health and decreases crime. We support supervised injection sites because they decrease the risk of death and disease for those living with addiction and mental illness, reduce crime, and protect public health and safety. (Gainey 2015)

In January 2016, the Liberal-led federal government announced that the Dr. Peter Centre in Vancouver was approved (under the old criteria) to become Canada's second official supervised injection site.

Safer Inhalation Rooms

Health and service providers and drug users themselves have called for the establishment of safer inhalation programs. Similar to Insite, which provides supervised inject services, a safer inhalation room would provide a safe space for people to smoke crack cocaine or other substances. In fact, Insite planned to include a safer inhalation room at its inception. In a 2012 review of the safer inhalation program in Ottawa, the author, Dr. Lynne Leonard (2010: 95), noted what she called the "demonstrated capacity of individual Medical Officers of Health to prevent the full implementation of the program in their region." Reportedly one-third of public health units in Ontario do not distribute harm reduction supplies despite the inclusion of this requirement in the province's Public Health Standards. As Leonard notes, this non-distribution of harm reduction supplies has significant impacts on the sharing of drug use equipment (ibid).

Opioid Substitution Therapies

Pharmacotherapy for opioid dependence includes substitution medications like methadone and buprenorphine. In Canada, most provinces support some form of opioid substitution therapy, including methadone (and methadose) maintenance therapy (MMT) programs. Best practices for these programs typically suggest that a multidisciplinary approach is needed that includes physician prescribing, pharmacy dispensing and provision of psychosocial supports (such as counselling or housing), though the psychosocial support services are often in short supply. MMT requires pharmacist-observed daily dosing until a patient is stabilized, after which time take-home doses may be granted.

In Canada, the organization and implementation of opioid substitution therapies is plagued by several key problems (Luce and Strike 2011). Services can vary considerably from province to province; some offer more comprehensive services, including low-threshold, intensive and primary care services, and some do not. Low-threshold services remove barriers that can limit or delay access to MMT and usually have an open referral processes meaning people can be referred from many places in the system. Conversely, high-threshold services offer psychosocial supports and can be thus more limited by the availability of resources (Christie et al. 2013). As of 2012 there were approximately 65,000 people on opioid substitution therapy in Canada (Luce and Strike 2011; Ontario College of Physicians 2013; Provincial Health Officers 2013).

Some family physicians offer MMT and it is also available through private clinics and in prisons. Even within the same jurisdiction, services can vary considerably between urban and rural areas. In rural areas, lack of transportation to services, few pharmacies that dispense methadone and shorter pharmacy hours may affect the success of MMT treatment. Unlike most other health care services, in most jurisdictions, MMT is offered through a mix of public and private settings, meaning that some people must pay for this essential health service. In many cases, private providers are not integrated with other important services and supports in the health care system and beyond. But in some areas, private providers are the only source of services.

Methadone can only be made available by a prescriber who has an exemption to the CDSA. To receive this exemption prescribers must obtain specialized physician training usually offered by provincial Colleges of Physicians and Surgeons or in Ontario by the Centre for Addiction and Mental Health. Not all provinces and territories provide this training, thus decreasing the number of available prescribers. This exacerbates the problem of already long wait lists for services in some regions. At the same time, opportunities to access opioid substitution therapy in settings like emergency rooms and primary care can be limited by a lack of accredited prescribers.

MMT programs are plagued by a lack of public accountability for the implementation of psychosocial supports, the role of physicians and pharmacists in the system and oversight of physician services and billing and pharmacy dispensing fees.

Retention rates in treatment can vary considerably both within and between jurisdictions. Retention rates are affected by how services are organized and by issues like discrimination. Clients report that the attitudes of some health professionals can be shaming and that practices like mandatory and observed urine screening effectively treat individuals as criminals rather than people in need of health care (Reist 2011: 16). Likewise, in some cities and towns, proposals for methadone services have been met with community hostility due to discrimination against people who use drugs. This can even take the form of discrimination against prescribers of methadone.

Most jurisdictions do not cover the costs of buprenorphine, except for patients who cannot tolerate methadone. Buprenorphine may be an appropriate approach for some people because the risk of overdose is less than with methadone and it does not always require daily dosing. But recent reanalysis of research comparing these medications indicates further research is needed to determine the comparable safety risks between methadone and buprenorphine (Luce and Strike 2011; see also Cavacuiti and Selby 2003; Mattick, Kimber, Breen and Davoli 2007). Clearly there is an urgent need to streamline the opioid substitution system and address the concerns expressed by patients and service providers.

Harm Reduction Case Study: Heroin-Assisted Treatment in Canada

Heroin-assisted treatment (HAT) as a treatment modality for drug dependence can be very challenging for some people who advocate only for abstinence-based services. But several research trials, along with the continued existence of programs that provide pharmaceutical-grade heroin, have demonstrated clear benefits. Recognizing that methadone maintenance therapies and abstinence-based treatments programs do not work for some people, Switzerland implemented HAT in several cities in the 1990s. The U.K. has long had heroin prescription as part of their treatment services and the success of the Swiss program led other countries, including Germany, the Netherlands, Spain, Belgium and Denmark, to adopt similar models. There is now a large evidence base on the safety and effectiveness of HAT (Blanken et al. 2010; Strang, Groshkova, and Metrebian 2012). In 1998, the first North American Opiate Medication Initiative (NAOMI) Working Group was formed to conduct a HAT trial in the U.S. and Canada. In 2005, NAOMI began enrolling people in the DTES Vancouver and Montreal (the U.S. site did not open).

The target population for NAOMI included individuals over the age of 25 who were "chronic, opioid dependent, daily" injection drug users and who had previously been unsuccessful with methadone maintenance and other treatment modalities. Researchers randomized participants in the NAOMI study to one of two groups: one received injections of diacetylmorphine (heroin) or hydromorphone (Dilaudid, a licensed medication) and the other received oral methadone. The NAOMI study provided heroin/hydromorphone for twelve months, followed by a three-month transition period (NAOMI Study Team 2008).

People in the heroin arm of the NAOMI study experienced marked health and other improvements, including decreased use of illicit "street" heroin, decreased criminal activity, decreased money spent on drugs and improved physical and psychological health (The NAOMI Study Team 2008). Yet, NAOMI patients were not kept on HAT following the study's termination. Canada is the only country that did not continue to provide HAT to its patients following its clinical trial; rather, they were returned to methadone or other conventional treatments — treatments that had not worked for them in the past (Boyd and NPA 2013).

In December 2011, another clinical trial, the Study to Assess Longer-term Opioid Medication Effectiveness (SALOME) opened its doors in the DTES. This study compared the effectiveness of six months of injectable diacetylmorphine (heroin) with six months of injectable hydromorphone (Dilaudid) and the effects of switching from injectable to oral heroin or Dilaudid. Participants were in the study for one year, followed by a one-month transition period where they were encouraged to, once again, take part in conventional treatments such as methadone maintenance, drug-free treatments and detox programs (treatments that have proven to be ineffective for these participants) (SALOME 2012). Like the NAOMI study, the repeated failure of other treatment efforts for participants is, in fact, part of the criteria for selection of participants in SALOME.

In response to Vancouver HAT clinical trials failing to incorporate plans for permanent programs, in January 2011, Dave Murray, a participant in the NAOMI trial, organized a group of participants from the heroin stream of the NAOMI clinical trial. The independent group, NAOMI Patients Association (NPA), held its meetings every Saturday at the VANDU offices in the DTES. In 2012, many SALOME participants joined the NPA and in 2013 the group changed their name to SNAP (SALOME/NAOMI Association of Patients) to better reflect their membership. SNAP has been at the forefront of advocating for permanent HAT programs to be set up in Canada (Boyd and NPA 2013; Boyd and SNAP 2013). From the perspective of people who had been enrolled in one or both of the HAT research trials (NAOMI and/or SALOME), ending the trials without the implementation of a permanent program was responsible for significant declines in health and social status of some participants (ibid.). SNAP argues if this was any other health issue, people would not be denied access to an effective treatment and that by not putting in place an adequate exit strategy — that is, the setting up of a permanent program following the end of the study — participants were left unsupported and without the benefit of the drug that proved effective. SNAP continues to raise these concerns because the evidence base for HAT is well established, and members experienced the benefits of HAT. They advocate for HAT research trials to stop and for permanent HAT programs to be set up in Canada. In order to facilitate this change SNAP has spoken at public events, national and international harm reduction conferences and met with researchers, policy makers and the media. SNAP's mission statement highlights their purpose and goals:

> SNAP is a unique group of people who were participants in the NAOMI and/or SALOME heroin-assisted therapy (HAT) clinical trials in Vancouver, BC. We are an independent group dedicated to supporting each other and educating peers, researchers, government, and the public. We advocate for the human rights of people who use opiates, the establishment of permanent HAT programs in Canada and an end to drug prohibition.

In 2013, SNAP decided to meet with Pivot Legal Society, a non-profit society in the DTES to consult about HAT and their situation. This event was followed by two doctors who worked in the SALOME study submitting Special Access Requests to Health Canada requesting injectable heroin for some patients exiting the SALOME study. In May 2013, Providence Health Care of B.C. stepped in and approved providing oral Dilaudid for some patients exiting the SALOME clinical trial. On September 20, 2013, for the first time since heroin was criminalized, Health Canada approved twenty-one Special Access Requests for addiction treatment for SALOME patients. A number of SNAP members' Special Access Requests were approved, meaning that at that time twenty-one former SALOME patients could receive legally prescribed heroin as a substitution drug in a clinical setting.

However, before the SNAP members could celebrate their victory, "Kafta-like" events unfolded. On the same day as SNAP members received the news their Special Access Request was approved, the federal Health Minister at that time, Rona Ambrose, publicly announced that her government would stop Special Access Requests for heroin. Within two weeks, Ambrose announced new regulations for Health Canada Special Access Program — diacetylmorphine (heroin) was no longer accessible (along with other criminalized drugs) for treatment of addiction.

Terribly disappointed but not defeated, SNAP and others continued to press for HAT. In November 2013, five plaintiffs (four regular members of SNAP, all SALOME patients) with co-plaintiff, Providence Health Care of B.C., filed a constitutional challenge in the B.C. Supreme Court to overturn the federal government's decision to prevent further Special Access Requests for HAT. They argue that the new federal regulations are unconstitutional and infringe on the Charter rights of SALOME patients. Lawyers from Pivot Legal Services are representing the five plaintiffs and Joe Arvay is representing Providence Health Care.

In May of 2014, Chief Justice Hinkson of the B.C. Supreme Court granted an injunction to the participants in the SALOME study. In affect, he approved an exemption from the new federal regulations for former SALOME patients. Thus, until the Charter challenge is decided in the Supreme Court, former SALOME patients can receive HAT if their doctor deems it the best treatment option for them. Meanwhile, the SALOME trial ended and Providence Health Care is providing oral hydromorphone (Dilaudid) to some former SALOME patients, including injection hydromorphone in the Opiate Assisted Therapy program. Finally, at the end of November 2014, some SNAP applicants began receiving HAT through Providence Health Care at Crosstown Clinic in the newly formed Opiate Assisted Therapy interim program. The Charter challenge will not be heard until October 2016. Thus, the fight for HAT continues, unless the Liberal-led federal government decides to support the setting up of permanent HAT programs in Canada. Meanwhile, SNAP celebrated its fourth year of support and advocacy for its members and support-ers by hosting a party in March 2015. It is now over five years since the members of SNAP began to meet and advocate for HAT. They continue to meet at VANDU every Saturday.

Overdose Prevention and Response

Unfortunately, overdose prevention and response in Canada is not fully addressed. Some effective harm reduction programs have been established that counter drug overdose deaths, such as Insite and Dr. Peter's Centre, both in Vancouver. However, a national prevention program does not exist. Across Canada innovative initiatives have emerged; yet more needs to be done to prevent overdose deaths. Though no comprehensive national data exists on overdoses, pockets of research have illustrated a growing problem in Canada. For people who inject illegal opioids, the annual rate of fatal overdoses is estimated to be between 1 percent and 3 percent per year (Milloy et al. 2008). Between 2002 and 2010 there were 1654 fatal overdoses attributed to illegal drugs in B.C. and between 2002 and 2009 there were 2,325 illegal drug-related overdose hospitalizations (Vallance et al. 2012). In Ontario, it is believed that opiate-related overdose rates rose by "242 per cent between 1991 and 2010" (Ubelacker 2014). Between 2000 and 2013, it is estimated that more than 5000 people in Ontario died of an opioid overdose. The majority of these deaths were unintentional (MDSCNO 2015)

Unintentional opiate overdose among people who use opioids (both illegal and legally prescribed opioids) contributes significantly to the illness and death of Canadians. The tragedy is that many of these deaths could have been prevented. Clearly, policy changes and interventions aimed at improving these disturbing statistics are urgently needed.

Similar to the U.S., alarm about the increasing use of non-medical prescription opioids has increased in Canada in recent years, due to increases in the use of prescribed opioids (Fischer, Jones, Krahn and Rehm 2011). Research in the U.S. suggests that there is a strong correlation between increased prescribing of these drugs and an increase in harms, such as overdose injury, death and treatment admissions (Fischer et al. 2008). A Canadian study pointed to the correlation between high doses of opioid drugs and overdose deaths (Gomes et al. 2014: 831). In Ontario, for example, regions with a high incidence of opioid-related deaths per capita had high rates of prescription opioid use (Maladi et al. 2013: 1). In response to these concerns, seven provinces removed OxyContin (an opioid drug) from provincial drug formularies in 2012. These changes were meant to suppress the widespread use of these drugs by limiting their supply.

However, as the United Nations Office on Drugs and Crime reports, if the use of one drug is controlled by reducing supply, suppliers and users may move on to another drug with similar psychoactive effects, but of greater potency and purity (Count the Costs 2012b; Van Hout and Brennan 2012). As Oxy products have been removed from many of the provincial and federal formularies in Canada, some people have switched to equally strong prescribed drugs or are seeking other illegal alternatives. Data and anecdotal evidence suggest that the non-medical use of prescription opioids has become more prevalent than heroin use (Davis and Johnson 2008; Fischer et al. 2006). With the removal of OxyContin from many provincial drug formularies and the federal drug plan, illegal substitutes such as heroin and fentanyl analogues could be making a resurgence as cheap, available alternatives to OxyContin (Ontario Health Promotion E-Bulletin. 2013). OxyContin can be crushed and injected; and it was identified as contributing to addiction and overdoses and deaths. OxyNeo is no different pharmacologically than OxyContin; however, it is designed so that the drug can no longer be injected or snorted. Since OxyContin became less available, the province of Alberta has experienced a steep increase in fentanyl overdose deaths (Southwick 2015). Responding to these deaths, the newly elected NDP provincial government announced in 2015 that they would develop a provincial overdose prevention strategy.

Data suggest that rates of overdose are unacceptably high in Canada, especially since overdose can be prevented. Overdose can occur during the use of illegal drugs, non-medical use of prescription opioids and even when opioids are used as prescribed. Community-based programs that provide training on how to recognize the signs of overdose and treat overdose have been shown to be highly successful at preventing death and injury.

These programs teach drug users, friends and families how to administer naloxone, a drug that counters opioid-related overdose. They also provide naloxone. Laura Shaver, a board member of VANDU, describes the first time she injected naloxone to a fellow drug user when she was camping outside of Nelson, B.C. Fellow campers woke her up because one of their friends had overdosed on methadone. Shaver grabbed her naloxone, a clean syringe and a flashlight, and went to help. Luckily for the overdose victim, Laura Shaver had just completed training by the B.C. Centre for Disease Control "on how to intervene in opioid drug overdoses. Since 2012, the B.C. Take Home Naloxone program has trained more than 575 opioid drug users, family and friends and service providers and distributed more than 440 kits to prevent overdose deaths" (Eggertson 2014: 17). Due to Shaver's expertise and having naloxone on hand, her fellow camper did not die of an overdose.

Take-home programs were pioneered in Canada by Streetworks in Edmonton in 2005. The Works (a harm reduction program at Toronto Public Health) began a peer-based program in 2011. This program dispensed 610 kits since its inception and peers have reported 65 administrations of naloxone (personal communication, Susan Sheperd). In 2012 Ontario launched a provincial program to provide naloxone education and kits through harm reduction services. B.C.'s program, which began in 2012, is modelled on these pre-existing initiatives and combines education on prevention, identification and response to overdose, with take-away naloxone kits for people who are using opioids. These training programs combined with the availability of naloxone help people to be prepared in the event of an opioid overdose (Eggertson 2014).

Naloxone, a safe and simple medication that reverses opioid overdoses, has been used in emergency settings for over forty years in Canada and is on the WHO List of Essential Medicines. The B.C. ambulance service administered naloxone 2,367 times in 2011 (B.C. Provincial Harm Reduction Program 2012). Unfortunately, efforts to increase the reach of this drug in Canada are hindered by legal and jurisdictional issues. Naloxone is not covered by provincial drug plans; nor is this drug as widely available due to its cost, even though its patent has run out. And naloxone is a regulated substance available only by prescription in most provinces. However, responding to overdose deaths in Canada, in January 2016 Health Canada announced that it put forward an amendment to the prescription drug list to allow "non-prescription use" of naloxone "specifically *for emergency used for opioid overdose outside hospital settings.*" Health Canada also initiated a consultation on the proposed changes and noted that product labeling would be revised and training sessions would be set up and required for those who might administer the drug (Health Canada 2016).

> ## Toronto Public Health: Education and Training to Prevent Overdose
>
> In spring 2012, Toronto Public Health (The Works) created educational webinars on peer-based naloxone training, prescription and distribution to supplement its already existing peer-based training program on overdose prevention and treatment. Staff at community health centres, hospitals, prisons, First Nations communities and methadone programs across Ontario viewed these webinars. Training and consultation were also provided for agency administrators. This action came in response to concerns about the potential impact of OxyContin's removal from the market in Ontario and the increased risk of overdose as people transition to other, potentially more harmful opiates such as fentanyl. In addition, The Works and the Toronto Harm Reduction Task Force also partnered to produce a short film, entitled *The First 7 Minutes*, which promotes developing and implementing overdose protocols at agencies that serve marginalized populations. The video can be used in combination with a broader, peer-based overdose prevention curriculum in trainings with peer workers, people who use drugs and frontline workers. Eight training sessions have been conducted since spring 2010 with a total of 223 participants (TDSIP 2012).

Unlike Canada, the U.S. has over 180 Take Home Naloxone programs to train friends and family to resuscitate overdose victims and administer naloxone. Evaluations of these programs have demonstrated that they are effective at reducing overdose deaths (Walley et al. 2013). Several U.S. jurisdictions also have best-practice policies for physicians to support co-prescribing naloxone with any opioid for people at risk of an overdose (Project Lazarus 2013).

Reducing the Barriers to Calling 911

Most overdoses occur in the presence of other people (Eggertson 2014). The chance of surviving an overdose, like that of surviving a heart attack, is almost entirely dependent on how fast one receives emergency medical services (EMS). Though witnesses to heart attacks rarely hesitate to call 911, witnesses to an overdose too often waver on whether to call for help, or in many cases simply don't make the call. Many overdose deaths occur because those who witness overdoses are fearful of arrest and will avoid calling even in urgent cases where emergency medical services are needed for a friend or family member who is overdosing. Anecdotal reports from across the country have also found that victims of overdose will often ask friends not to call 911 because they fear police interaction and/or because they are on parole or do not want to go to jail. In addition, amendments to Canada's CDSA stipulate mandatory minimum prison sentences for some drug-related offences. These provisions unquestionably intensify fear of prosecution for witnesses of drug overdose and increase rates of preventable overdose deaths.

The more practical solution to encourage overdose witnesses to seek medical help is to provide exemption from criminal prosecution, an approach commonly referred to as "911 Good Samaritan Immunity" legislation. In general, this law could provide protection from arrest and prosecution for drug use and possession charges if the evidence is gained as a result of the person calling 911.

911 Good Samaritan legislation is a step toward saving lives and urgent action is needed to enact this legislation in Canada (Fischer et al. 2006). States south of the border — California, New Mexico, Colorado, Washington, Illinois, New York, Rhode Island, Connecticut, Massachusetts and Florida — have all passed Good Samaritan legislation in the last six years. In New York and Florida, support for these laws was bipartisan and these bills passed nearly unanimously. These laws send the message that accidental drug overdose is a health issue, and that fear of criminal justice involvement should not be a barrier to calling 911 in the event of an overdose.

The CCSA, in conjunction with the National Advisory Council on Prescription Drug Misuse, released a strategy on this topic that calls for action to address the increasing harms associated with prescription medication use (National Advisory Council on Prescription Drug Misuse 2013). The strategy focuses on opioids, sedative-hypnotics (such as Diazepam) and stimulants and makes a series of recommendations to government to ameliorate the harms of these substances. The strategy also attempts to address the harms of prescription drug use while acknowledging their beneficial medical purposes especially for the relief of pain. The strategy includes fifty-eight recommendations focused on prevention, treatment, education, monitoring and surveillance (data collection). While the strategy makes excellent recommendations about the need to collect better data and address prescribing practices and educate prescribers, patients and family on the appropriate use of medications, it does not give significant attention to two key activities that can help prevent overdose. Though mention is made of the need to review the evidence for community-based take-home naloxone programs (ibid. mp. 33, Recommendation 8), the strategy does not recommend a comprehensive health and human rights approach to overdose prevention and treatment; nor does it call for improved access to naloxone or the need for federal 911 Good Samaritan legislation.

Prisoners, Syringes and Harm Reduction in Canada

People do not surrender their human rights when they enter prison. Instead, they are dependent on the criminal justice system to uphold their human rights — including their right to health. Prison health is public health.

The statement above may seem self-evident to some, but the right to adequate health care services is the basis of a legal case brought against the Canadian federal government. Prison syringe exchange programs are a crucial component of a comprehensive strategy to prevent the spread of infectious diseases but the federal correctional service does not permit this life-saving health service in Canada's federal prisons. To challenge this policy, the Canadian HIV/AIDS Legal Network, Prisoners with HIV/AIDS Support Action Network, CATIE (Canada's source for HIV and hepatitis information), the Canadian Aboriginal AIDS Network and Steven Simons, a former federal prisoner, launched a lawsuit in September 2012 against the Government of Canada over its failure to protect the health of people in prison through its ongoing refusal to implement new clean needle and syringe programs. In fact, this case challenges Canada's federal correctional system to ensure that incarcerated persons are provided with equivalent access to health care as other Canadians (Canadian HIV/AIDS Legal Network 2012a).

Drug use in prisons is a reality. A 2007 survey by the Correctional Service of Canada (CSC) revealed that 16 percent of men and 14 percent of women had injected drugs while in prison (Correctional Service of Canada 2010b). Some prisoners are not ready to partake in treatment, treatment may be unavailable or treatment may not be appropriate. Despite the fact that drug use and possession is illegal in prison and despite efforts to prevent drugs from entering the prisons, drugs remain widely available. In fact, no prison system in the world has been able to keep drugs completely out. Sharing syringes is an efficient way of sharing blood-born illnesses. In a 2007 nationwide survey by the CSC, the rates of HIV and hepatitis C (HCV) among federally imprisoned women were 5.5 and 30.3 percent, compared to 4.5 and 30.8 percent among federally incarcerated men. Aboriginal women reported the highest rates of HIV and HCV, at 11.7 and 49.1 percent, respectively (Canadian HIV/AIDS Legal Network 2012b). This means that people in prison have rates of HIV and HCV that are *at least* ten and thirty times higher than the population as a whole and much of this infection is occurring because prisoners do not have access to sterile injection equipment (Canadian HIV/AIDS Legal Network 2012a).

This legal case challenges the belief that people revoke their rights when they enter a prison and are thus not entitled to equitable access to health care. In fact, prisoners retain all the human rights that people in the community have, except those that are necessarily restricted by incarceration. This includes the right to the highest attainable standard of health, a right enshrined in several U.N. treaties and conventions. This right encompasses measures, such as syringe exchanges, that have been shown repeatedly to prevent the transmission of diseases (UNODC, WHO, UNAIDS 2009).

These services are available in many parts of the world and evaluations have found that they reduce needle sharing, do not lead to increased drug use or injecting, help reduce drug overdoses, facilitate referrals of users to drug treatment programs and have not resulted in needles or syringes being used as weapons against staff. When these services were introduced in Swiss prisons, staff were initially reluctant, but because syringe exchange reduced the likelihood of a needle stick (accidently being poked by a needle) they realized that distribution of sterile injection equipment was in their own interest and felt safer than before the distribution started (Lines et al. 2006).

The vast majority of prisoners eventually return to the community, so illnesses that are acquired in prison do not necessarily stay in prison. This means that when we protect the health of prisoners we protect the health of everyone in our communities. Prisoners are part of Canadian life — they are mothers, fathers, brothers, sisters, friends and loved ones.

Harm Reduction: The Case of Ecstasy

On any given night in Canada, thousands of young people are attending dance events or parties held in clubs or private homes. A significant number of these party goers will choose to use substances to enhance their experience, including alcohol, cannabis, ecstasy and other mood-altering substances, some illegal and some legal. One of the more popular substances used at these parties is ecstasy, a street name for MDMA (methylenedioxymethamphetamine). Since illegal psychoactive substances used for non-medical purposes are not subject to government regulations for safe manufacture and distribution, ecstasy created in clandestine laboratories is often tainted with potentially damaging chemicals. In 2011 and 2012, five people in B.C. died as a result of ingesting ecstasy, causing uproar in the health and enforcement community about how to best respond to this situation. Toxicology results showed that the MDMA purchased by these people was tainted with PMMA (paramethoxy-metamphetamine) (B.C. Coroner's Service 2012). These deaths created a new and a familiar dilemma: we know that, despite drug prohibition, people will use ecstasy on a regular basis and we know that this drug will be purchased from an unregulated market; thus the quality of the drug and strength is unknown. Unbeknownst to buyers, other drugs, such as PMMA, may be included or sold as ecstasy. Given these realities, how do we best respond to minimize or significantly reduce the risks associated with the act of ingesting ecstasy of unknown potency, composition and quality that has been purchased from an unregulated source within an illegal unregulated market?

To date, drug prohibition and criminalization of people who possess drugs are touted as methods to ensure that drugs are not available to young people. Security services and policing efforts attempt to make events drug and dealer free. Despite these efforts, drugs like ecstasy are often available at dance events, clubs and private parties, or they may be purchased in advance of the event. Some efforts have been made by non-profit volunteer organizations to either test pills using rudimentary tests that determine if MDMA or other drugs are present in substances that are supposed to be ecstasy (Dancesafe 2013).

It may be time to acknowledge that young people in our society will continue to experiment with ecstasy, and that to better protect these people pill-testing services should be a part of our monitoring and early warning system. More robust testing services recognize the reality of drug use but prioritize health effects and outcomes. The Dutch have had a system of pill testing available to people who use drugs for many years and attribute their extremely low rate of injury and death from "bad" drugs at dance parties to the increased knowledge that young people have of the risks of ecstasy and their desire to test what they buy on the street before they use it. They also maintain that testing these pill products helps to "clean up" the illegal market in that dealers who sell toxic, dangerous or poor products are quickly exposed, which rewards those in the business who sell safer drugs (Benschop, Rabes and Korf 2002).

A comprehensive street drug testing service is an important part of a continuum of harm reduction responses to illegal drug use. Drug testing that provides feedback to clients allows them to make better-informed decisions, which contributes to improved self-determination and safety. Drug testing also gives health and other service providers a means to collect and assess information about illegal drug markets, the monitoring and surveillance of which are otherwise notoriously difficult. A street drug testing service that provides quick feedback to clients creates some accountability between the consumers of street drugs and those who supply them. When consumers of street drugs are able to have their drugs tested for purity and quality, or to test them themselves, they are empowered to boycott those dealers who sell poor-quality or heavily adulterated products.

In a comprehensive review of street drug testing, the European Monitoring Centre on Drugs and Drug Addiction concluded that street drug testing is an important source of information on new substances and consumption trends, including ecstasy. It stressed that testing should be closely linked to the provision of safer use messages through a wide range of information supports (ibid.).

The tragic outcome of drug policies that perpetuate a strict prohibition on assisting young people to determine the safety of their drugs, is that some will needlessly be injured or die as a result of tainted, unregulated and untested products. Prohibitionist policies rely on the sacrifice of some young people in an attempt to keep drugs out of their hands and to create the perception that taking illegal drugs is always a high-risk activity.

It appears that we have a choice to make as a society: since we know that drug taking by young people will continue to occur, we can continue to perpetuate enforcement and prevention messages that rely on scare tactics — such as the anti-drug media campaigns by the Conservative-led federal

---

The 595 Prevention Team in Winnipeg

The 595 Prevention Team is a network of over one hundred member organizations — such as Manitoba Area Network of Drug Users, The Mothering Project and Aboriginal Youth Opportunities — interested in harm reduction and addressing the determinants of health and preventing the transmission of sexually transmitted infections and blood borne infections (STBBIS), primarily HIV and HCV, in Manitoba. The 595 works with peers, network members, policy makers and community leaders to make recommendations regarding the development, implementation and evaluation of STBBI-prevention initiatives based on evidence and best practice with priority populations. Core values of The 595 include client-centred and non-judgemental care, relationship building and creating supportive environments for people who use drugs. The 595 believes in best practice, especially when working with underserved populations. They offer a selection of workshops in conjunction with a consultation process that includes communities, participants and service providers. Workshops such as "Define 'Harm Reduction' and discuss the principles and components of the Harm Reduction model"; "Review risk-taking and risk assessment"; and "HIV/HCV prevention, treatment, and care" are just a few of those offered. All workshops have a foundation of consistent core information and are tailored to ensure that specific community needs are addressed. Workshops have been delivered throughout Manitoba as far north as Thompson and are thoroughly evaluated. Since 2008 they have trained over 1200 service providers (595 Prevention Team 2015).

government discussed in Chapter 5 that discourage this activity from taking place — or we can implement a system that will help young people gain knowledge of what they are buying, the associated risks of drug use and safer practices in taking those drugs and, at the same time, put dealers and producers on notice that they will be exposed if their products are tainted.

Community Organizations

Community organizations in Canada support harm reduction initiatives and increasingly work together to educate peers, frontline health and service providers, and researchers about innovative harm reduction practices. For example, since 2000, the Alberta Harm Reduction conference has been held annually and now every two years to bring together harm reduction practitioners from across Canada and the U.S. to discuss the work they are doing. The conference is hosted by Alberta's needle exchange/harm reduction programs throughout the province, including Safeworks, Central Alberta AIDS Network, HIV North, HIV West Yellowhead, HIV Community Link, HIV Connection and Streetworks. In addition to conferences, organizations such as 595 Prevention Team in Winnipeg network with over one hundred other organizations, providing workshops on harm reduction and related topics.

OBSTACLES TO HARM REDUCTION

In the sections above, we highlight many effective harm reduction services in Canada that seek to reduce drug related harms. We also discuss programs that need to be expanded. Though many municipalities, provinces and territories provide some form of support for harm reduction, the range of harm reduction services varies considerably across the country. Harm reduction services are also plagued by a number of obstacles, such as a lack of integration into existing services, or "siloing."

Harm Reduction Services Are Siloed

The "siloing" of harm reduction in HIV policy and program areas continues. Provincial and health authority funding arrangements for harm reduction services usually flow from programs to prevent the transmission of blood-borne pathogens, such as HIV and HCV, and are not integrated with other substance-related program areas (that is, drug treatment). These funding arrangements partly originate in the historical development of harm reduction services in Canada. Due to the slowness of government response to the HIV epidemic in the 1980s, peer-based and other community groups created harm reduction services to respond to this crisis. But due to a lack of leadership on the part of governments, services for the prevention of blood-borne pathogens remained isolated from other drug-related services. This separation occurs at multiple levels and sites, including in policy, funding, information flow, approaches to admission to services and varying philosophical approaches to treatment and recovery. These programmatic arrangements have been partly responsible for a failure to fully integrate harm reduction services into the overall system of health care. They also perpetuate the notion that harm reduction is somehow the opposite of abstinence-based services rather than both being seen as part of a continuum of care.

The result is that many jurisdictions still treat harm reduction as simply "supply distribution" for the prevention of HIV and other blood-borne pathogens, such as only supplying clean needles rather than other social and health supports. As the numerous harm reduction services across the country have demonstrated, harm reduction is much more than distributing needles or other supplies; because of its philosophical underpinnings in non-judgemental, client-centred care, it is also an exemplary practice of health engagement that could potentially be a model for other health issues.

Meeting a Wide Range of Important Needs

Because harm reduction services draw on non-judgemental and accessible approaches to care, clients routinely request assistance with other issues like housing and income support. But because harm reduction is still seen as "supply distribution," many harm reduction services remain grossly underfunded to meet the full range of client needs, such as stable housing, employment, access to income support programs, prenatal and antenatal care and childcare. Provincial and/or health authority funding mechanisms for harm reduction services do not always recognize the broader services provided by harm reduction programs; nor do provincial policy and funding mechanisms recognize the broader needs of clients. In fact, social assistance rates are not adequate for people to find and keep stable housing and meet basic needs such as nutritious foods. The lack of adequate social supports undermines the ability of some Canadians to live healthy and safe lives (MacKinnon 2011).

Good Relationships Can Change

Successful and effective harm reduction service providers are often dependent upon good relationships with provincial government and/or health authority counterparts for the continued funding of their services. This is a concern because relationships can change as people change employment, or as political and policy priorities change. Managers in health authorities who support harm reduction services may move to other positions and new mangers may not support existing programs or the establishment of new ones.

More Rural and Remote Services Are Needed

In many places in Canada there is no comprehensive plan to recognize the harm reduction needs of people living in rural areas. In many rural contexts, harm reduction supplies (needles, alcohol swabs, screens/filters and so on) are either not available or are available only through secondary or "natural helper" distribution. Natural helpers refers to people who use harm reduction services and who also distribute equipment received there to friends and associates (Sharp Advice Needle Exchange 2013). These forms of distribution are often reliant on unpaid helpers and are vulnerable because of a lack of formal mechanisms to provide these services. The scale-up of services in rural and remote areas is also hindered by discrimination against people who use drugs.

Centralized Supply Purchasing Creates Efficiencies

Only three provinces, B.C., Ontario and, most recently, Alberta, have centralized purchasing and distributing harm reduction supplies. Centralized mechanisms for supply distribution (such as syringes and alcohol swabs) are cost-effective ways of purchasing and distributing supplies. Centralized services can collect data on the amount and type of supplies distributed and can assess shifts in supply requirements that may signal emerging drug use issues. In the absence of these centralized mechanisms, harm reduction providers must make arrangements with local health authorities or others to access cost-effective supplies and staff time must be allocated to purchasing supplies (Buxton et al. 2008).

Women, Pregnancy and Harm Reduction

Despite improvements, Canada lacks a comprehensive system of harm reduction supports for pregnant women who use drugs. A harm reduction approach to pregnancy and drug use draws on the pragmatic approach discussed earlier but also focuses on providing basic needs, such as prenatal and antenatal care, housing and nutrition. This approach recognizes that discrimination against pregnant and mothering women who use drugs drives them away from prenatal and antenatal care. Most harm reduction programs are not funded to provide these services and, in some jurisdictions, services simply do not exist for pregnant and mothering women who use drugs. (See discussion above for examples of existing programs.)

Harm Reduction is Still Profoundly Misunderstood by Some

Media reports and some key politicians still claim that harm reduction services operate in opposition to abstinence-based and other drug treatment programs (see Ambrose 2013; CBC News 2015a; Robson 2013; Wente 2008; Woo 2013). In fact, media reports are not sufficiently critical of the suggestion that funding for harm reduction services detracts from drug treatment programs. These claims pit harm reduction programs against the rest of the system of supports for drug use. It cannot be emphasized enough that harm reduction services are part of a larger continuum of care that includes other low-threshold services, treatment and aftercare. Media coverage of backlash against these services can exacerbate tensions between people who use drugs and other community members. This backlash and subsequent media reporting can reinforce common myths and stereotypes that contribute to exclusionary public policies. Following the federal government's refusal to grant a continuation of the legal exemption to Insite in 2007, and the subsequent legal challenge that went all the way to the Supreme Court in 2008, Margaret Wente, a columnist for the *Globe and Mail,* wrote a four-part series on drug policy and harm reduction. Her articles attacked harm reduction programs and Canadian researchers who have evaluated them. Having never visited Insite herself or examined the research evaluating the program, Wente presented a distorted picture of Insite and other harm reduction initiatives (Wente 2008). Politicians, such as former Health Minister Rona Ambrose, have also released misinformation about harm reduction programs. In 2013, then Health Minister Ambrose demonized providing legally prescribed heroin administered by doctors for patients following the SALOME study (discussed earlier in this chapter). She claimed that giving heroin to heroin users is in opposition to the "government's anti-drug policy." She also noted that it is the government's policy to "take heroin out of the hands of addicts, not to put it into their arms" (Ambrose 2013). This resistance is fed by lack of understanding — or the resistance to understanding — the effectiveness of these services and by discriminatory attitudes and behaviours against people who use drugs.

Unfortunately, since 2007, the federal government of Canada has been a major force in obstructing the establishment of some harm reduction programs and contributing to misunderstanding about harm reduction. Harm reduction was seen, as former Health Minister Rona Ambrose made clear above, as in opposition to the Conservative-led federal government's anti-drug policy.

MISINFORMED AND DISINFORMED: RESISTANCE TO HARM REDUCTION PROGRAMS

Harm reduction programs in Canada are sometimes on the receiving end of public backlash. Resistance by the federal government, community groups, municipalities and even medical health officers can lead to delays or denial of harm reduction services. Even when provinces have clearly articulated provincial-level policy frameworks that support harm reduction, this does not guarantee that all municipalities or health authorities will support harm reduction services. Municipalities have become another site for public conflicts over the provision of harm reduction and methadone services. Since 2005, some municipalities in B.C. have become involved in regulating illegal substances through the use of bylaws and residential inspection programs. These activities have focused mainly on using municipal bylaws to control the cultivation of marijuana and the production of methamphetamines (Boyd and Carter 2014). But bylaws and zoning provisions have also been used to restrict the availability of harm reduction services. In 2012, Mission, B.C., passed a bylaw that prevents the establishment of pharmacies in its downtown area effectively preventing methadone dispensing in their Core Commercial Downtown Zones (Bernstein and Bennett 2013). In 2005, Abbotsford, B.C. passed an amendment to its zoning bylaws that restricts harm reduction services (needle exchanges, mobile dispensing vans, supervised injection sites) in its municipality. In Coquitlam, B.C., a 1996 bylaw restricts the location of methadone clinics and another bylaw designates methadone clinics as "undesirable businesses" (ibid.). Abbotsford's restrictive zoning bylaws were challenged by Pivot Legal Society in 2013:

> Pivot filed a lawsuit and human rights complaint on behalf of three people who use drugs in Abbotsford and the BC/Yukon Association of Drug War Survivors, challenging the Abbotsford zoning bylaw, which prohibits all harm reduction uses anywhere in the municipality. In early 2014, the City of Abbotsford voted to amend the Bylaw before the case went to court. (Pivot Legal Society 2013)

Pivot states that, "this is a huge victory of drug users in the City of Abbotsford and for human rights in this province."

In Ontario, resistance to harm reduction services and opioid maintenance programs has occurred in several communities in recent years, sometimes spearheaded by local politicians. Several municipalities — for example, Windsor, Pembroke and Oshawa — have also passed bylaws or land-use requirements that restrict methadone clinics (City of Windsor 2013; City of Pembroke 2013; City of Oshawa 2013).

HARM REDUCTION OUT OF THE NADS

In 2007, the federal government eliminated harm reduction from the NADS and until the federal election in fall 2015, it had been either indifferent or hostile to harm reduction services. Many Canadians were concerned about this hostility to a well-established health practice supported by global organizations, such as the United Nations Office on Drugs and Crime, UNAIDS and the World Health Organization (WHO, UNODC and UNAIDS 2009). For example, the B.C. Ministry of Health, the Quebec Ministry of Health, the City of Toronto and the City of Vancouver support and fund harm reduction initiatives. The lack of federal government support for harm reduction undermined efforts to establish new harm reduction services from 2007 to 2015 and to more fully integrate and expand currently existing programs into the health care system. In fact, when the CCSA released a strategy to address "prescription drug misuse" in Canada, the document avoided the use of the term "harm reduction" altogether though it nods in several places to the need to address the harms of prescribed drug use by drawing on an evidence-based public health approach. The strategy recommends, for example, that Health Canada and the Public Health Agency of Canada "develop and promote risk reduction programs for individuals who use prescription drugs" (National Advisory Council on Prescription Drug Misuse 2013: 32), though no specifics about the nature of these "risk reduction" programs are provided. Unfortunately the open hostility of the prior Conservative-led federal government to harm reduction made it increasingly difficult for both federal agencies and groups funded by the federal government to openly discuss the merits of this important health care service (ibid.). This then emphasizes the importance of this chapter's discussion of harm reduction initiatives that are effective in Canada, places for improvement and advocacy for change, especially now that a change in federal government has occurred.

10

DRUG POLICY
IN THE FUTURE

In this book we discuss important areas of drug policy and innovations that are taking place in Canada. We also introduce readers to critical sociological and feminist perspectives, and critical addiction frameworks. In the first chapter of this book we asked how ideas about substances and the people who use them shape policy. We also asked what solutions and policies are advanced to solve the problem of illegal drugs. Then we set out to provide some answers to these questions by providing a brief history of Canada's drug laws and policies, drug use rates in Canada and federal drug policy under the NADS. Following these chapters we introduced services for people who use drugs and harm reduction programs, some of which are threatened by federal drug policies. We also examined why punitive prohibitionist drug policies are a failure and discussed the global movement to end drug prohibition. This book calls for a review of the overall use of the criminal law in responding to the use of illegal substances and drug-related problems.

The findings of this book, drawing on interviews with change-makers and service providers and a review of policy documents and research, reveals that Canada is at a crossroads when it comes to drug laws and policies. A new direction in drug policy is required. We can continue to work within the paradigm of drug prohibition or we can begin to explore alternative approaches and chart a new course that can help save lives, will respect human rights and foster social inclusion and will be more cost effective.

Fortunately, drug policies and law are not unchanging. In fact, sweeping change, such as the end of cannabis prohibition and the legal regulation of the substance, and the decriminalization of possession of all drugs, has occurred around the world. Sometimes, drug reform is incremental. At other times, small policy shifts slowly evolve over time to form a larger change. With the election of a Liberal-led federal government in the fall of 2015, Canada's drug policies are about to change dramatically if the Liberal promise to end cannabis prohibition is enacted into law.

As we write, Canada still relies on the criminal law to curb illegal drug use and stem the growth of illegal drug markets. Canada also spends enormous amounts of money annually to prevent the illegal purchase, use and distribution of illegal drugs both inside Canada and beyond its borders. The Conservative-led federal government allocated $527.8 million for the NADS for 2012–17, much of it on enforcement related activities. It is too soon to know how the allocation of funds will be prioritized in the next federal budget, especially if cannabis prohibition ends and a legal regulatory framework is created in its place. However, the NADS strategy only accounts for a portion of government spending on drug control. Activities such as provincial, municipal and RCMP drug enforcement, national drug interdiction efforts and the use of military personnel in international drug control efforts, drive up policing, military and border security budgets.

Cannabis remains a key target of these policing activities — cannabis possession charges numbered 59,965 in 2013, a rate of 168 per 100,000 people in Canada. The rate of police-reported incidents of cannabis possession are far higher than for any other illegal drug (at 22 per 100,000 for cocaine possession and a rate of 32 per 100,000 for all other illegal drugs combined) (Boyce, Cotter and Perreault 2014: Table 5). The rate of cannabis possession offences has more than doubled since 1991 (Cotter, Greenland and Karam 2015: 7). Cannabis remains a lucrative market — annual retail expenditures on this substance are estimated to be about $357 million per year in B.C. alone. Cannabis is a popular drug and its harmful effects are certainly less than alcohol and tobacco. Thus, the Liberal-led federal government plans to move forward to set up a legal framework to regulate and tax cannabis. However, what will this legal framework look like? Will small and local cannabis dispensaries become part of the framework? Will adults be allowed to grow a few cannabis plants for personal use? Will cannabis arrests cease now rather than waiting until after the new framework is implemented? Will people with past cannabis convictions be pardoned?

One of the most urgent issues affecting Canadians is discrimination against people who use illegal drugs. Poor and racialized women and men, especially First Nations peoples, are discriminated against in the criminal justice system (policing, courts and prison systems) and in social welfare and health services. In fact, poor and marginalized people bear the brunt of our prohibitionist drug policies. This discrimination and the hostility towards people who use drugs can be seen in the derogatory statements that appear routinely in media reports of public debates about services. Even with cannabis reform, legal discrimination against people who use other criminalized drugs may continue. In addition, people who sell small amounts of criminalized drugs may be further demonized. Thus, a reconsideration of all drug policies would be beneficial.

Therefore, there is also a need for urgent change in three key areas: drug law reform, discrimination, services and supports. In order to move forward, we recommend the reform of Canada's legislative, policy and regulatory frameworks that address psychoactive substances. We call for the replacement of the NADS with one focused on health and human rights, social inclusion and the legal regulation of all drugs for personal use (and any step forward, such as decriminalization and the elimination of criminal penalties for personal possession), and the immediate creation of a regulatory system for adult cannabis use as the Liberal-led federal proposes to do. In addition, we remind readers that most drug use is not problematic; rather, drug use is a social and cultural practice. Thus, not all drug use needs to be treated (or criminalized). However, we advocate the scaling-up of comprehensive health and social services, including housing and treatment services that engage people with drug problems. In addition, we advocate increased support for efforts to reduce the harms of substance use, which includes robust educational programs about safer drug use, programs for distributing new supplies for injection and crack cocaine use, safer consumption services, opioid substitution therapies and heroin-assisted treatment. We argue that these services are part of larger social and public health approach to substance use that respects the human rights of people who use drugs. In addition, we also advocate that social and economic supports accompany drug reform. We also support expanded efforts to implement research-based and social approaches to eliminate stigma and discrimination and social and health inequities that affect people who use drugs.

Canada has many good people working at every level from frontline services and organizations to provincial and federal ministries, whose efforts are severely hampered by fear, lack of leadership and poorly informed policies based on outdated ideas and beliefs about drugs, addiction and the people who use, produce and sell substances. At the same time, critics in Canada assert that drug prohibition causes more harm than the drugs and the people it attempts to regulate. Eugene Oscapella, in his report with the Canadian Drug Policy Coalition Policy Working group, *Changing the Frame: A New Approach to Drug Policy in Canada*, stresses that there is "no substantial evidence that the criminal law significantly deters drug use" (Oscapella 2012: 12). In addition, a global movement of sitting and former political leaders is emerging that acknowledges that the over-reliance on the criminal law in addressing drug problems is causing more harm than good. In 2011, the Global Commission on Drug Policy stated:

The global war on drugs has failed, with devastating consequences for individuals and societies around the world. Fifty years after the initiation of the U.N. Single Convention on Narcotic Drugs ... fundamental reforms in national and global drug control policies are urgently needed. (Global Commission on Drug Policy 2011: 2)

The Commission recommends an end to the discrimination and marginalization of people who use currently criminalized drugs. They also recommend that governments implement models of legal regulation.

As drug users themselves and service and health providers continue to operate innovative harm reduction and drug services in Canada, and press for municipal, provincial and national reform, others, such as the Canadian Drug Policy Coalition, the Global Commission on Drug Policy, Transform Drug Policy Foundation and Drug Policy Alliance (to name a few organizations), are also pressing for change at the international level, including organizing national and international discussions and meetings prior to the United Nations General Assembly Special Session (UNGASS) in 2016 that will take place in New York. As we discussed in Chapter 7, UNGASS is a special deliberation by the General Assembly to discuss a pressing issue of the day relating to health, gender or, in this case, the world's drug control priorities. The previous special session on drugs, held in 1998, adopted a plan to make the world "drug-free" by 2008. This plan has not been realized. UNGASS 2016 is seen as an opportunity to craft a more realistic and constructive plan.

UNGASS 2016 was precipitated by an aligned and resolute group of reform-minded Latin American countries. But calls for reform are also emanating from Europe, and even the U.S. — traditionally one of the world's staunchest proponents and architects of the war on drugs — recognizes the need for more flexible interpretations of U.N. drug treaties.

The number of U.N. member states advocating for new approaches to drug policy is unprecedented. As we highlighted in the pages of this book, globally, unparalleled drug reform is taking place. In a short span of time cannabis prohibition ended in Uruguay, four U.S. states and the District of Columbia; the decriminalization of personal use of all drugs took place in Portugal, and Bolivia opted to allow the chewing of coca leaves. These are only a few of the many drug reform shifts going on around the world. Along with drug reform is a commitment to harm reduction initiatives and diverse drug treatment programs, supported by economic and social supports, such as housing.

With so many governments and citizens ready for change, UNGASS 2016 represents an unprecedented opportunity to put an end to the war on drugs, and instead prioritize health, human rights and safety. Now that the Conservative-led federal government, which opposed putting an end to punitive prohibitionist approaches, no longer dominates Parliament, Canada has a chance to join with reformist voices at the U.N.

The irony is that despite the past federal government's opposition to harm reduction and drug policy reform, Canada is known internationally for its innovation in this area. This is thanks to many of the municipal-level initiatives that we describe in the pages of this book. Following the federal election in the fall of 2015, drug policy reform is more likely to occur if Canadians demand change. We hope that this book contributes to ongoing dialogues in Canada about drug prohibition and that it provides a framework for understanding drug policies and possibilities for change.

LIST OF ACRONYMS

ADHD	attention deficit and hyperactivity disorder
CADUMS	Canadian Alcohol and Drug Use Monitoring Survey
CAMH	Centre for Addiction and Mental Health
CCRA	*Corrections and Conditional Release Act*
CDSA	*Controlled Drugs and Substances Act*
CIC	Correctional Investigator of Canada
CSC	Correctional Service of Canada
CCSA	Canadian Centre on Substance Abuse
DARE	Drug Abuse Resistance Program
DOCAS	Drugs and Organized Crime Awareness Service (RCMP)
DSCIF	Drug Strategies Community Initiatives Fund
DTC	drug treatment court
DTES	Downtown Eastside (Vancouver)
DTFP	Drug Treatment Funding Program
EMS	emergency medical services
HCV	hepatitis C virus
HAT	heroin-assisted treatment
HIV	human immunodeficiency virus
INCB	International Narcotics Control Board
MDMA	methylenedioxymethamphetamine (sometimes known as ecstasy though ecstasy does not necessarily contain MDMA)
MDSCNO	Municipal Drug Strategy Co-ordinator's Network of Ontario
MMPR	Marihuana for Medical Purposes Regulations
MMT	methadone maintenance therapy
NADS	National Anti-Drug Strategy
NAOMI	North American Opiate Medication Initiative

NAF	Narcotic Addiction Foundation of B.C
NNADAP	National Native Alcohol and Drug Abuse Program
NPA	NAOMI Patients Association
PUPL	Personal Use Production Licences
RCMP	Royal Canadian Mounted Police
SALOME	Study to Assess Longer-Term Opioid Medication Effectiveness
SIS	supervised injection site
SSCA	*Safe Streets and Communities Act*
STBBI	sexually transmitted infections and blood borne infections
TDS	Toronto Drug Strategy
UCR	Uniform Crime Reporting Survey
UNGASS	United Nations General Assembly Special Session
UNODC	United Nations Office on Drugs and Crime
VANDU	Vancouver Area Network of Drug Users
VPD	Vancouver Police Department
WRCPC	Waterloo Region Crime Prevention Council
WHO	World Health Organization

REFERENCES

Acker, C. 2002. *Creating the American Junkie: Addiction Research in the Classic Era of Narcotic Control*. Baltimore: Johns Hopkins University Press.

Adlaf, E., and A. Paglia-Boak. 2007. *Drug Use Among Ontario Students: OSDUHS Highlights 1977–2007*. Centre for Addiction and Mental Health.

Alberta Health. 2011. *Creating Connections: Alberta's Mental Health and Addictions Strategy, 2011*. <http://www.health.alberta.ca/documents/Creating-Connections-2011-Strategy.pdf>.

Alford, D., P. Compton and J. Samet. 2006. "Acute Pain Management for Patients Receiving Maintenance Methadone or Buprenorphine Therapy." *Annals of Internal Medicine* 144: 127–134.

Allard, P., T. Lyons, and R. Elliot. 2011. *Impaired Judgment: Assessing the Appropriateness of Drug Treatment Courts as a Response to Drug Use in Canada*. Toronto: Canadian HIV/AIDS Legal Network. <http://www.aidslaw.ca/site/wp-content/uploads/2013/09/DTCs-Oct11-E.pdf>.

Ambrose, R. 2013. Statement—Minister Ambrose. Ottawa: Minister of Health. September 20.

Angus Reid. 2011. *British Columbians Link Gang Violence to Illegal Cannibis Market*. Poll commissioned by Stop the Violence BC. September. <http://stoptheviolencebc.org/2011/10/26/poll-britishcolumbians-link-gang-violence-to-illegal-cannabis-market/>.

____. 2012. *Most Americans and Canadians Are Ready to Legalize Marijuana*. Angus Reid Public Opinion, November 29. <http://www.angus-reid.com/polls/47901/most-americans-and-canadians-are-ready-to-legalize-marijuana/>.

Bacchi, C. 1999. *Women, Policy and Politics: The Construction of Policy Problems*. London: Sage Publications.

____. 2009. *Analysing Policy: What's the Problem Represented To Be?* French Forest, Australia: Pearson.

____. 2012. "Why Study Problematizations? Making Politics Visible." *Open Journal of Political Science* 2, 1: 1–8. <http://dx.doi.org/10.4236/ojps.2012.21001>.

Balfour, G., and E. Comack (eds). 2006. *Criminalizing Women: Gender and (In) justice in Neo-liberal Times*. Halifax: Fernwood Publishing.

____. 2014. *Criminalizing Women: Gender and (In)Justice in Neo-Liberal Times* 2nd edition. Winnipeg: Fernwood Publishing.

Barrett, D., R. Lines, R. Scheifer, R. Elliot, and D. Bewley-Taylor. 2008. *Recalibrating the Regime: The Need for a Human Rights-Based Approach to International Drug Policy*. Beckley Foundation Drug Policy Programme. <http://www.ihra.net/contents/552>.

B.C. Coroner's Service. 2012. *Coroners Service Confirms Chemical Linked to Ecstasy Deaths*. <http://www2.news.gov.bc.ca/news_releases_2009-2013/2012PSSG0004-000029.htm>.

B.C. Corrections, Ministry of Justice. 2014. "Data on Women Who Received a Jail Sentence with British Columbia Corrections." Email communication with C. Gress, Director of Research & Planning, February 17.

B.C. Mental Health and Substance Use Project. 2007. *Cross-Jurisdictional Review: Mental Health and Substance Use Policies*. <http://www.nshrf.ca/sites/default/files/bc_report_referenced_in_rfps_05.01.12.pdf>.

B.C. Ministry of Health. 2010. "Healthy Minds, Healthy People: A Ten-Year Plan to Address Mental Health and Substance Use in British Columbia." <http://www.health.gov.bc.ca/library/publications/year/2010/healthy_minds_healthy_people.pdf>.

____. 2012. "Guidance Document for Supervised Injection Services." <http://www.health.gov.bc.ca/cdms/pdf/guidance-document-for-sis-in-bc.pdf>.

B.C. Ministry of Health Services. 2004. "Every Door Is the Right Door: A British Columbia Planning Framework to Address Problematic Substance Use and Addition." Victoria, BC. <http://www.health.gov.bc.ca/library/publications/year/2004/framework_for_substance_use_and_addiction.pdf>.

B.C. Partners for Mental Health Addictions Information. 2013. "Learn About Tobacco, Alcohol and Other Drugs." Vancouver: Heretohelp. <http://www.heretohelp.bc.ca/sites/default/files/images/drugs.pdf>.

B.C. Provincial Harm Reduction Program. 2012. "Take-Home Naloxone: Backgrounder." <http://towardtheheart.com/naloxone/>.

BCCDC (BC Centre for Disease Control). 2012. *Toward the Heart: Study — Crack Cocaine Users*. <http://towardtheheart.com/news/perceptions-of-people-who-smoke-crack-cocaine-in-vancouver>.

____. 2013. "Opioid Use and Overdose in British Columbia." <http://towardtheheart.com/assets/naloxone/opioid-use-in-bc--final_99.pdf>.

Beasley, E., R. Jesseman, D. Patton, and National Treatment Indicators Working Group. 2012. *National Treatment Indicators Report, 2012*. Ottawa: Canadian Centre on Substance Abuse.

Bell, M., C. Dell, and R. Duncan. 2011. *Alcohol and Substance Use in Saskatoon: Emerging Trends. A Canadian Community Epidemiology on Drug Use Inaugural Site Report*. Saskatoon: CCENDU. <http://www.addictionresearchchair.ca/wp-content/uploads/FINAL-SUBMITTED-CCENDU-Report-Saskatoon-2011-April-4.2011.pdf>.

Belle-Isle, L., and A. Hathaway. 2007. "Barriers to Access to Medical Cannabis for

Canadians Living with HIV/AIDS." *AIDS Care* 19, 4: 500–06.

Benschop, A., M. Rabes, and D.J. Korf. 2002. "Pill Testing, Ecstasy and Prevention: A Scientific Evaluation in Three European Cities." Amsterdam: Rozenberg Publishers.

Bernstein, S., and D. Bennett. 2013. "Zoned Out: 'NIMBYism,' Addiction Services and Municipal Governance in British Columbia." *International Journal of Drug Policy* 24: e61–e65.

Berridge, V. 2013. *Demons: Our Changing Attitudes to Alcohol, Tobacco, & Drugs.* New York: Oxford University Press.

Best, J. 1995. *Random Violence: How We Talk About New Crimes and New Victims.* Berkeley: University of California Press.

Blanken, P., et al. 2010. "Heroin-Assisted Treatment in the Netherlands: History, Findings, and International Context." *European Neuropsychopharmacology* 20 (Suppl 2): S105–S158.

Blickman, T. 2013. *Objections to Bolivia's Reservation to Allow Coca Chewing in the UN Conventions.* TNI: Drug Law Reform in Latin America. <http://druglawreform.info/en/weblog/item/4245-objections-to-bolivias-reservation-to-allow-coca-chewing-in-the-un-conventions>.

Bronskill, J. 2015. "Tax Revenue from Legalized Pot Should Fund Addiction Programs, Trudeau Says." *The Brandon Sun*, December 17. <http://www.brandonsun.com/national/breaking-news/taxation-of-legalized-pot-wont-be-a-government-cash-cow-trudeau-says-362833511.html?thx=y>.

Boyce, J., A. Cotter, and S. Perreault. 2014. "Police-Reported Crime Statistics in Canada, 2013." *Juristat.* Ottawa: Canadian Centre for Justice Statistics.

Boyd, J., S. Boyd, and T. Kerr. 2015. "Visual and Narrative Representations of Mental Health and Addiction by Law Enforcement." *International Journal of Drug Policy* 26, 7: 636–44.

Boyd, N. 1984. "The Origins of Canadian Narcotics Legislation: The Process of Criminalization in Historical Context." *Dalhousie Law Journal* 8: 102–36.

____. 2013. *The Enforcement of Marijuana Possession Offences in British Columbia: A Blueprint for Change.* <http://sensiblebc.ca/wp-content/uploads/2013/02/Blueprint-for-Change.pdf>.

Boyd, S. 2006. "Representations of Women in the Drug Trade." In G. Balfour and E. Comack (eds.), *Criminalizing Women.* Halifax: Fernwood Publishing.

____. 2013. "A Canadian Perspective on Documentary Film: *Drug Addict.*" *International Journal of Drug Policy* 24, 6: 589–96.

____. 2014. "The Criminal Addict: Canadian Radio Documentary Discourse, 1957–1969." *Contemporary Drug Problems* 41, 2: 201–32.

____. 2015. *From Witches to Crack Moms: Women, Drug Law and Policy,* 2nd edition. Durham: Carolina Academic Press.

Boyd, S., and C. Carter. 2014. *Killer Weed: Marijuana Grow Ops, Media, and Justice.* Toronto: University of Toronto Press.

Boyd, S., J. Johnson, and B. Moffat. 2008. "Opportunities to Learn and Barriers to Change: Crack-Cocaine Use and Harm Reduction in the Downtown Eastside of Vancouver." *Harm Reduction Journal* 5, 34: 1–12.

Boyd, S., B. Osborn, and D. MacPherson. 2009. *Raise Shit! Social Action Saving Lives.*

Halifax: Fernwood Publishing.

Boyd, S., and NPA (NAOMI Patients Association). 2013. "Yet They Failed to Do So: Recommendations Based on the Experiences of NAOMI Research Survivors and a Call for Action." *Harm Reduction Journal* 10, 6: 1–13

Boyd, S., and SNAP. 2013. "SNAP: *Telling Our Stories, Heroin-Assisted Treatment and Advocacy*." Vancouver, November 30. <http://www.drug policy.ca/>.

Bracke, H., K. Bailey, S. Marshall, and P. Plourde. 2012. *Safer Crack Use Kit Distribution in the Winnipeg Health Region*. Winnipeg: Population and Public Health Program, Winnipeg Regional Health Authority.

Brecher, E., and the Editors of Consumer Reports. 1972. *Licit & Illicit Drugs*. Boston: Little, Brown and Company.

Brennan, S. 2012. *Police Reported Crime Statistics in Canada, 2011*. Ottawa: Statistics Canada. <http://www.statcan.gc.ca/pub/85-002-x/2012001/article/11692-eng. htm>.

Bungay, V., J. Johnson, et al. 2010. "Women's Health and Use of Crack Cocaine In Context: Structural and 'Everyday' Violence." *International Journal of Drug Policy* 21, 4: 321–29.

Buxton, J.A., E.C. Preston, et al. 2008. "More Than Just Needles: An Evidence-Informed Approach to Enhancing Harm Reduction Supply Distribution in British Columbia." *Harm Reduction Journal* 5, 37.

CADUMS (Canadian Alcohol and Drug Use Monitoring Survey). 2012. *Summary of Results for 2012*. Health Canada. <http://www.hc-sc.gc.ca/hc-ps/drugs-drogues/ stat/_2012/summary-sommaire-eng.php>.

Calcaterra, S., J. Glanz, and I. Binswaner. 2012. "National Trends in Pharmaceutical Opioid Related Overdose Deaths Compared to Other Substance Related Overdose Deaths: 1999–2009." *Drug and Alcohol Dependence* 131: 263–70.

CAMH Population Studies eBulletin. 2008. Vol. 9, 2. Public Health and Regulatory Policy Research Unit, CAMH.

Campbell, N. 2007. *Discovering Addiction: The Science and Politics of Substance Abuse Research*. Ann Arbor: University of Michigan Press.

Campbell, N., and E. Ettorre. 2011. *Gendering Addiction: The Politics of Drug Treatment in a Neurological World*. New York: Palgrave Macmillan.

Canadian Association of Nurses. 2011. *Harm Reduction and Currently Illegal Drugs: Implications for Nursing Policy, Practice, Education and Research*. <https://cna-aiic. ca/~/media/cna/page-content/pdf-en/harm_reduction_2011_e.pdf>.

Canadian Bar Association. 2009. *Canadian Bar Association Favours Judge's Discretion over Mandatory Minimums for Drug-Related Offences*. <http://www.cba.org/cba/ news/2010_releases/2010-10-27-MandatoryMin.aspx>.

Canadian Bar Association, National Criminal Law Section. 2009. *Bill C-15 — Controlled Drugs and Substances Act Amendments*. <http://www.cba.org/CBA/submissions/ pdf/09-27-eng.pdf>.

Canadian Council on Social Development. 2014. *Children and Youth: Crime Prevention Through Social Development*. <http://www.ccsd.ca/resources/CrimePrevention/ index.htm>.

Canadian HIV/AIDS Legal Network. 2005. *"Nothing About Us Without Us": Greater,*

Meaningful Involvement of People Who Use Illegal Drugs: A Public Health, Ethical, and Human Rights Imperative. <http://www.aidslaw.ca/Maincontent/issues/druglaws/greater_involvement.html>.

_____. 2012a. *Lawsuit Filed Against Government of Canada for Failing to Protect the Health of Federal Prisoners.* <http://www.aidslaw.ca/publications/interfaces/downloadDocumentFile.php?ref=1316>.

_____. 2012b. *Women in Prison, HIV and Hepatitis C.* <http://www.aidslaw.ca/publications/publicationsdocEN.php?ref=1281>.

Canadian Medical Association. 2012. MD *Role in the Use of Medical Marijuana Baffles Many Doctors: Survey.* October 11. <http://www.cma.ca/md-role-medical-marijuana-baffles>.

Canadian Network of Substance Abuse and Allied Professionals. N.D. *Essentials of ... Trauma Informed Care.* <http://www.bccewh.bc.ca/news-events/documents/PT-Trauma-informed-Care-2012-01-en.pdf>.

Carstairs, C. 2006. *Jailed for Possession: Illegal Drug use, Regulation, and Power in Canada, 1920–1961.* Toronto: University of Toronto Press.

Carter, C., and B. Graham. 2013. *Opioid Overdose Prevention in and Response in Canada.* Vancouver, BC: Canadian Drug Policy Coalition. <http://drugpolicy.ca/wp-content/uploads/2014/07/CDPC_OverdosePreventionPolicy_Final_July2014.pdf>.< http://drugpolicy.ca/wp-content/uploads/2014/07/CDPC_OverdosePreventionPolicy_Final_July2014.pdf

Cavacuiti, C., and P. Selby. 2003. "Managing Opioid Dependence: Comparing Buprenorphine with Methadone." *Canadian Family Physician* 49: 876–77.

CBC News. 2007. "Tories Plan Get-Tough National Drug Strategy." Sept. 29. <http://www.cbc.ca/news/canada/story/2007/09/29/drug-strategy.html>.

_____. 2011. "Calgary Addicts No Longer Given Crack Pipes." August 19. <http://www.cbc.ca/news/canada/calgary/story/2011/08/19/calgary-crack-pipes-street-health.html>.

_____. 2015a. "Canada's Health Minister Says Dispensaries Normalize Marijuana Use." April 25. <http://www.cbc.ca/news/canada/british-columbia/canada-s-health-minister-says-dispensaries-normalize-marijuana-use-1.3048543>.

_____. 2015b. "Federal Medical Marijuana Raids Not Part of Vancouver Police Plans." September 11. <http://www.cbc.ca/news/canada/british-columbia/federal-medical-marijuana-raids-not-part-of-vancouver-police-plans-1.3224111>.

_____. 2015c. "Fentanyl Suspected in Death of Vancouver Teen." August 3. <http://www.cbc.ca/news/canada/british-columbia/fentanyl-suspected-in-death-of-vancouver-teen-1.3177987>.

CCSA (Canadian Centre on Substance Abuse). 2007. *A Drug Prevention Strategy for Canada's Youth.* Ottawa: CCSA. <www.ccsa.ca/2007%20CCSA%20Documents/ccsa-011522-2007-e.pdf>.

_____. 2008. *A Systems Approach to Substance Use in Canada: Recommendations for a National Treatment Strategy.* Ottawa: CCSA. <http://www.ccsa.ca/Resource%20Library/nts-systems-approach-substance-abuse-canada-2008-en.pdf>.

_____. 2011. *Cross Canada Report on Student Alcohol and Drug Use, Technical Report.* Ottawa: CCSA. <http://www.ccsa.ca/Eng/Priorities/Research/StudentDrugUse/

Pages/default.aspx>.

____. 2012. *A Systems Approach to Substance Use in Canada.* <http://www.ccsa.ca/ Resource%20Library/nts-developing-systems-approach-to-substance-use-2012-en. pdf>.

____. 2012b. *National Alcohol Strategy: Reducing Alcohol-Related Harm in Canada.* <http://www.ccsa.ca/Eng/Priorities/Alcohol/Pages/default.aspx>.

____. 2014. *National Treatment Indicators Report, 2011–2012.* <http://www.ccsa.ca/ Resource%20Library/NTS-2014-National-Treatment-Indicators-Report-en.pdf>.

____. 2015. "MDMA." Ottawa: CCSA. <http://www.ccsa.ca/Resource%20Library/CCSA-MDMA-Drug-Summary-2015-en.pdf>.

CDPC (Canadian Drug Policy Coalition). 2013. *Voices of the Drug War: Mexico and Canada.* <http://drugpolicy.ca/2013/10/ voices-of-the-drug-war-mexico-and-canada/>.

Centre for Addiction and Mental Health. 2010. *Do You Know... Prescription Opioids.* <http://www.camh.ca/en/hospital/health_information/a_z_mental_health_and_ addiction_information/oxycontin/Pages/opioids_dyk.aspx>.

____. 2011. *Development of Needs Based Planning Models for Substance Use Services and Supports in Canada – Current Practices.* <http://needsbasedplanningmodels. wordpress.com/about/>.

Centres for Disease Control and Prevention. 2013. *Morbidity and Mortality Weekly Report.* <http://www.cdc.gov/mmwr/preview/mmwrhtml/mm6226a3. htm?s_cid=mm6226a3_w>.

Chan, W., and D. Chunn. 2014. *Racialization, Crime, and Criminal Justice in Canada.* Toronto: University of Toronto Press.

Chandler, R. 2008. *Best Practices for British Columbia's Harm Reduction Supply Distribution Program.* Vancouver: BC Centre for Disease Control. <http://www. health.gov.bc.ca/cdms/harmreduction.html>.

Christie, T., A. Murugesan, D. Manzer, M. O'Shaughnessy, and D. Webster. 2013. "Evaluation of a Low-Threshold/High Tolerance Methadone Maintenance Treatment Clinic in Saint John, New Brunswick, Canada: One Year Retention Rate and Illicit Drug Use." *Journal of Addiction,* doi.org/10.1155/2013/753409.

Chu, Sandra. 2012. "Thrown Under the Omnibus: Implications of the Safe Streets and Communities Act." Presentation to OHRDP 2012, The Current Political Environment: Implications for Harm Reduction and Supervised Consumption. January 30. <http://www.ohrdp.ca/conference/2012-conference/>.

CIC (Correctional Investigator of Canada). 2012. *Annual Report of the Office of Correctional Investigator, 2011/12.* <http://www.oci-bec.gc.ca/rpt/index-eng.aspx>.

City of Oshawa. 2013. Zoning By-law Number 60-94 as Amended: <http://www. oshawa.ca/documents/ZoningBylawNo.6094.pdf>.

City of Pembroke. 2013. Zoning Bylaw. <http://www.pembrokeontario.com/download. php?dl=YToyOntzOjI6ImlkIjtzOjM6IjU3MiI7czozOiJrZXkiO2k6MTt9>.

City of Windsor. 2013. Bylaw 8600, see INDEX OF BY-LAWS AMENDING BY-LAW 8600, p. 21.12. <http://www.citywindsor.ca/cityhall/by-laws-online/ documents/8600.pdf>.

CMAJ News. 2012. "Prescription Drug Abuse Rising Among Aboriginal Youths." *CMAJ*

184, 12 (Sept. 4). <http://www.cmaj.ca/content/184/12/E647.full>.

Collins, C. 2006. *Substance Abuse Issues and Public Policy in Canada: I. Canada's Federal Drug Strategy.* Ottawa: Library of Parliament.

Collins, S., and A. Marlatt. 2012. "Seeing the Writing on the Wall: A Lesson in Harm Reduction." In A. Marlatt, M. Larimer, and K. Witkiewitz (eds.), *Harm Reduction: Pragmatic Strategies for Managing High-Risk Behaviors,* 2nd edition. New York: Guilford Press.

Comack, E. 1986. "We Will Get Some Good Out of This Riot Yet: The Canadian State, Drug Legislation and Class Conflict." In S. Brickey and E. Comack (eds.), *The Social Basis of Law: Critical Readings in the Sociology of Law.* Toronto: Garamond.

____. 1996. *Women in Trouble.* Halifax: Fernwood Publishing.

Comack, E., and G. Balfour. 2004. *The Power to Criminalize: Violence, Inequality and the Law.* Halifax: Fernwood Publishing.

Commission of Inquiry into the Non-Medical Use of Drugs. 1973. *Final Report.* Ottawa: Information Canada.

Compton, M. 1994. "Cold-Pressor Pain Tolerance in Opiate and Cocaine Abusers: Correlates of Drug Type and Use Status." *Journal of Pain and Symptom Management* 9: 462–73.

Conrad, P., and K.K. Barker. 2010. "The Social Construction of Illness: Key Insights and Policy Implications." *Journal of Health and Social Behaviour* 51: S67–S79.

Coomber, R., and N. South, N. 2004. *Drug Use and Cultural Contexts 'Beyond the West': Tradition, Change and Post-Colonialism.* London: Free Association Press.

Cooperstock, R., and J. Hill. 1982. *The Effects of Tranquillization: Benzodiazepine Use in Canada.* Ottawa: Health and Welfare Canada.

Correctional Service of Canada. 2009. *Evaluation Report: Correctional Service Canada's Safer Tattooing Practices Pilot Initiative.* Ottawa. <http://www.csc-scc.gc.ca/text/pa/ev-tattooing-394-2-39/index-eng.shtml>.

____. 2010a. *Statistics: Key Facts and Figures.* Ottawa. <http://www.csc-scc.gc.ca/text/pblct/qf/41-eng.shtml>.

____. 2010b. *Summary of Emerging Findings from the 2007 National Inmate Infectious Diseases and Risk-Behaviours Survey.* <http://www.csc-scc.gc.ca/text/rsrch/reports/r211/r211-eng.shtml#Toc253473348>.

Correctional Services Program. 2015. *Adult Correctional Statistics in Canada, 2013/2014.* Statistics Canada. <http://www.statcan.gc.ca/pub/85-002-x/2015001/article/14163-eng.htm>.

Cotter, A., J. Greenland, and M. Karam. 2015. "Drug-Related Offences in Canada, 2013." *Juristat.* Ottawa: Canadian Centre for Justice Statistics.

Count the Costs of the War on Drugs. 2012a. *Creating Crime, Enriching Criminals.* <http://www.countthecosts.org/seven-costs/creating-crime-enriching-criminals>.

____. 2012b. *The Alternative World Drug Report: Counting the Costs of the War on Drugs.* <http://www.countthecosts.org/>.

Coyle, J. 2013. "Rob Ford: What He Could Expect in Rehab." *Toronto Star,* Nov. 9. <http://www.thestar.com/news/gta/2013/11/09/rob_ford_what_he_could_expect_in_rehab.html>.

Csete, J. 2012. *Overhauling Oversight: Human Rights at the INCB.* London: LSE Ideas.

<http://www2.lse.ac.uk/IDEAS/publications/reports/SR014.aspx>.

Csete, J., and R. Pearshouse. 2007. *Dependent on Rights: Assessing Treatment of Drug Dependence from a Human Rights Perspective.* Toronto: Canadian HIV/AIDS Legal Network.

Csete, J., and D. Tomasini-Joshi. 2015. *Drug Courts: Equivocal Evidence on a Popular Intervention.* New York: Open Society Foundations. <http://www.opensocietyfoundations.org/reports/drug-courts-equivocal-evidence-popular-intervention>.

CTV News. 2015. "Bill Adding New Safe-Injection Requirements Receives Royal Assent." June 22. <http://www.ctvnews.ca/politics/bill-adding-new-safe-injection-requirements-receives-royal-assent-1.2434656>.

Cuijers, P. 2003. "Three Decades of Drug Prevention Research." *Drugs Education Prevention and Policy* 10, 1: 7–20.

Culhane, D. 2003. "Their Spirits Live Within Us: Aboriginal Women in Downtown Eastside Vancouver Emerging into Visibility." *American Indian Quarterly* 27, 3/4: 593–606.

Currie, J., and BC Centre of Excellence for Women's Health. 2004. "Manufacturing Addiction: The Over-Prescription of Tranquilzers and Sleeping Pills to Women in Canada." *Canadian Women's Health Network* 6, 7 (4/1). <http://www.cwhn.ca/en/node/39526>.

Curry, B. 2014. "Opposition MPs Accuse Conservatives of Whitewashing Marijuana Report." *Globe and Mail,* Oct. 21. <http://www.theglobeandmail.com/news/politics/opposition-mps-accuse-conservatives-of-whitewashing-marijuana-report/article21216302/>.

Dancesafe in Seattle. 2013. Seattle, Washington. <http://dancesafe.org/products/testing-kits/complete-adulterant-screening-kit-0>.

Davis, W., and B. Johnson. 2008. "Prescription Opioid Use, Misuse, and Diversion Among Street Drug Users in New York City." *Drug and Alcohol Dependence* 92: 267–76.

de Leeuw, S., M. Greenwood, and E. Cameron. 2010. "Deviant Constructions: How Governments Preserve Colonial Narratives of Addictions and Poor Mental Health to Intervene into the Lives of Indigenous Children and Families in Canada." *International Journal of Mental Health and Addictions* 8, 2: 282–95.

DeBeck, K., E. Wood, et al. 2006. "Canada's 2003 Renewed Drug Strategy: An Evidence Based Review." *HIV/AIDS Policy and Law Review* 11, 2/3: 5–12.

____. 2009. "Canada's New Federal 'National Anti-Drug Strategy': An informal Audit of Reported Funding Allocation." *International Journal of Drug Policy* 20, 2: 188–91.

Degenhardt, L., W.T. Chiu, et al. 2008. "Toward a Global View of Alcohol, Tobacco, Cannabis, and Cocaine Use: Findings from the WHO World Mental Health Surveys." *PLoS Med* 5, 7: e141. <http://www.plosmedicine.org/article/info:doi/10.1371/journal.pmed.0050141>.

Degenhardt, L., and W. Hall. 2012. "Extent of Illicit Drug Use and Dependence, and Their Contribution to the Global Burden of Disease." *Lancet* 379, 9810: 55–70. <http://dx.doi.org/10.1016/S0140-6736(11)61138-0 Medline:22225671>.

Dell, CA., G. Roberts, J. Kilty, K. Taylor, M. Daschuk, C. Hopkins, and D. Dell. 2012.

"Researching Prescription Drug Misuse among First Nations in Canada: Starting from a Health Promotion Framework." *Substance Abuse: Research and Treatment* 2012(6): 23–31.

Department of Justice, Canada. 2012. *Backgrounder — Safe Streets and Communities Act: Targeting Serious Drug Crime.* <http://www.justice.gc.ca/eng/news-nouv/nr-cp/2012/doc_32809.html>.

Dorn, N., and N. South. 1993. "After Mr. Bennett and Mr. Bush: U.S. Foreign Policy and the Prospects for Drug Control." In F. Pearce and M. Woodiwiss (eds.), *Global Crime Connections: Dynamics and Control.* Toronto: University of Toronto Press.

Drug Policy Alliance. 2012. *The UN General Assembly Approves Resolution Presented by Mexico on International Cooperation Against Drugs.* November 27. <http://www.drugpolicy.org/resource/un-general-assembly-approves-resolution-presented-mexico-international-cooperation-against->.

DSCIF (Drug Strategy Community Initiatives Funding). 2015. Ottawa: Health Canada. <http://www.hc-sc.gc.ca/hc-ps/drugs-drogues/dscif-ficsa/index-eng.php#fproj>.

Durlak, J.A., R.P. Weissberg, A.B. Dymnicki, R.D. Taylor, and K.B. Schellinger. 2011. "The Impact of Enhancing Students' Social and Emotional Learning: A Meta-Analysis of School-Based Universal Interventions." *Child Development* 82: 405–32

Easton, S.T. 2004. *Marijuana Growth in British Columbia. Public Policy Sources: A Fraser Institute Occasional Paper.* Vancouver: The Fraser Institute.

Edgewood. 2015. "Addiction Treatment Fee Structure." <http://www.edgewood.ca/addiction-treatment-fees-structure>.

EDOSPPM (Evaluation Division Office of Strategic Planning and Performance Measurement). 2010. *National Anti-Drug Strategy: Implementation Evaluation.* <http://canada.justice.gc.ca/eng/pi/eval/rep-rap/10/nasie-snaef/index.html>.

Eggertson, E. 2014. "Take-Home Naloxone Kits Preventing Overdose Deaths." CMAJ 186, 1: 17.

Elliot, E. 2011. *Security, with Care: Restorative Justice and Healthy Societies.* Halifax: Fernwood Publishing.

Emont, S.L., W.S. Choi, et al. 1993. "Clean Indoor Air Legislation, Taxation, and Smoking Behaviour in the United States: An Ecological Analysis." *Tobacco Control* 2, 1: 13.

Erickson, P. 1992. "Recent Trends in Canadian Drug Policy: The Decline and Resurgence of Prohibitionism." *Daedalus* 121, 3A: 247–66.

Erickson, P., and E. Hyska. 2010. "Four Decades of Cannabis Criminals in Canada, 1970–2010." *Amsterdam Law Forum* 2, 4: 14.

Ettorre, E. 1992. *Women and Substance Use.* New Brunswick, N.J.: Rutgers University Press.

Farooqt, U., and C. Guy. 2012. "The Movement for Peace and Justice in Mexico." *The Nation,* June 5. <http://www.thenation.com/article/movement-peace-and-justice-mexico/>.

Ference, Weicker and Company. N.D. *Evaluation of the National Anti-Drug Strategy.* Obtained under the Access to Information Act.

First Nations Health Authority, BC Ministry of Health, Health Canada. 2013. *A Path Forward: BC First Nations and Aboriginal People's Mental Wellness and Substance*

Use — 10 Year Plan: A Provincial Approach to Facilitate Regional and Local Planning and Action. <http://www.health.gov.bc.ca/library/publications/year/2013/First_Nations_Aboriginal_MWSU_plan_final.pdf>.

Fischer, B., K. Ala-Leppilampi, E. Single, and A. Robins. 2003. "Cannabis Law Reform in Canada: Is the 'Saga of Promise, Hesitations and Retreat' Coming to an End?" *Canadian Journal of Criminology and Criminal Justice* 45, 3: 265–98. <http://dx.doi.org/10.3138/cjccj.45.3.265>.

Fischer, B., and E. Argento. 2012. "Prescription Opioid Related Misuse, Harms, Diversion and Interventions in Canada: A Review." *Pain Physician* 15: ES191–203.

Fischer, B., M. Bibby, M. Argento, T. Kerr, and E. Wood. 2012. "Drug Law and Policy in Canada: A Review of History, Evidence, and Interventions Torn Between Criminal Justice and Public Health." In K. Ismali, J. Sprott, and K. Varma (eds.), *Canadian Criminal Justice Policy: Contemporary Perspectives.* Toronto: Oxford University Press.

Fischer, B., M. Bibby, and M. Bouchard. 2010. "The Global Diversion of Pharmaceutical Drugs: Non-Medical Use and Diversion in North America: A Review of Sourcing Routes and Control Measures." *Addiction* 105: 2063.

Fischer, B., W. Jones, M. Krahn, and J. Rehm. 2011. "Differences and Over-Time Changes in Levels of Prescription Opioid Analgesic Dispensing from Retail Pharmacies in Canada, 2005–2010." *Pharmacoepidemiology and Drug Safety* 20: 1269–77.

Fischer, B., and A. Keates. 2012. "'Opioid Drought,' Canadian Style? Potential Implications of the 'Natural Experiment' of Delisting Oxycontin in Canada." *International Journal of Drug Policy* 23: 495–97.

Fischer, B., S. Popova, J. Rehm, and A. Ivsins. 2006. "Drug-Related Overdose Deaths in British Columbia and Ontario, 1992–2004." *Canadian Journal of Public Health* 97, 5: 384–87.

Fischer, B., J. Rehm, B. Goldman, and S. Popova. 2008. "Non-Medical Use of Prescription Opioids and Public Health in Canada: An Urgent Call for Research and Interventions Development." *Canadian Journal of Public Health* 99, 3: 182–84.

Fischer, B., J. Rehm, and W. Hall. 2009. "Cannabis Use in Canada: The Need for a 'Public Health' Approach." *Canadian Journal of Public Health* 100, 2: 101–103.

Fischer, B., J. Rehm, J. Patra, and M. Firestone Cruz. 2006. "Changes in Illicit Opioid Use Profiles Across Canada." *Canadian Medical Association Journal* 175: 1–3.

Fischer, B., et al., 2005. "Illicit Opioid Use in Canada: Comparing Social, Health, and Drug Use Characteristics of Untreated Users in Five Cities." *Journal of Urban Health* 82: 250–66.

595 Prevention Team. 2015. <http://the595.squarespace.com/about>.

Flavin, J. 2009. *Our Bodies, Our Crimes: The Policing of Women's Reproduction in America.* New York: New York University Press.

Ford, A., and D. Saibil (eds.). 2010. *The Push to Prescribe: Women & Canadian Drug Policy.* Toronto: Women's Press.

Forget, P. 2011. "Law Enforcement Detachments and the Canadian Navy: A New Counter-Drug Capability." *Canadian Naval Review* 7, 2: 6–11.

Fraser, S., and D. Moore. 2011a. "Constructing Drugs and Addiction." In S. Fraser and D. Moore (eds.), *The Drug Effect: Health, Crime and Society.* New York: Cambridge

University Press.

____. 2011b. "Governing Through Problems: The Formulation of Policy on Amphetamine-Type Stimulants (ATS) in Australia." *International Journal of Drug Policy* 22, 6: 498–506.

Fraser, S., k. valentine, and C. Roberts, C. 2009. "Living Drugs." *Science as Culture* 18, 2: 123–31.

Friedman, S., et al. 2007. "Harm Reduction Theory: Users' Culture, Micro-Social Indigenous Harm Reduction, and the Self-Organization and Outside-Organizing of Users' Groups." *International Journal of Drug Policy* 18, 2: 107–17.

Gabor, T., and N. Crutcher. 2002. *Mandatory Minimum Penalties: Their Effects on Crime, Sentencing Disparities and Justice System Expenditures.* Ottawa: Research and Statistics Branch.

Gainey, A. 2015. President of Liberal Party of Canada's Response to CDPC Questionnaire about Drug Policy. September 11. <http://drugpolicy.ca/2015/10/questionnaire/>.

Giffen, P.J., S. Endicott, and S. Lambert. 1991. *Panic and Indifference: The Politics of Canadian Drug Laws.* Ottawa: Canadian Centre on Substance Abuse.

Global Commission on Drug Policy. 2011. *War on Drugs: Report of the Global Commission on Drug Policy.* <http://www.globalcommissionondrugs.org/reports/>.

____. 2014. *Taking Control: Pathways to Drug Policies That Work.* Retrieved September 9, 2015. <http://www.globalcommissionondrugs.org/>.

Gomes, T., M. Mamdan, I. Dhalla, S. Cornish, J. Paterson, and D. Juurlink. 2014. "The Burden of Premature Opioid-related Mortality." *Addiction* 109: 1482–88.

Government of Canada. 2012a. "Marihuana for Medical Purposes Regulations." *Canada Gazette* 146, 5 (December 15). <http://gazette.gc.ca/rp-pr/p1/2012/2012-12-15/html/reg4-eng.html>.

____. 2012b. *National Defence and the Canadian Forces: Operation Caribbe.* <http://www.cjoc.forces.gc.ca/cont/caribbe/index-eng.asp>.

Grace, J. 1958. "A Survey of the Women's Division, Oakalla Prison Farm, B.C., 1958: The Beginning of a Treatment Program." Unpublished master's thesis, School of Social Work, University of British Columbia, Canada.

Grayson, K. 2008. *Chasing Dragons: Security, Identity, and Illicit Drugs in Canada.* Toronto: University of Toronto Press.

Grindspoon, L. 1998. "Medical Marihuana in a Time of Prohibition." *International Journal of Drug Policy* 10, 2: 145–56.

Hadland, S., T. Kerr, K. Li, J.S. Montaner, and E. Wood. 2009. "Access to Drug and Alcohol Treatment Among a Cohort of Street-Involved Youth." *Drug and Alcohol Dependency* 1, 101: 1–7.

Haines-Saah, R., J. Johnson, R. Repta, A. Ostry, M. Young, J. Shoveller, J., et al. 2013. "The Privileged Normalization of Marijuana Use — An Analysis of Canadian Newspaper Reporting, 1997–2007." *Critical Public Health.* DOI:10.1080/09581596.2013.771812.

Harris, K. 2009. "Prison Tattoo Program Cut Risk of HIV: Report." *Sudbury Star*, April 15. <http://www.thesudburystar.com/2009/04/15/prison-tattoo-program-cut-risk-of-hiv-report-7>.

Health Canada. 2016. "Health Canada Statement on Change in Federal Prescription

Status of Naloxone." Ottawa: Government of Canada. <http://news.gc.ca/web/article-en.do?nid=1027679>.

———. 2012. *Canadian Alcohol and Drug Monitoring Use Survey (CADUMS), 2012.* <http://www.hc-sc.gc.ca/hc-ps/drugs-drogues/stat/_2012/tables-tableaux-eng.php#t1>.

———. 2013. *Transition and the Marihuana for Medical Purposes Regulations.* <http://www.hc-sc.gc.ca/dhp-mps/marihuana/transition-eng.php>.

———. 2015. *Medical use of Marihuana.* <http://www.hc-sc.gc.ca/dhp-mps/marihuana/index-eng.php>.

Health Canada and the Canadian Centre on Substance Abuse. 2007. *Answering the Call: National Framework for Action to Reduction the Harms Associated with Alcohol and Other Drugs and Substances in Canada.* <http://www.nationalframework-cadrenational.ca/detail_e.php?id_top=1>.

Health Canada and the National Native Addictions Partnership Foundation. 2011. *Honouring Our Strengths: A Renewed Framework to Address Substance Use Issues Among First Nations People in Canada.* <http://nnadaprenewal.ca/>.

Health Council of Canada. 2012. *Empathy, Dignity and Respect: Creating Cultural Safety for Aboriginal People in Urban Health Care Settings.* Toronto. <http://www.healthcouncilcanada.ca/rpt_det_gen.php?id=437&rf=2>.

Health Officers Council of British Columbia. 2011. *Public Health Perspectives for Regulating Psychoactive Substances: What We Can Do About Alcohol, Tobacco and Other Drugs.* <http://drugpolicy.ca/solutions/research-and-statistics/hocreport/>.

Henderson, S., C. Stacey, and D. Dohan. 2008. "Social Stigma and the Dilemmas of Providing Care to Substance Users in a Safety-Net Emergency Department." *Journal of Health Care for the Poor and Underserved* 19: 1336–49.

Here to Help. 2013. *Understanding Substance Use: A Health Promotion Perspective.* Vancouver: BC Partners for Mental Health and Addictions. <http://www.heretohelp.bc.ca/sites/default/files/understanding-substance-use-a-health-promotion-perspective.pdf>.

Hughes, C., and A. Stevens. 2010."What Can We Learn From the Portuguese Decriminalization of Illicit Drugs?" *British Journal of Criminology* 50, 6: 999–1022.

Human Rights Watch. 2008. *Targeting Blacks: Drug Law Enforcement and Race in the United States.* New York: Human Rights Watch.

Hyshka, E. 2013. "Applying a Social Determinants of Health Perspective to Early Adolescent Cannabis Use — An Overview." *Drugs: Education, Prevention and Policy* 20, 2: 110–19.

Hyshka, E., J. Butler-McPhee, et al. 2012. "Canada Moving Backwards on Illegal Drugs." *Canadian Journal of Public Health* 103, 2: 125–27. <http://canadianharmreduction.com/sites/default/files/Backwards.pdf>.

Ialomiteanu, A.R., E.M. Adlaf, H. Hamilton, and R.E. Mann. 2012. *CAMH Monitor eReport: Addiction and Mental Health Indicators Among Ontario Adults, 1977–2011.* Toronto: Centre for Addiction and Mental Health. <http://www.camh.ca/en/research/news_and_publications/Pages/camh_monitor.aspx>.

Iftene, A., and A. Manson. 2012. "Recent Crime Legislation and the Challenge for Prison Health Care." *CMAJ*, Nov. 5.

INCB (International Narcotics Control Board). 2012. *Report of the International Narcotics*

Control Board, 2011. <http://www.incb.org/incb/en/publications/annual-reports/annual-report.html>.

____. 2014. *Report of the International Narcotics Control Board, 2014.* <https://www.incb.org/incb/en/publications/annual-reports/annual-report-2014.html>.

International Drug Policy Consortium. 2012. IDPC *Advocacy Note: The United Nations Drug Control System: A Time for Carefully Planned Reform.* <http://idpc.net/publications/2012/12/idpc-advocacy-note-the-un-drug-control-system-a-time-for-carefully-planned-reform>.

International Harm Reduction Association. 2010. *What Is Harm Reduction? A Position Statement from the International Harm Reduction Association.* <http://www.ihra.net/files/2010/08/10/Briefing_What_is_HR_English.pdf>.

Isvins, A., E. Roth, et al. 2001. "Uptake, Benefits of and Barriers to Safer Crack Use Kit (SCUK) Distribution Programmes in Victoria, Canada — A Qualitative Exploration." *International Journal of Drug Policy* 22, 4: 292–300.

Johnson, J., et al. 2008. *Lessons Learned from the* SCORE *Project: A Document to Support Outreach and Education Related to Safer Crack Use.* <http://canadianharmreduction.com/node/2300>.

Johnson, T.P., and M. Fendrich. 2007. "Homelessness and Drug Use: Evidence From a Community Sample." *American Journal of Preventive Medicine* 32, 6 (Supplement 1): S211–18.

Jürgens, R. 2002. "House of Commons Committee Releases Report on Canada's Drug Strategy." HIV AIDS *Policy Law Review* 7, 2–3: 9–12.

____. 2004. "Facing Up to an Epidemic: Drug Policy in Canada." Paper presentation at Moving Harm Reduction Policy Forward, Kiev, Ukraine, October 4–6.

Keane, H. 2002. *What's Wrong with Addiction?* New York: New York University.

Kensy, J., C. Stengel, M. Nougier, and R. Birgin. 2012. "*Drug Policy and Women: Addressing the Negative Consequences of Harmful Drug Control.*" London: International Drug Policy Consortium. <http:// ssrn.com/abstract+2186004>.

Kerr, T., W. Small, and E. Wood. 2005. "The Public Health and Social Impacts of Drug Market Enforcement: A Review of the Evidence." *International Journal of Drug Policy* 16, 4: 210–20.

Kilmer, B., J.P. Caulkins, R.L. Pacula, and P. Reuter. 2012. *The U.S. Drug Policy Landscape: Insights and Opportunities for Improving the View.* Santa Monica: RAND Drug Policy and Research Centre.

Kilmer, B., and R.L. Pacula. 2009. *Estimating the Size of Global Drug Market: A Demand-Side Approach.* Santa Monica: RAND Europe.

Lancaster, K., and A. Ritter. 2014. "Examining the Construction and Representation of Drugs as a Policy Problem in Australia's National Drug Strategy Documents 1985 to 2010." *International Journal of Drug Policy* 25, 1: 81–87.

Lart, R. 1998. "Medical Power/Knowledge: The Treatment and Control of Drugs and Drug Users." In R. Coomber (ed.), *The Control of Drugs and Drug Users: Reason or Reaction?* Amsterdam: Harwood Academic Publishers.

Le Dain, G. 1973. *Final Report of the Commission of Inquiry into the Non-Medical Use of Drugs.* Ottawa: Information Canada.

Leonard, L. 2010. *Ottawa's Safe Inhalation Program: Final Evaluation Report.* Ottawa:

Somerset West Community Health Centre. <http://www.medecine.uottawa.ca/ epidemiologie/assets/ documents/Improving%20Services%20for%20People%20 in%20Ottawa%20who%20smoke%20crack.pdf>.

Leonard, L., et al. 2007. "'I Inject Less as I Have Easier Access to Pipes': Injecting and Sharing of Crack-Smoking Materials Decline as Safer-Crack Smoking Resources are Distributed." *International Journal of Drug Policy* 19, 3: 255–64.

Lepard, D. 2015. *Service and Policy Complaint #2015-112 Regarding Enforcement against Marihuana Dispensaries.* Vancouver Police Department. September 1. <http:// vancouver.ca/police/policeboard/agenda/2015/0917/1509C01-2015-112- Marijuana-Dispensaries.pdf>.

Levy, D.T., F. Chaloupka, and J. Gitchell. 2004. "The Effects of Tobacco Control Policies on Smoking Rates: A Tobacco Control Scorecard." *Journal of Public Health Management and Practice* 10, 4: 338.

Lewit, E.M., A. Hyland, N. Kerrebrock, and K.M. Cummings. 1997. "Price, Public Policy and Smoking in Young People." *British Medical Journal* 6 (Suppl 2): S17.

Lines, R., R. Jürgens, G.I. Betteridge, H. Stöver, D. Laticevshi, and J. Nelles. 2006. *Prison Needle Exchange: Lessons from a Comprehensive Review of International Evidence and Experience.* <http://www.aidslaw.ca/publications/interfaces/downloadFile. php?ref=1173>.

London School of Economics. 2014. *Ending the Drug Wars.* May. Report of the LSE Expert Group on the Economics of Drug Policy. London: Author.

Lucas, P. 2012. "It Can't Hurt to Ask: A Patient-Centred Quality of Service Assessment of Health Canada's Medical Cannabis Policy and Program." *Harm Reduction Journal* 9, 2: 436–41.

Luce, J., and C. Strike. 2011. *A Cross-Canada Scan of Methadone Maintenance Treatment Policy Developments.* Ottawa: Canadian Executive Council on Addictions. <http:// www.ccsa.ca/ceca/activities.asp>.

Lupick, T. 2015. "Corporations Move in on Canada's Medicinal Cannabis Industry." *The Georgia Straight*, March 18. <http://www.straight.com/news/413966/ corporations-move-canadas-medicinal-cannabis-industry>.

MacKinnon, S. 2011. ccpa *Review: Poverty Reduction and the Politics of Setting Social Assistance Rates.* Manitoba Office: Canadian Centre for Policy Alternatives. <http://www.policyalternatives.ca/publications/commentary/ ccpa-review-poverty-reduction-and-politics-setting-social-assistance-rates>.

MacPherson, D., and N. Klassen. 2015. "Vancouver Buyers Club." *Walrus* 12, 4. <http:// thewalrus.ca/vancouver-buyers-club/>.

MacPherson, D., Z. Mulla, and L. Richardson. 2006. "The Evolution of Drug Policy in Vancouver, Canada: Strategies for Preventing Harm from Psychoactive Substance Use." *International Journal of Drug Policy* 17: 127–32.

Mahony, T. 2011. *Women and the Criminal Justice System.* Statistics Canada: Ministry of Industry.

Maladi, P., D. Hildebrandt, A.E. Lauwers, and G. Koren. 2013. "Characteristics of Opioid-Users Whose Death Was Related to Opioid-Toxicity: A Population-Based Study in Ontario, Canada." plos *One* 8, 4: E60600.

Mallea, P. 2010. *The Fear Factor: Stephen Harper's "Tough on Crime" Agenda.* Ottawa:

Canadian Centre for Policy Alternatives. <http://www.policyalternatives.ca/sites/default/files/uploads/publications/National%20Office/2010/11/Tough%20on%20Crime.pdf>.

Manning, P. 2007. "Introduction." In P. Manning (ed.), *Drugs and Popular Culture: Drugs, Media and Identity in Contemporary Society* (3-6). Cullompton: Willan.

Mares, A. 2011. *The Rise of Femicide and Women in Drug Trafficking.* Council on Hemispheric Affairs. <http://www.coha.org/the-rise-of-femicide-and-women-in-drug-trafficking/>.

Marlatt, G., M. Larimer, and K. Witkiewitz (eds.). 2012. *Harm Reduction: Pragmatic Strategies for Managing High-Risk Behaviors.* New York: Guilford Press.

Martel, M. 2006. *Not this Time: Canadians, Public Policy, and the Marijuana Question 1961–1975.* Toronto: University of Toronto Press.

Mattick, R., J. Kimber, C. Breen, and M. Davoli. 2007. "Buprenorphine Maintenance Versus Placebo or Methadone Maintenance for Opioid Dependence." *Cochrane Database of Systematic Reviews* 4. Art. No.: CD002207.

McGregor, G. 2014. "Doctors Pull Out of Conservative Government's Anti-Pot Ads." *Ottawa Citizen,* August 17. <http://ottawacitizen.com/news/national/doctors-pull-out-of-conservative-governments-anti-pot-ads>.

MDSCNO (Municipal Drug Strategy Co-ordinator's Network of Ontario). 2015. *Prescription for Life.* <http://www.drugstrategy.ca>.

Million, D. 2013. *Therapeutic Nations: Healing in an Age of Indigenous Human Rights.* Tucson, AZ: University of Arizona Press.

Milloy, M., T. Kerr, M. Tyndall, J. Montaner, and E. Wood. 2008. "Estimated Drug Overdose Deaths Averted by North America's First Medically-Supervised Safer Injection Facility." *PLoS ONE* 3, 10: e3351.

Mills, C. Wright. 1975. *The Sociological Imagination.* New York: Oxford Press.

Milloy M., E. Wood, C. Reading, D. Kane, J. Montaner, and T. Kerr T. 2010. "Elevated Overdose Mortality Rates among First Nations Individuals in a Canadian Setting: A Population-based Analysis." *Addiction* 105: 1962–70.

Mintzes, B. 2010. "'Ask Your Doctor': Women and Direct to Consumer Advertising." In A. Ford and D. Saibil (eds.), *The Push to Prescribe: Women & Canadian Drug.* Toronto: Women's Press.

Moore, D. 2008. "Erasing Pleasure from Public Discourse: On the Creation and Reproduction of an Absence." *International Journal of Drug Policy* 19, 5: 353–58.

Moreira, M., B. Hughes, C. Storti, and F. Zobel. 2011. *Drug Policy Profiles — Portugal.* Luxembourg: European Monitoring Centre for Drugs and Drug Addiction. <http://www.emcdda.europa.eu/publications/drug-policy-profiles/portugal>.

Mosher, C. 1998. *Discrimination and Denial: Systemic Racism in Ontario's Legal and Criminal Justice Systems, 1892–1961.* Toronto: University of Toronto Press.

Murkin, G. 2014. *Drug Decriminalisation in Portugal: Setting the Record Straight.* London: Transform Drug Policy Foundation. <http://www.tdpf.org.uk>.

Musto, D. 1987. *The American Disease: Origins of Narcotic Control* (expanded ed.). New York: Oxford University Press.

NAOMI Study Team. 2008. *Reaching the Hardest to Reach — Treating the Hardest-to-Treat: Summary of the Primary Outcomes of the North American Opiate Medication Initiative*

(NAOMI). <http://www.naomistudy.ca/ documents.html>.

National Advisory Council on Prescription Drug Misuse. 2013. *First Do No Harm: Responding to Canada's Prescription Drug Crisis*. Ottawa: Canadian Centre on Substance Abuse.

National Collaborating Centre for Aboriginal Health. 2011. *The Aboriginal Health Legislation and Policy Framework in Canada*. <http://www.nccah-ccnsa.ca/en/ publications.aspx?sortcode=2.8.10&searchCat=5>.

National Treatment Strategy Working Group. 2008. *A Systems Approach to Substance Use in Canada: Recommendations for a National Treatment Strategy*. Ottawa: National Framework for Action to Reduce the Harms Associated with Alcohol and Other Drugs and Substances in Canada.

Nolin, P., and C. Kenny. 2002. *Cannabis: Our Position for Canadian Public Policy: Report of the Senate Special Committee on Illegal Drugs*. Ottawa: Canadian Senate. <http:// www.parl.gc.ca/Content/SEN/Committee/371/ille/rep/repfinalvol2-e.pdf>.

Nosyk, B., D.L. Marhsalla, B. Fischer, J.S.G. Montaner, E. Wood, and T. Kerr. 2012. "Increases in the Availability of Prescribed Opioids in a Canadian Setting." *Drug and Alcohol Dependence* 126: 7–12.

Nova Scotia. 2011. *Nova Scotia Public Health Standards 2011–2016*. <http://novascotia. ca/dhw/publichealth/documents/Public_Health_Standards_EN.pdf>.

____. 2012. *Together We Can: The Plan to Improve Mental Health and Addictions Care in Nova Scotia*. <http://www.gov.ns.ca/health/mhs/reports/together_we_can.pdf>.

Nutt, D., L. King, and L.Phillips. 2010. "Drug Harms in the UK: A Multicriteria Decision Analysis." *The Lancet* 376, 9752: 1558–65.

Office of the Correctional Investigator. 2012. *Spirit Matters: Aboriginal People and the Corrections and Conditional Release Act*. <http://www.oci-bec.gc.ca/rpt/pdf/oth-aut20121022-eng.pdf>.

Office of the Prime Minister. 2007. "Prime Minister Pledges Crackdown on Drug Criminal, Compassion for Their Victims." Speech, October 4. Ottawa: Government of Canada. <http://www.pm.gc.ca/eng/news/2007/10/04/ pm-pledges-crackdown-drug-criminals-compassion-their-victims>.

Office of the Provincial Health Officer (B.C.). 2013. *Health, Crime and Doing Time: Potential Impacts of the Safe Streets and Communities Act (Former bill C10) on the Health and Well-being of Aboriginal People in BC*. <http://www.health.gov.bc.ca/pho/ pdf/health-crime-2013.pdf>.

Office of the Sentencing Council. 2011. *Drug 'Mules': Twelve Case Studies*. London: Sentencing Council of England and Wales. <http://sentencingcouncil.judiciary.gov. uk/facts/ research-and-analysis-publications.htm>.

Ontario. 2011. *Open Minds Healthy Minds: Ontario's Comprehensive Mental Health and Addictions Strategy, 2011*. <http://www.health.gov.on.ca/en/common/ministry/ publications/reports/mental_health2011/mentalhealth.aspx>.

Ontario College of Physicians and Surgeons. 2013. "Methadone Maintenance Treatment Program: Answers to Frequently Asked Questions." <http://www.cpso.on.ca/ uploadedFiles/homepage/homepageheadlines/MethadoneFactSheet%281%29. pdf>.

Ontario Drug Treatment Funding Program, Ontario Systems Projects. N.D. *What is the*

DTFP? <http://ontariodtfp.wordpress.com/>.

Ontario Expert Group on Narcotic Addiction. 2012. *The Way Forward: Stewardship for Prescription Narcotics in Ontario.* <http://www.health.gov.on.ca/en/public/publications/mental/docs/way_forward_2012.pdf>.

Ontario Health Promotion E-Bulletin. 2013. "Opioid overdose prevention training and community-based naloxone distribution in Ontario." Feb. <http://www.ohpe.ca/node/14023>.

Oscapella, E., with Canadian Drug Policy Coalition Policy Working Group. 2012. *Changing the Frame: A New Approach to Drug Policy in Canada.* Vancouver, BC: Canadian Drug Policy Coalition. <http://www.drugpolicy.ca>.

Paltrow, L., and J. Flavin. 2013. "Arrests of and Forced Interventions on Pregnant Women in the United States, 1973–2005: Implications for Women's Legal Status and Public Health Journal of Health Politics." *Policy and Law* 38, 2: 299–343.

Paulus, I. 1966. *History of Drug Addiction and Legislation in Canada.* Vancouver: Narcotic Addiction Foundation of British Columbia.

Pauly, B., K. MacKinnon, and C. Varcoe. 2009. "Revisiting 'Who Gets Care?': Health Equity as an Arena for Nursing Action." *Advances in Nursing Science* 32, 2: 119–27.

Peachy, J., and T. Franklin. 1985. "Methadone Treatment of Opiate Dependence in Canada." *British Journal of Addiction* 80: 291–99.

Pfohl, S. 1994. *Images of Deviance and Social Control: A Sociological History,* 2nd edition. New York: McGraw-Hill.

Pirie, T., and National Treatment Indicators Working Group. 2015. *National Treatment Indicators Report: 2012–2013 Data.* Ottawa: Canadian Centre on Substance Abuse.

Pivot Legal Society. 2013. "Health and Drug Policy: City of Abbotsford Strikes Down Anti-Harm Reduction Bylaw." <http://www.pivotlegal.org/health_and_drug_policy>.

Pocock, J. 2011. *Drug and Alcohol Trends in Ottawa: Ottawa Site Report for the Canadian Community Epidemiology Network on Drug Use (CCENDU).* <http://www.ccsa.ca/Eng/Priorities/Research/CCENDU/pages/2010-report-summaries.aspx#ottawa>.

Poole, N., and L. Greaves (eds.). 2012. *Becoming Trauma Informed.* Toronto: CAMH.

Poole, N., C. Urquhart, and C. Talbot. 2010. *Women-Centred Harm Reduction, Gendering the National Framework Series* (Vol. 4). Vancouver, BC: British Columbia Centre of Excellence for Women's Health.

Popova, S., J. Patra, S. Mohapatra, B. Fischer, and J. Rehm. 2009. "How Many People in Canada Use Prescription Opioids Non-Medically in General and Street-Drug Using Populations?" *Canadian Journal of Public Health* 100, 2: 104–08.

Potter, G., et al. 2015. "Global Patterns of Domestic Cannabis Cultivation: Sample Characteristics and Patterns of Growing across Eleven Countries." *International Journal of Drug Policy* 26, 3: 226–37.

Project Lazarus. 2013. <http://projectlazarus.org/doctors/nc-medical-board>.

Provincial Health Officers. 2013. *BC Methadone Maintenance Systems: Performance Measures, 2011/12.* <http://www.health.gov.bc.ca/pho/pdf/methadone-2011-12.pdf>.

Public Health Agency of Canada. 2010. *Population Specific HIV/AIDS Report: Aboriginal Peoples.* Ottawa: PHAC. <http://www.phac-aspc.gc.ca/aids-sida/publication/ps-pd/

index-eng.php>.

____. 2013. *I-Track: Enhanced Surveillance of* HIV, *Hepatitis C and Associated Risk Behaviours among People Who Inject Drugs in Canada. Phase 2 Report.* Centre for Communicable Diseases and Infection Control, Infectious Disease Prevention and Control Branch. Ottawa: Public Health Agency of Canada.

____. 2014. *Summary of Key Findings from I-Track Phase 3 (2010–2010).* Centre for Communicable Diseases and Infection Control, Infectious Disease Prevention and Control Branch. Ottawa: Public Health Agency of Canada.

Public Safety Canada. 2012. *Corrections and Conditional Release Statistical Overview 2012.* <http://www.publicsafety.gc.ca/cnt/rsrcs/pblctns/2012-ccrs/2012-ccrs-eng.pdf>.

Rachlis, B.S., T. Kerr, et al. 2009. "Harm Reduction in Hospitals: Is It Time?" *Harm Reduction Journal* 6, 19. doi:10.1186/1477-7517-6-19.

Razack, S. (ed.). 2002. *Race, Space, and the Law: Unmapping a White Settler Society.* Toronto: Between the Lines.

RCMP. 2013. *Drug Awareness.* <http://www.rcmp-grc.gc.ca/ns/prog_services/community-policing-police-communautaire/drug-awareness-sensibilisation-drogues/index-eng.htm>.

Redding, C. and F. Wien. 2009. *Health Inequities and Social Determinants of Aboriginal Peoples' Health.* National Collaborating Centre on Aboriginal Health. <http://www.nccah-ccnsa.ca/docs/social%20determinates/NCCAH-loppie-Wien_report.pdf>.

Reinarman, C., and R. Granfield. 2015. "Addiction Is Not Just a Brain Disease: Critical Studies of Addiction." In R. Granfield and C. Reinarman (eds.), *Expanding Addiction: Critical Essays.* New York: Routledge.

Reinarman, C., and H. Levine. 1997. "The Crack Attack: Politics and Media in the Crack Scare." In C. Reinarman and H. Levine (eds.), *Crack in America: Demon Drugs and Social Justice.* Berkeley: University of California Press.

____. 2000. "Crack in Context: Politics and Media in the Making of a Drug Scare." In R. Cruthchfield, G. Bridges, J. Weis, and C. Kubrin (eds.), *Crime Readings,* 2nd edition. Thousand Oaks, CA: Pine Forge Press.

Reinarman, R. 2011. "Cannabis in Cultural and Legal Limbo: Criminalisation, Legalisation and the Mixed Blessing of Medicalization in the USA." In S. Fraser and D. Moore (eds.), *The Drug Effect: Health, Crime and Society.* New York: Cambridge.

Reist, D. 2011. *Methadone Maintenance Treatment in British Columbia, 1996–2008.* Victoria: Centre for Addictions Research of BC. <http://www.health.gov.bc.ca/cdms/methadone.html>.

Rhodes, T. 2009. "Risk Environments and Drug Harms: A Social Science for Harm Reduction Approach." *International Journal of Drug Policy* 20: 193–201.

Robson, G. 2013. "Harm Reduction Doesn't Fit All Sizes." *Maple Ridge Pitt Meadows Times,* March 26: 10.

Room, R., T. Babor, and J. Rehm. 2005. "Alcohol and Public Health." *Lancet* 365, 9458: 519.

Room, R., B. Fischer, et al. 2008. *Cannabis Policy: Moving Beyond Stalemate.* Oxford: Oxford University Press.

Room, R., and P. Reuter. 2012. "How Well Do International Drug Conventions Protect Public Health?" *Lancet* 379, 9810: 84–91.

Rosmarin, A., and N. Eastwood. 2012. *A Quiet Revolution: Drug Decriminalization Policies in Practice Across the Globe*. London: Release Legal Emergency and Drug Services. <http://www.release.org.uk/publications/quiet-revolution-drug-decriminalisation-policies-practice-across-globe>.

Royal Commission on Aboriginal Peoples. 1996. *Highlights from the Report of the Royal Commission on Aboriginal Peoples*. <http://www.aadnc-aandc.gc.ca/eng/110010001 4597/1100100014637>.

Rush, B. 2012. A Look into a National DTFP project, The Development of a Needs-Based Planning Model for Substance Use Services and Supports in Canada. EEnet, Evidence Exchange Network Webinar, Dec. 19. <http://eenet.ca/wp-content/uploads/2012/12/EENet_NBP-Webinar-Presentation_19Dec12FINAL.pdf>

Rush, B., B. Fogg, L. Nadeau, and A. Furlong. 2008. *On the Integration of Mental Health and Substance Use Services and Systems. Main Report.* Ottawa: Canadian Executive Council on Addictions.

Rush, B., and L. Nadeau. 2011. "Integrated Service and System Planning Debate." In D. Cooper (ed.), *Responding in Mental Health — Substance Use*. Milton Keynes, UK: Radcliffe Health.

Rush, B., et al. 2012. *Development of a Needs-Based Planning Model for Substance Use Services and Supports in Canada (Draft)*. Toronto: Centre for Addictions and Mental Health, Health Systems and Health Equity Research Group.

SALOME. 2012. "About SALOME." <http://www.providencehealthcare.org/salome/about-us.html>

SAMHSA (Substance Abuse and Mental Health Services Administration), Office of Applied Studies. 2012. *Results from the 2011 National Survey on Drug Use and Health: National Findings.* <http://www.samhsa.gov/data/sites/default/files/Revised2k11NSDUHSummNatFindings/Revised2k11NSDUHSummNatFindings/NSDUHresults2011.htm>.

Sapers, H. 2013. *Annual Report of the Office of the Correctional Investigator 2012–2013.* Office of the Correctional Investigator, Government of Canada. <http://www.oci-bec.gc.ca/cnt/rpt/annrpt/annrpt20122013-eng.aspx>.

____. 2014. *Annual Report of the Office of the Correctional Investigator 2013–2014.* Office of the Correctional Investigator, Government of Canada. <http://www.ocibec.gc.ca/cnt/rpt/pdf/annrpt/annrpt20132014-eng.pdf>.

Saskatchewan Ministry of Health. 2010. *Saskatchewan's HIV Strategy, 2010–2014.* <www.health.gov.sk.ca/hiv-strategy-2010-2014>.

Sharp Advice Needle Exchange. 2013. *The Natural Helper Model: A Rural Remedy: A Guide to Reaching Rural Injection Drug Users. AIDS Coalition of Cape Breton.* <http://www.catie.ca/en/resources/natural-helper-model-rural-remedy-guide-reaching-rural-injection-drug-users>.

Shepherd, S. (Toronto Drug Strategy). Personal Communication.

Siren, A.H., and B.K. Applegate. 2006. "Intentions to Offend: Examining the Effects of Personal and Vicarious Experiences with Punishment Avoidance. *Journal of Crime and Justice* 29, 20: 25–50.

Small, W., N. Van Borek, N. Fairbairn, E. Wood, and T. Kerr. 2009. "Access to Health and Social Services for IDU: The Impact of a Medically Supervised Injection Facility."

Drug and Alcohol Review 28, 4: 341–46.

Smart, C., and B. Smart. 1978. "Women and Social Control: An Introduction." In C. Smart and B. Smart (eds.), *Women, Sexuality and Social Control*. London: Routledge & Kegan Paul.

Solomon, R., and M. Green. 1988. "The First Century: The History of Nonmedical Opiate Use and Control Policies in Canada, 1870–1970." In J. Blackwell and P. Erickson (eds.), *Illicit Drugs in Canada* (pre-publication ed.). Toronto: Methuen.

Southwick, R. 2015. "Deadly Painkiller Linked to Rising Number of Alberta Deaths." *Calgary Sun*, January 27. <http://calgaryherald.com/news/crime/deadly-painkiller-linked-to-rising-number-of-alberta-deaths>.

Spittal, P., et al. 2002. "Risk Factors for Elevated HIV Incidence Rates Among Female Injection Drug Users in Vancouver." *Canadian Medical Association Journal* 166, 7: 894–98.

Statistics Canada. 2013. *Aboriginal Peoples in Canada: First Nations People, Métis and Inuit. National Household Survey, 2011*. Ministry of Industry. <http://www12.statcan.gc.ca/ nhs-enm/2011/as-sa/99-011-x/99-011-x2011001-eng.cfm>.

____. 2014. "Table 252-0051. Incident-Based Crime Statistics, by Detailed Violations, Annual, 1998–2013." <http://www5.statcan.gc.ca/subject-sujet/result-resultat.actio n?pid=2693&id=2102&lang=eng&type=ARRAY&pageNum=1&more=0>.

Steinberg, N. 2013. *Mexico's Disappeared: The Enduring Cost of a Crisis Ignored*. Human Rights Watch. <http:// www.hrw.org>.

Stevenson, G., L. Lingley, G. Trasov, and H. Stansfield. 1956. "Drug Addiction in British Columbia: A Research Survey." Unpublished manuscript, University of British Columbia, Vancouver.

Stockwell, T., B. Pakula, S. Macdonald, J. Buxton, J. Zhao, A. Tu, D. Reist, G. Thomas, A. Puri, and C. Duff. 2007. "Alcohol Consumption in British Columbia and Canada: A Case for Liquor Taxes that Reduce Harm." *CARBC Statistical Bulletin* 3: 1–8. University of Victoria, British Columbia. <http://www.uvic.ca/research/centres/carbc/assets/docs/bulletin3-alcohol-consumption-in-bc.pdf>.

Strang, J., T. Groshkova, and N. Metrebian. 2012. *New Heroin-Assisted Treatment: Recent Evidence and Current Supervised Injectable Heroin Treatment in Europe and Beyond*. Luxemburg: Insights, European Monitoring Centre for Drugs and Drug Addiction.

Sudbury, J. (ed.). 2005. *Global Lockdown: Race, Gender, and the Prison-Industrial Complex*. London: Routledge.

Taylor, M. 2015. December 18. Personal communication.

TDSIP (Toronto Drug Strategy Implementation Panel). 2012. *The Toronto Drug Strategy Report 2012*. <www.toronto.ca/health/drugstrategy>.

Terry, C., and M. Pellens. 1970. *The Opium Problem*. Montclair, NJ: Patterson Smith.

Ti, L., Buxton, J., Wood, E., Shannon, K., Zhang, R., Montaner. J., Kerr, T. 2012. "Factors associated with difficulty accessing crack cocaine pipes in a Canadian setting." *Drug and Alcohol Review*, 31, 890-896.

Tickner, A., and C. Cepeda. 2012. "The Role of Illegal Drugs in Colombian-U.S. Relations." In A. Gaviria and D. Mejia (eds.), *Anti-Drugs Policies in Colombia: Successes, Failures and Wrong Turns*. Universidad de los Andes (uncorrected Proof).

Tonry, M. 2009. "The Mostly Unintended Effects of Mandatory Penalties: Two

Centuries of Consistent Findings." In M. Tonry (ed.), *Crime and Justice: A Review of Research*, Volume 38. Chicago: University of Chicago Press.

Tornsey, P. (House of Commons, Canada). 2002. *Working Together to Redefine Canada's Drug Strategy: Report of the Special Committee on the Non-Medical use of Drugs.* <http://www.parl.gc.ca/HousePublications/Publication.aspx?Language=E&Mode =1&Parl=37&Ses=2&DocId=1032297&File=0>.

Toronto Drug Strategy. 2010. *Stigma, Discrimination and Substance Use: Experiences of People Who Use Alcohol and Other Drugs in Toronto.* <http://www.toronto.ca/health/ drugstrategy/pdf/stigma_discrim_summ.pdf>.

Toronto Public Health. 2011. *Alcohol and Other Drug Use: A Research Summary.* <http:// www.ccsa.ca/Eng/Priorities/Research/CCENDU/pages/2010-report-summaries. aspx#toronto>.

Toumbourou, J., T. Stockwell, C. Neighbors, C., G. Marlatt, J. Sturge, and J. Rehm. 2007. "Interventions to Reduce Harm Associated with Adolescent Substance Use." *The Lancet* 369, 9570: 1390–401.

Transform Drug Policy Foundation. 2014. *Ending the War on Drugs: How to Win the Global Drug Policy Debate.* <http://www.tdpf.org.uk/sites/default/files/Global-Drug-Policy-Debate_0.pdf>.

Transnational Institute, Drug Law Reform. 2012. "Objections to Bolivia's Reservation to Allow Coca Chewing in the UN Conventions: The United States, United Kingdom, Sweden, Italy and Canada Notified Their Objections." <http://druglawreform.info/ en/weblog/item/4245-objections-to-bolivias-reservation-to-allow-coca-chewing-in-the-un-conventions>.

Treasury Board of Canada, Department of Justice Supplementary Tables, Horizontal Initiatives. 2007/08, 2012/13. Data on budgets for the 2007–12 period can be found at <http://www.tbs-sct.gc.ca/hidb-bdih/plan-eng.aspx?Org=37&Hi=28&Pl=164>. Data for the 2012–2017 period can be found at <http://www.tbs-sct.gc.ca/hidb-bdih/plan-eng.aspx?Org=37&Hi=28&Pl=447>.

Trevethan, S., and C.J. Rastin. 2004. *A Profile of Visible Minority Offenders in the Federal Canadian Correctional System.* Research Branch, Correctional Service of Canada. <www.csc-scc.gc.ca/text/rsrch/reports/r144/r144_e.pdf>.

Tupper, K.W. 2008. "The Globalization of Ayahuasca: Harm Reduction or Benefit Maximization?" *International Journal of Drug Policy* 19, 4: 297–303

Ubelacker, S. 2014. "Deaths from Opioid Overdose on the Rise in Ontario." *Global News* July 7. <http://globalnews.ca/news/1435867/ deaths-from-opioid-overdoses-on-the-rise-in-ontario/>.

U.S. Department of Health and Human Services, Substance Abuse & Mental Health Services Administration. 2012. *National Survey on Drug Use & Health 2011.* Washington: U.S. Department of Health and Human Services.

UNICEF. 2013. *Child Well-Being in Rich Countries: A Comparative Overview.* <http://www. unicef.org.uk/Images/Campaigns/FINAL_RC11-ENG-LORES-fnl2.pdf>.

Union of BC Municipalities. 2012. "Member Release – 2012 Resolutions Disposition." <http://www.ubcm.ca/EN/main/resolutions/resolutions/resolutions-responses. html>.

United Nations. 1961. "United Nations Single Convention on Narcotic Drugs, as

Amended by the 1972 Protocol Amending the Single Convention on Narcotic Drugs, Article 4, General Obligations." <https://treaties.un.org/pages/ViewDetails. aspx?src=TREATY&mtdsg_no=VI-17&chapter=6&lang=en>.

____. 1988. "United Nations Convention Against Illicit Traffic in Narcotic Drugs and Psychotropic Substances." <https://treaties.un.org/Pages/ViewDetails. aspx?src=IND&mtdsg_no=VI-19&chapter=6&lang=en>.

United Nations Office on Drugs and Crime. 2013. *World Drug Report, 2012.* <http:// www.unodc.org/documents/data-and-analysis/WDR2012/WDR_2012_web_ small.pdf>.

Urban Health Research Institute. N.D. *Insight into Insite.* Vancouver: BC Centre for Excellence in HIV/AIDS. <http://uhri.cfenet.ubc.ca/images/Documents/insight_ into_insite.pdf>.

Vallance, K., et al. 2012. *Overdose Events in British Columbia: Trends in Substances Involved, Contexts and Responses.* Victoria: Centre for Addiction Research of BC. <http://www.carbc.ca/Portals/0/propertyagent/558/files/180/carbc_bulletin8. pdf>.

Valverde, M. 1998. *Diseases of the Will: Alcohol and Dilemmas of Freedom.* Cambridge: Cambridge University Press.

Van Hout, M.C., and R. Brennan. 2012. "Curiosity Killed the M-Cat: A Post Legislative Study on Mephedrone Use in Ireland." *Drugs: Education, Prevention and Policy* 19, 2: 156–62.

Vancouver Coastal Health. 2013. *Evaluation Report: Vancouver Coastal Health Safer Smoking Pilot Project.* <http://www.vch.ca/media/safer-smoking-pilot-2013.pdf>.

____. 2015. "Harm Reduction." <http://www.vch.ca/your-health/health-topics/ harm-reduction/harm-reduction>.

VANDU Women's Care Team. 2009. *"Me, I'm living it": The Primary Health Care Experiences of Women Who Use Drugs in Vancouver's Downtown Eastside.* Vancouver: Author.

Vienna Declaration. 2010. <http://www.viennadeclaration.com/>.

Walley, A., et al. 2013. "Opioid Overdose Rates and Implementation of Overdose Education and Nasal Naloxone Distribution in Massachusetts: Interrupted Time Series Analysis." *British Medical Journal* 346, f174. DOI: 10.1136/bmj.f174.

Wente, M. 2008. "We Still Await the Scientific Proof of Harm Reduction's Success." *Globe and Mail,* July 15. <http://www.theglobeandmail.com/news/national/ we-still-await-the-scientific-proof-of-harm-reductions-success/article714998/>.

Werb, D., T. Kerr, B. Nosyk, S. Strathdee, J. Montaner, and E. Wood. 2013. "The Temporal Relationship Between Drug Supply Indicators: An Audit of International Government Surveillance Systems." *BMJ* 3, 9: doi: 10.1136/bmjopen-2013-003077.

Werb, D., B. Nosyk, T. Kerr, B. Fischer, J. Montaner, and E. Wood. 2012. "Estimating the Economic Value of British Columbia's Domestic Cannabis Market: Implications for Provincial Cannabis Policy." *International Journal on Drug Policy* 23, 6: 436–41. <http://dx.doi.org/10.1016/j.drugpo.2012.05.003 Medline: 23085258>.

Werb, D., G. Rowell, G. Guyatt, T. Kerr, J. Montaner, and E. Wood. 2010. *Effect of Drug Law Enforcement on Drug Related Violence: Evidence From a Scientific Review.* Vancouver: International Centre for Science in Drug Policy. <http://www.icsdp.org/

Libraries/doc1/ICSDP-1_-_FINAL_1.sflb.ashx>.

____. 2011. "Effect of Drug Law Enforcement on Drug Market Violence: A Systematic Review." *International Journal on Drug Policy* 22, 2: 87–94.

White, W., and W. Miller. 2007. "The Use of Confrontation in Addiction Treatment: History, Science and Time for Change." *Counselor* 8, 4: 12–30.

WHO, UNODC & UNAIDS. 2009. *Technical Guide for Countries to Set Targets for Universal Access to HIV Prevention, Treatment and Care for Injecting Drug Users.* <www.unodc.org/documents/eastasiaandpacific//Publications/DrugsAndHIV/WHO_UNODC_UNAIDS__IDU_Universal_Access_Target_Setting_Guide_-_FINAL_-_Feb_09.pdf>.

Willis, E. 1992. *No More Nice Girls: Countercultural Essays.* Hanover, NH: University Press of New England.

Winstock, A., L. Mitcheson, and J. Marsden. 2010. "Mephedrone: Still Available and Twice the Price." *Lancet* 376: 1537.

Woo, A. 2013. "Debate Over Harm Reduction Simmers in Abbotsford." *Globe and Mail.* Jan. 30. <http://www.theglobeandmail.com/news/british-columbia/debate-over-harm-reduction-simmers-in-abbotsford/article8029819/>.

____. 2015. "Ottawa Warns Against Plan to Regulate Vancouver Pot Dispensaries." *Globe and Mail*, April 23. <http://www.theglobeandmail.com/news/british-columbia/health-minister-warns-vancouver-not-to-regulate-illegal-marijuana-dispensaries/article24090887/>.

Wood, A., P. Zettel, and W. Stewart. 2003. "Dr. Peter Centre: Harm Reduction in Nursing." *Canadian Nurse* 99, 5: 20–24.

Wood, E., M. McKinnon, R. Strang, and P.R. Kendall. 2012. "Improving Community Health and Safety in Canada Through Evidence-Based Policies on Illegal Drugs." *Open Medicine* 6, 1: 37.

World Health Organization. 1986. *The Ottawa Charter for Health Promotion.*

Wortley, S. 2004. "Hidden Intersections: Research on Race, Crime and Criminal Justice in Canada." *Canadian Ethnic Studies Journal* 35, 3: 99–17.<http://www.who.int/healthpromotion/conferences/previous/ottawa/en/index.html>.

Yalkin, T.R., and M. Kirk. 2012. *The Fiscal Impact of Changes to Eligibility for Conditional Sentences of Imprisonment in Canada.* <http://www.pbo-dpb.gc.ca/files/get/publications/23?path=%2Ffiles%2Ffiles%2FPublications%2FConditional_sentencing_EN.pdf>.

Zedillo, E. 2012. "Overview." In E. Zedillo and H. Wheeler (eds.), *Rethinking the "War on Drugs" through the US-Mexican Prism.* New Haven, CT: Yale Centre for the Study of Globalization.